Songs of Hestia
Five Plays from the 2010 San Francisco Olympians Festival

Aphrodite
A Romance in Infomercials
by Nirmala Nataraj

Hermes
by Bennett Fisher

Hera
or Juno en Victoria
by Stuart Eugene Bousel

Demeter's Daughter
by Claire Rice

Hephaestus
and the Three Golden Robots
by Evelyn Jean Pine

Songs of Hestia
Five Plays from the 2010 San Francisco Olympians Festival

Edited by Stuart Eugene Bousel
Copyright © 2011 by Stuart Eugene Bousel
All rights reserved

Aphrodite: A Romance in Infomercials © 2010 Nirmala Nataraj
Demeter's Daughter © 2010 Claire Rice
Hephaestus and the Three Golden Robots © 2010 Evelyn Jean Pine
Hermes © 2010 Bennett Fisher
Hera, or Juno en Victoria © 2010 Stuart Eugene Bousel
Introduction © 2011 Marissa Skudlarek

Published by EXIT PRESS
Assistance for this publication was provided by the
Kenneth R. Rainin Foundation

Book design by Richard Livingston
Cover design by Cody Rishell

CAUTION: Professionals and amateurs are hereby warned that the plays represented in this book are subject to a royalty. All rights of every kind to the plays included in this collection belong to their authors.
Please direct performance inquiries to
Stuart Eugene Bousel
www.horrorunspeakable.com

ISBN: 978-0-9774684-5-4

EXIT PRESS
156 Eddy Street
San Francisco, CA 94102-2708
mail@theexit.org

First Edition: May 2012

For Marissa Skudlarek

   our unsung goddess of punctuation,
   grammar and good taste.

Contents

Introduction
by Marissa Skudlarek vii
Aphrodite: A Romance in Infomercials
by Nirmala Nataraj 1

Hermes
by Bennett Fisher 75

Hera, or Juno en Victoria
by Stuart Eugene Bousel 129

Demeter's Daughter
by Claire Rice 195

Hephaestus and the Three Golden Robots
by Evelyn Jean Pine 231

Writers and Artists 271

No Nude Men Productions 277

Introduction

In July 2010, I served as box-office manager for the first San Francisco Olympians Festival. As a result, I was present to witness the staged readings of twelve stimulating new plays by Bay Area writers. I couldn't be more pleased that EXIT Press is now publishing five of these plays, and I am honored to have the opportunity to introduce them to a wider audience.

The success and appeal of the Olympians Festival, in 2010 and beyond, is the result of two main factors. First, the Bay Area contains a wealth of talented playwrights, actors, and directors. Second, Greek mythology is full of rich possibilities for writers. More than any other pantheon, the Greek gods possess human emotions and traits. When we write about them, we are really writing about ourselves: our hopes, fears, and values.

Stuart Eugene Bousel, the Festival's founder, always emphasizes that the purpose of the Festival is to show how these gods and myths remain relevant today. While many Festival plays contain allusions and in-jokes that will delight mythology experts, the writers do not pledge fidelity to the Ancient Greek source material. Rather, they reinterpret these stories and themes according to their own perspectives.

This collection is called *Songs of Hestia*, and the logo for the 2010 Festival was a hearth fire, because Hestia, goddess of the hearth, appears in each play. Hestia was one of the original twelve Olympian deities, but later gave up her throne to Dionysus, god of wine and theater. If you interpret mythology as metaphor, there is a lovely symbolism to this story. Before theater existed, the hearth was the place where people came together to share warmth and community and a drink or two. And, above all, the Olympians Festival believes that theater can bring people together – forging new connections between Bay Area theater artists, as well as between artists and audience.

In order to honor Hestia's sacrifice and highlight the importance of this neglected goddess, Bousel ruled that every 2010 Olympians play should include Hestia as a character. To examine each play's portrayal of Hestia is to see how every Olympians playwright interprets mythology in a distinctive and personal way. In this collection, Hestia is variously an ex-nun who runs a Hollywood hot dog cart (*Aphrodite*); a barista who serves as the play's moral conscience (*Hermes*); a sharp-tongued spinster (*Hera*); a crazed, childlike wraith (*Demeter*); and a nurturing but ultimately ineffectual goddess (*Hephaestus*). These writers' depictions of other mythological figures are equally innovative.

Aphrodite: A Romance in Infomercials, by Nirmala Nataraj, is a contemporary satire set in modern-day Los Angeles. Like the best satire, from Aristophanes onward, it is animated by a deeply felt sense of anger and injustice. Here, Nataraj directs her anger toward the way Hollywood and the media co-opt and pervert our ideas of love and beauty – Aphrodite's areas of influence. Love and beauty ought to be the most wonderful things in the world, but for too many people, particularly for women, they cause anxiety and self-loathing.

Nataraj's heroine, Psyche Pendleton, is a washed-up reality-TV star reduced to doing infomercials and fretting about her weight and wrinkles. Although she is unhappy, Psyche feels powerless to change her life or rid herself of people who are clearly not good for her, such as her deadbeat boyfriend Ned. Then, through her encounters with handsome plastic surgeon Dr. Eros and eccentric ex-nun Hestia, Psyche learns that a seductive surface may conceal an ugly truth and a homely face may coexist with a beautiful soul. The goddess Aphrodite also visits Psyche in her sleep. Over the course of the play, Aphrodite transforms from a terrifying reminder of everything that Psyche is not, into an inspirational vision showing her what she could be.

While *Aphrodite: A Romance in Infomercials* has a serious message to impart, its tone is offbeat and quirky, featuring loopy humor, dream sequences, Hollywood in-jokes, and even a Judd Apatow movie about bees. Its allusions to our reality-TV-obsessed, tabloid-reading pop culture may be up-to-the-minute, but its theme is as eternal as Aphrodite herself. As Oscar Wilde wrote in 1894, "To love oneself is the beginning of a lifelong romance."

Bennett Fisher's *Hermes* is another contemporary satire, this time motivated by anger at the greed, selfishness and mercenary attitudes that have led to the current financial crisis. Often, we think of Hermes as a pleasant figure: the trustworthy, speedy messenger of the gods. However, Hermes is the Greeks' trickster god, ruling over commerce, fraud, thieves and liars. In the words of the Homeric Hymn to Hermes, quoted in Fisher's play, he is a god "of many shifts, blandly cunning, a robber, a cattle driver, a bringer of dreams, a watcher by night, a thief at the gates."

Fisher wanted to highlight these aspects of Hermes' persona and originally planned to write a play dealing with American corporate fraud. But in the early months of 2010, when a debt crisis arose in Greece (Greece, of all places!), Fisher changed his tack. The result is one of the timeliest plays that I have ever had the privilege to see. It was absolutely exhilarating to sit in the audience at the Olympians Festival reading of *Hermes* on July

15, 2010, and hear references to events that had happened just two or three months earlier. The eruption of the Eyjafjallajökull volcano in April 2010 and the "flash" stock market crash of May 6, 2010 are woven into the fabric of the play.

Over one year later, *Hermes* remains relevant. As I write this in December 2011, debt crises have spread to other European economies and the future of the euro is in doubt. Furthermore, greed and selfishness are unlikely to disappear any time soon. Thus, Fisher's witty, fast-paced play, and his characterization of Hermes as an obnoxious frat boy, speak directly to our present moment. Even the Greeks agree. A Greek-language version of *Hermes*, translated by Dimitris Kontos, has been workshopped at the National Theatre of Northern Greece.

The Olympians Festival's mandate to show how these gods and myths relate to contemporary life does not necessitate that all Festival plays take place in the present day. *Hera, or Juno en Victoria*, by Stuart Eugene Bousel, is a sparklingly witty drawing-room comedy set in 1850s England, portraying Hera as the lady of a country estate. Hera is the Greek goddess of marriage, and, for better or worse, Western societal attitudes about marriage and gender roles remain heavily rooted in Victorian traditions. Thus, though set in the past, *Hera, or Juno en Victoria* speaks to our time. And, as the only play in this collection that does not contain supernatural elements, it places mythology on a very human and relatable scale.

In *Hera, or Juno en Victoria*, Hera oversees the wedding of her daughter Hebe to railroad baron Heracles, while also confronting intimations that her husband, Zeus, is up to his old philandering ways. Zeus never appears onstage in this play, which focuses squarely on the domestic realm, Hera's realm. While Hera is often portrayed as a jealous, nagging shrew, Bousel presents a fresh interpretation of her character. In this play, Hera is a good-humored hostess, a delightful conversationalist, a loving mother. Meanwhile, Bousel depicts Hestia as a meddling busybody, albeit due to her concern for her sister Hera. As such, the play provides new twists on mythological archetypes, and on archetypes of Victorian literature such as the marriageable ingénue, the spinster sister, the Cockney servants, and the "angel in the house" matriarch.

While the three-act structure of *Hera, or Juno en Victoria* is tidy and the plot is skillfully constructed, the play also raises provocative questions. Is it better to fight against a difficult situation, or to rise above it? Is Hera a victim or a heroine? How much compromise is required in a marriage?

Claire Rice's play *Demeter's Daughter* also deeply explores women's lives. In this drama, Louisa, a young American widow, travels to Greece to seek spiritual guidance from the old gods. Louisa's husband was killed in the Greek Civil War of the late 1940s and her baby daughter is very ill. On a blasted battlefield, Louisa encounters Hera, Hestia, and Demeter — old crones forced to wander the earth because humans no longer perform the rites that consecrate them as goddesses. Persephone is trapped in the underworld and cannot rejoin her mother Demeter for her allotted six months of the year. Thus, Demeter has withdrawn into a state of mourning and the earth no longer bears fruit. When Louisa arrives, the goddesses see in her their last chance to regain their divinity.

Though *Demeter's Daughter* takes place in the winter of 1949, it feels timeless. Its subject is not the specific circumstances of the Greek Civil War, but the way that history repeats itself, in cycles akin to the cycle of the seasons. Throughout the ages, men have died in wars, and women like Louisa have buried their bodies and wept for them. Throughout the ages, women have experienced motherhood as a profound mystery, and have found comfort and strength in thinking of their foremothers and the patterns of life.

The ancient Greeks drew deep spiritual meaning from the myth of Demeter and Persephone (it formed the basis of the Eleusinian Mysteries) and Rice's play taps into some of that same spiritual, and ritual, power. Taking place at the end of the bloodiest decade of the twentieth century, *Demeter's Daughter* warns us of what will happen when we are no longer in touch with nature or with the gods who govern it. Yet, Rice proposes, there is always a glimmer of hope. The winter may seem long but spring always comes.

Finally, on the last night of the 2010 Festival, Evelyn Jean Pine's *Hephaestus and the Three Golden Robots* took us back to the mythological past and the creation of humanity. The play features three fire-gods: Hephaestus, god of volcanoes, who uses fire as a tool in his forge; Hestia, whose cooking-hearth is also a tamed, domesticated form of fire; and Prometheus, the rebel who created humans and then stole the gods' fire to give to them. Exiled for his crime, Prometheus makes Hephaestus promise to look after humanity and protect it from Zeus's anger. We can guess why Prometheus chose Hephaestus for this task. The lame, cuckolded, put-upon Hephaestus has always been one of the most sympathetic and human of the Olympian gods.

Hephaestus has created three golden robots in the image of his unfaithful wife, Aphrodite, to help him with his work in the forge. When he "upgrades" the robots to grant them more autonomy and intelligence, they, too, start to rebel. They persuade Hephaestus to create a human woman, Pandora; they suggest to Pandora that she open the infamous box; finally, they leave Hephaestus and go join the humans. Already a poignant figure, Hephaestus gains an extra pathos when we realize that, as a god, he cannot change or break out of his appointed role. Humans and even robots can evolve, but gods cannot, and that gives humans a power that the gods themselves lack.

Hephaestus and the Three Golden Robots is thus a paean to humanity: our curiosity, our enthusiasm, our talent for growth and transformation. It reminds us that fire is not only a symbol of warmth and community, but also represents inspiration and knowledge, the "creative spark."

All of the playwrights of the Olympians Festival, disparate though their plays may be, abound in imagination, creativity, curiosity and passion. They've adapted some of Western culture's oldest stories to illuminate our present-day concerns. They've written plays that ask the hard questions. They've explored our humanity through exploring the myths that make us who we are.

Marissa Skudlarek
San Francisco
December 2011

Aphrodite
A Romance in Infomercials

by Nirmala Nataraj

Aphrodite
A Romance in Infomercials

Aphrodite: A Romance in Infomercials was first produced in reading on July 23, 2010 at EXIT Stage Left in San Francisco, California as part of the San Francisco Olympians Festival. The play was directed by Cassie Powell with the following cast:

Psyche	Leigh Shaw
Aphrodite/Cytherea	Molly Gazay
Eros	Ross Pasquale
Hestia	Jan Marsh
Ned	Kai Morrison
Aletheia	Jenni Gebhardt
Stage Directions	Cassie Powell

Characters

PSYCHE, *a washed-out infomercial actress – self-assured and glamorous on the surface, insecure and miserable to all those who know her*
APHRODITE*, *the beautiful, menacing goddess who haunts Psyche's dreams*
EROS, *a top Hollywood plastic surgeon with movie-star good looks who has fallen in love with Psyche*
NED, *Psyche's self-involved, noncommittal actor boyfriend*
CYTHEREA*, *Psyche's whip-cracking producer*
HESTIA, *an elderly devout nun and Psyche's accidental spiritual confidante*
ALETHEIA, *Psyche's caustic yet lovable best friend and therapist*
* *Aphrodite and Cytherea should be played by the same actress.*

Minor Characters

CAMERAMAN *on infomercial set*
DEXTER, *a flaming homosexual product representative*
THE GRACES, *Aphrodite's beautiful attendants*
TOUR GUIDE *on a reality TV tour bus*
WOMAN *in West Hollywood tearoom*
MEDICAL ASSISTANT *in Eros' office*
VOICE ON RECEIVER, *presumably Ned's agent*
JUDD APATOW, *the movie director*

TOM COLICCHIO, *the chef and television personality*
MEL GIBSON, *the actor*
MICHAEL PATRICK KING, *the lead writer for* Sex and the City
LUCY PEARL, *a reality TV show contestant*
MAKEUP PERSONS *on infomercial set*
CHLOE, MONA, AND LAYLA, *women offering infomercial testimonials*
Random infomercial characters, voiceovers, and talking advertisements

Act 1

Scene 1

The play opens on an infomercial set – a kitchen. PSYCHE, an attractive woman in her mid-30s, stands awkwardly in the middle of a kitchen, leaning against a four-foot-long island. She sinks into the island, her forearm extended against the granite counter, inches from an immaculately hand-blown glass pitcher and a five-inch-tall glass with imprints of daisies. Above her, a crystal and plastic lighting fixture reaches down from an indeterminate ceiling, while behind her a stainless-steel electric range sits half-open and a translucent yellow vacuum cleaner stands in front of a sparkling refrigerator with French doors. Suddenly, lights floods through the previously blackened windows, and PSYCHE turns into little more than a silhouette. When she strains forward, flash lighting pops into her face and she puts her hands in front of her eyes, momentarily taken aback.

CAMERAMAN Okay, we're ready. We'll overlay this with product info voiceover in post-production. Let's roll.

PSYCHE arches her back, plasters on a smile, and looks into an undefined distance. As she goes through the motions, we hear her internal monologue – her instructions to herself as she poses and preens for the camera.

PSYCHE *(internal monologue)* You are the quintessential American woman. Flip your hair and smile here.

PSYCHE giggles, flipping her hair back and looking straight into the audience as light bulbs continue to flash, illuminating her face.

(internal monologue) You are beautiful yet maternal, sexy yet nurturing. Your kids idolize you. Your husband desires you. Friends and strangers seek you out. You are confident. You are brash! You are completely and

fully self-realized. You are also thirsty, and want to drink a glass of fresh lemonade.

> *PSYCHE quickly turns around and walks to the back of the island, half-tipping the pitcher into an empty glass. The lighting switches, and the backlight from the windows, meant to replicate the sun, fades and is replaced by a beam of greenish-yellow light from stage right, giving her a sickly appearance that is reinforced by her lost, directionless expression.*

(internal monologue) Smile again. Laugh. Your two children are still at school. Your husband took the day off work just to join you. You just finished a ravishing love-making session, and you're preparing for a pedicure, trying on that brand-new outfit that you bought in the boutique downtown. Your husband tells you he loves you, reminds you of your prowess beneath the sheets, commenting on the fullness of your breasts, the softness of your lips, how your hips swayed when he pinned you against the floor. Blush. In the light of day, you act as if you are embarrassed, but you are also thrilled, happy to have pleased him, content that your body is hypnotic, all-powerful, capable of bringing powerful men to their knees, that your smile can move the earth, that your...

DEXTER Cut. Cut! Cut!

> *The lighting returns to normal, as PSYCHE'S smile recedes and she exhales and sets the pitcher down.*

PSYCHE What's wrong? I was getting into the rhythm.

> *NED, CYTHEREA, and DEXTER enter the stage. NED is Psyche's boyfriend, a nondescript, slightly paunchy man in his late 30s, with an animated face and plenty of nervous energy. CYTHEREA is Psyche's producer, a distinguished-looking Amazon of a woman with a face that's as severe as it is beautiful. She holds a martini glass in one hand, and a strained smile is plastered across her face. DEXTER wears a pink cashmere scarf, with his hair teased into a bird's nest on top of his head. He is obviously gay, and speaks with an overextended lisp. NED is making small talk with a distracted-looking CYTHEREA.*

NED *(to CYTHEREA)* It's a laugh-out-loud romantic comedy about single women and the insects that love them. It's called *To Bee or Not to Bee*. Awesome title, huh? I can totally give you some flyers. Opening night is in a couple weeks.

DEXTER Baby girl, it isn't your rhythm that I was concerned about. Your rhythm is impeccable. Graceful like a ballerina. You could be on *Dancing* *with the Stars*, for all I care. It isn't your rhythm, it isn't your poses. It's you.

PSYCHE Me?

DEXTER Yes, *you*. You aren't *you*, darling. At least not the *you* we paid for. What happened to *Princess of the Parade* or *The Suburban Stunner*? That Pysche had an eternal beauty, impeccable form. This Psyche's been running on empty for too long now. Caffeine and alcohol might perk you up, darling, but let me tell you, they haven't been doing your complexion many favors of late. Ever considered getting some *work* done?

PSYCHE *(taken aback)* You mean plastic surgery???

DEXTER Don't get your panties in a wad, sweetheart. I know some surgeons that are so good they make it look like *play*. You can finally say buh-bye to turkey wattles and muffin tops. *(takes out iPhone)* Want a referral?

> *NED is very overtly sizing up two nubile, 20-something production assistants as he keeps one ear attuned to the conversation at hand.*

NED *(noncommittally)* Don't speak to my girlfriend like that.

CYTHEREA Surely, Dex, you're being just a tad harsh here. This is the woman who consistently made every Most Beautiful People in the World top ten in the early part of the millennium! You and the other product reps agreed at all the meetings that she gives good face, didn't you?

PSYCHE Please don't talk about me as if I'm not standing here.

DEXTER I'm just not sure that this will work. Certain stipulations are in your contract – clauses and asterisks, darling. Conditions and opt-outs. I mean, look at the flab beneath your biceps. Sweet Jesus. It makes me want to snort a line of cranberry.

> *A gaggle of interns and stagehands rushes onto the set and begin polishing the kitchenware. They are young, blonde, and beautiful. NED turns away from PSYCHE and smiles at one of them.*

PSYCHE *(coldly)* This is an ad for facial cream, not a swimsuit shoot.

DEXTER And thank God for that. I don't want to be a bigger queen than I already am.

PSYCHE *(visibly flustered as NED chats up a young intern)* I – I don't deserve to be treated like this. I'm a star.

DEXTER This isn't 2003, honey. You're a spokeswoman, not a star.

> *PSYCHE turns away from DEXTER and pulls on CYTHEREA'S arm.*

PSYCHE *(to CYTHEREA)* How could you have gotten me involved with this product? I'm making half of what I did for one episode of *Princess* and I have to put up with him?

CYTHEREA Stop being histrionic, Psyche. Play nice. If you want to take that trip to Cancun this fall, you need the money. *(takes a huge swig from her martini and turns to DEXTER)* What if we give her a pushup bra? Maybe soften the lighting a bit to render her with a more ethereal look? And, as far as her arms, she could wear longer sleeves.

DEXTER More clothes?!? We're not selling this stuff to nunneries, honey bee. This is for the modern woman. The elegant cougar.

CYTHEREA *(continues as if she isn't listening)* With more cleavage, darker lipstick.

PSYCHE *(raises her hand, exasperated)* Still here!

DEXTER *(in disbelief)* Holy fading beauty, Christ and Liza. I guess we'll give it a shot. No promises on final approval. In other words, don't hold your breath for that infomercial spot.

CYTHEREA Wonderful, wonderful. I'm glad we could work this out, Dexter. Great to do business with you. *(to PSYCHE)* Young lady, we are going to have a looooong sit-down after this is over.

> *PSYCHE scowls and the stage goes dark. When the lighting returns, PSYCHE is alone on the stage. Her face is crumpled. She looks uncomfortable in her clothes, and she puckers her lips, dispersing the violet lipstick as she readjusts her breasts, trying to push them higher.*

PSYCHE *(internal monologue)* You are the perfect woman. *(breathes heavily)* Beautiful. Serene. Sexy. Women want to be you. Men want to be with you.

> *The stage lights gradually lower in sync with the shots of the camera. At first it's a low strobe effect over a half-darkened stage. And then the lights from the flashes grow brighter and more sustained.*

(internal monologue) You are happy, content, self-possessed. Fucking happy. Life has blessed you. Your smile is a welcoming beacon, your body supple and ever-youthful. Laugh, confidently. Fucking laugh, goddamnit!

> *PSYCHE suddenly looks sick. She closes her eyes. The strobe lighting has ceased and is replaced by stadium lighting that drowns out all detail. Then,, there's darkness, and behind her, a projection of APHRODITE, a celestially exquisite woman, appears, billowing, menacing. PSYCHE is in silhouette as she slowly turns around and stares at the image.*

> *At this point, a coterie of naked men and women trot out around the stage, wearing sandwich boards covered in advertisements peddling a plethora of colorful women's products. The boards are plastered with images of "perfect" women – smiling, coiffed, silicone-enhanced, and exuding an artificial happiness. The merchandise being peddled is plastered in advertisement kitsch and smarmy buzzwords. It ranges from anti-aging creams to cellulite reduction therapy to other absurd cosmetic miracle products, the kind that clutter billboards, women's magazines, and television commercials. As they parrot the advertisements they are adorned in, they flock around PSYCHE in a malevolent, sing-songy gaggle.*

ADVERTISEMENT 1 Look at meeeee! I'm fresh and young and beautiful. For just three installments of $99.99, I'll let you in on my little secret.

ADVERTISEMENT 2 Do you want the keys to your sexy confidence and feminine radiance placed right in the palm of your hand? Join hundreds of women who are tuning into their sacred, sensual selves – and discover the keys to a more passionate and powerful you.

ADVERTISEMENT 3 What if I told you that for just two minutes a day, you could slim your entire neckline and get amazing results that take years off your appearance? And I'm not talking cosmetic surgery.

ADVERTISEMENT 4 Let me guess – you're busier than you've ever been, you know you should feel grateful for everything you have going on, but something *still* feels like it's missing. And when you think about getting naked for your man, you just want to sink into the ground and disappear. Can you say, serious self-doubt and zero confidence? Now, I know that's not what you want – and we both know it's not what you deserve.

> *At this point the advertisements coalesce into a mashup of cliché buzzwords and phrases that lose their coherence as they are uttered in frantic, overlapping waves.*

ADVERTISEMENTS *(variously)* Television's top reality stars!
Sexy glutes butt workout, with incredible exercises for your inner thighs...
Work those PC muscles and keep your man smiling!
Blame biology, but fix what Mother Nature gave you...

> *Altogether.*

ADVERTISEMENTS *(all together)* If you haven't picked up the phone yet, what are you waiting for? Just do it – we promise, you won't regret it.

> *PSYCHE screams as the advertisements surround her. The lights black out, and only the laughing projection of APHRODITE is left. The projection slowly fades.*

Scene 2

> *We open on a bedroom. PSYCHE is lying in bed next to NED, who is snoring loudly. PSYCHE shoots up from a dream, as she hears the phone ringing.*

PSYCHE Work, work, fucking work! Dragons, you're all dragons! Keep them away from me!

NED *(half-awake, also in the midst of a dream)* I love Tilda Swinton – she was so good in *Orlando!* Go, woolly mammoth!

PSYCHE *(waking up)* Huh?

NED *(stirred awake, yawns)* What time is it? Is that the phone? Can you get that, babe?

> *PSYCHE picks up the phone and summarily hangs it up.*

PSYCHE It's five in the morning. I just had a nightmare. Fuck!

NED Well, I was having a good dream. Go back to sleep.

> *NED unceremoniously turns on his side and resumes his loud snoring. But PSYCHE is obviously too disturbed by her dream to go back to sleep. She scratches her head and pulls the blankets tightly around her body. From the light that is just peeking in through the curtains, we can see that it's probably around the crack of dawn.*

PSYCHE *(mumbles to self)* Let's see if I can remember everything. There was… a fleet of winged baby angels holding a scroll that contained all the things I'd ever done in my life, good and bad. There they were, arrowing towards the earth, towards me, in a frenzy of divine accusation. I thought I was going to die! I told myself not to be afraid – I'm a Buddhist, so I don't believe in all this bullshit. But I had to ask myself, all the same – will I be called to task someday? God's probably kicking my ass for all those years of schlepping fad diets and non-FDA-approved beauty regimens. And let's not even talk about the reality TV years. *(pauses to reflect)*

> *The opposite corner of the stage lights up and we see APHRODITE, who gazes at herself in a mirror. She is surrounded by three women, THE GRACES, who mutely attend to her.*

There I was, crouching before the angels, begging them for mercy. And then I saw her. A woman so beautiful, she was terrifying. The harbinger of my death!

APHRODITE *(to PSYCHE, imperiously)* Bow down, slave!

PSYCHE Excuse me? Who the hell are you?

APHRODITE Why, silly, I'm Aphrodite, of course! The goddess of love and beauty? *(giggles)* Usually. But I have a bone to pick with you, and it's not going to be pretty.

PSYCHE I don't understand. Those angels – why are they here?

APHRODITE Those aren't angels. They are my minions. They do everything I ask, and then some.

PSYCHE But I'm a good person! I pay my taxes on time. I go to all the charity benefits I'm invited to. I recycle. I listen. I eat right. I'm a great friend.

APHRODITE You've been a bimbo and a birdbrain of a girl. A most foul and inadequate representative of the living goddess. A bumbling, fumbling ambassador of the divine Feminine.

PSYCHE *(flails helplessly as if she is beating off a formidable opponent)* I don't get it! Why are you letting them do this to me?

APHRODITE *(giggles)* Because you summoned me!

> *The side of the stage with APHRODITE and THE GRACES fades to black, and then PSYCHE'S alarm clock goes off. PSYCHE gasps, slowly lulled back into her reality.*

NED Fuck, I thought you said it was five in the morning! Why'd you set the alarm so early?

PSYCHE *(hits the snooze button)* I have an early photo shoot. Sorry, didn't mean to wake you again.

NED It's okay – I guess I'm already awake. Want me to come with? No rehearsals today, and I have to run a few errands anyway.

PSYCHE Really? That would be awesome! I've been having nightmares about this one.

NED You can't say I don't support my girl's career! Besides, I'm always looking to curry favor with high-level Hollywood fags. Dexter's going to be around, right?

PSYCHE *(sarcastically)* Yeah – really looking forward to that. It'll be so great to have you there. Cytherea's been a bitch lately.

NED *(interested)* Oh yeah?

PSYCHE She thinks our sponsors have been taking their business elsewhere because of my weight gain.

NED Ludicrous.

PSYCHE Well, I'm not exactly the same bombshell I was five years ago. *(tests NED's reaction)*

NED Yeah, but you *were* in the big leagues. You had a personal trainer. You had a makeup and hair team and all that behind-the-scenes help to keep you looking hot. And what are these assholes giving you now? You don't so much as get your own *dressing* room. How do they expect you to self-maintain without your own fucking *dressing* room?

PSYCHE *(visibly disappointed in his response)* So you don't think I'm the same bombshell I was five years ago?

NED Actually, I think you're even more combustible these days. *(begins to grope her)* Think you can help a guy out here?

PSYCHE Oh, honey, I really have to get ready right now.

NED It won't take long! You can always give me a blowjob.

PSYCHE That's romantic. *(NED continues to grope PSYCHE, and she playfully resists)* As much as I'd like to comply, I have a meeting with Cytherea at 7:30, then we have that test shoot at 8. Followed by lunch with Aletheia and a ton of client calls after. Shit, that means I have about an hour and a half to work out and shower before I high-tail it out of here.

NED It makes me hard when you talk logistics!

PSYCHE I'm serious, Ned! Not right now!

> *PSYCHE beats NED off with a pillow and proceeds to get out of bed and walk towards her closet to change into gym clothes.*

NED "Not right now, Ned." Seems to be your unconscious mantra. Sure it's not hormonal?

PSYCHE What? What isn't hormonal?

NED Well, you *are* pushing 40. Weight gain, sudden sharp decline in your sex drive. Dad says the same thing happened to Mom right before she hit menopause. It got ugly.

PSYCHE You're reaching, Ned. I'm thirty-frickin'-four years old, not a throwback to the dinosaurs! Excuse me. I have work I need to do.

NED Just trying to help…

> *PSYCHE storms out of the room and NED turns on the television. An infomercial for a women's libido-enhancing product fills the screen.*

VOICEOVER Need to reignite that sexual spark but don't know how? Yearning for the days you and your man used to go at each other like bunnies? Naturally, with kids, work, household chores, and bills to pay, staying sexy isn't at the top of your priority list. But here's an easy way to get in the mood and reclaim your natural desire.

NED Well, ain't this rich?

> *NED begins to masturbate as he watches the infomercial. The voiceover is set to a montage of romantic sequences with men and women, replete with candlelit dinners, horseback riding, and vacations in exotic locales. A middle-aged man and woman come onscreen, holding hands and glancing at each other empathetically as they take turns speaking.*

WOMAN After years of trying everything from sex toys to couples therapy, we were at our wits' end and on the brink of separating.

MAN *(nods sadly)* Everything else was going great, at least to the outside observer. We'd just refinanced our house, the kids had moved out to college. We thought we'd have more time for romance... but the bedroom stayed as cold as the Arctic Circle.

WOMAN My sex drive was at an all-time low. I felt unattractive and out of the mood 99% of the time. I didn't know what was wrong with me!

MAN Then we heard about this product that could turn all that around.

WOMAN Persephone's Box.

MAN I don't know all the science behind it, but I do know that magic happened. One minute, she was telling me she's not in the mood, and the next minute – wow! It was like someone flipped a switch, and there she was again, the passionate, sensual woman I fell in love with 20 years ago.

WOMAN Six months later, and we couldn't be happier!

MAN *(glances conspiratorially at his wife)* Now, our only issue seems to be trying not to wake the kids when they're home for the weekend.

WOMAN *(giggles and kisses her husband)* I love you, honey.

> *The TV screen fades to white, and PSYCHE comes on, the lights softly focused as she walks onto a stage with several chairs, talk-show-host style. PSYCHE gazes earnestly into the camera as she reads from a teleprompter.*

PSYCHE If you're a woman in your twenties, thirties, or forties, and you've suffered from thyroid issues, post-partum depression, or any disorders that affect your libido, this is a conversation you won't want to miss! Persephone's Box will help increase lubrication and blood flow to your genitals, and dramatically enhance your sexuality. And it will help you enjoy your life even more! Because you can fake an orgasm, but you can't fake intimacy.

NED *(excitedly, as he climaxes)* Yeah, I love it when you talk dirty!

PSYCHE *(from another room)* Did you say something?

NED Nothing, honey!

> *NED hops out of bed and heads toward the shower. Lights fade to black.*

Scene 3

> *PSYCHE and NED sit in a large double-decker tour bus emboldened with the words "Scenes from the Real." Around them, people excitedly hang out of the windows. Half are kitsch-addled queens, while the other half are tourists, outfitted in middle-American uniform: pink Crocs, university sweatshirts, and oversized tees with pictures of various pseudo-celebs etched in silver glitter. PSYCHE sits towards the back and is dressed in a purple velour sweat suit and a hat that reads "Zephyrus." NED, in his too-short tennis shorts and tucked-in polo, looks a bit like Hunter S. Thompson, if that author had survived fetal alcohol syndrome.*

PSYCHE Why did we have to take this bus?

NED 'Cause nobody walks in L.A. What, you're not interested in the essential landmarks of reality TV?

PSYCHE We should've taken a cab, or at least the cross-town.

TOUR GUIDE If you look to the left, you'll notice the condo that served as the set for *One Big Happy Family*. This is where Russell cheated on Amy with her brother, Alex, which sent Amy into a vicious rage, breaking the family pictures that hung throughout the apartment and causing Vanessa to cut her toe on a stray glass shard, which sent her to the hospital, where it was revealed that her husband, Theo, had been filching their healthcare payments in order to buy lingerie for the fabulously sexy au pair, Diana, whom you may remember as the star of the spin-off series, *From Diapers to Diamonds*. This sent Vanessa into the arms of lesbian super surgeon Dr. Olivia.

> *The tourists giddily flap their hands, and, with preternaturally bright smiles, look at one another in wonderment.*

NED Cheer up, hon. This is kind of fun.

> *PSYCHE shrugs.*

You've been a bit downcast ever since you found me masturbating to

Danielle Staub's sex tape.

PSYCHE Please, let's not relive that.

NED I'm sorry. *(puts his arm around her shoulder)* I thought that this tour would give you a chance to reconnect with your adoring public. You know, a boost to get your mind off things.

PSYCHE Yeah, well, that's the thing, isn't it? No one has recognized me yet.

NED I guess back in those days, you were different.

PSYCHE Thanks.

NED I don't mean it like that, babe. You were always half in the sack, mostly naked. Sipping champagne and martinis. Dior here, Fendi there. Slipping your nip on the red carpet or while stepping out of stretch limos.

PSYCHE I've seen better days, apparently.

NED Shit, you're really hung up on this Danielle Staub thing, aren't you? I have a need for habitual self-gratification. It's a form of therapy. It's not you. It's not her. It's me, babe.

>   *PSYCHE rolls her eyes.*

Guilt is a beta emotion.

TOUR GUIDE And on the right, you'll see the church where *Wholly Love* was filmed. Viewers will recognize the stairway where Andrew, the televangelist to the stars, fell for stagehand Anthony, sending him into a crisis of identity that resulted in a teary confession on national TV and a stint at the Get-Straight heterosexual reclamation clinic, headed by the infamous pastor Matty. If you remember, Anthony was revealed in the series finale to be an androgynous Democratic Party operative.

>   *The tourists look to the right, except for HESTIA, whose eyes stay plastered on PSYCHE. She is an elderly woman, her age exacerbated by her scarred, wart-ridden face and hunched frame.*

HESTIA *(whispering to PSYCHE)* I never bought that one.

PSYCHE *(staring, repulsed, at HESTIA)* Excuse me?

HESTIA That story. I used to be in the Church – a nun, in fact. Anthony was a little too old and butch for the clergymen I knew.

PSYCHE Well, it's never as real as advertised.

>   *HESTIA cocks her head back and takes stock of PSYCHE, and then holds her hands up to her mouth in an excited gesture.*

HESTIA *(excitedly)* Of course! I know who you are. You're Psyche Pendleton!

> *PSYCHE blushes and looks away, combing her hair in the reflection from the bus window.*

Oh, dear lord. I loved your work in *Luv Knuckles*. That was the definitive series on spousal abuse. You were very brave, dear.

PSYCHE That wasn't me. That was a show. And look at me now. Over the hill at 34. Forced to take a fucking bus to work. Pardon my French, sister.

HESTIA There's no shame in struggle, Psyche.

PSYCHE If you had to be a fly on the wall at my shoot today, you might change your tune. *(explains when she sees the confused look on HESTIA'S face)* It's a facial moisturizer made from caviar extract. Yes, I suppose it's a worthy product, but that isn't the problem. It isn't me the product or the sponsors want. They want the idea of me, the young starlet who turned heads on hit shows such as *Boardwalk Bordello*. I'm a different person now. Hell, I was a different person then.

HESTIA The past is like an anchor holding us back. You have to let go of who you were to become who you will be.

PSYCHE The Bible?

HESTIA No, *Sex and the City*. But the point is that there's always tomorrow, darling. Look at me, I just turned 73, and I'm just now learning how to live, and that's thanks to you.

PSYCHE Me?

HESTIA Let me tell you a story, Psyche. For 40 years, I served the Catholic Church, traveling the world to feed the needy and spread the word of God to the undernourished. I must have fed a million mouths, saved a thousand souls, but, somewhere along the line, I lost what was most important: my womanhood. That changed about a decade ago, around the turn of the millennium. I was sent to a Polish convent. It was the worst assignment I'd ever been given. The winters were absolutely unbearable, colorless and cold, with punishing blizzards and nothing to eat but Vienna sausages. The only other person that even spoke English was Sister Hazel, a firecracker of a nun from Eastern Tennessee. Sister Hazel had snuck in a few videotapes to keep us amused through those long winters – you know, the canon: *The Flying Nun*, *Sister Act*, and *The Exorcist* – but we ran through those quickly. It was a lonely, desperate time. But then, one night, by sheer luck, we discovered that between the hours of 10 and 1, the local Polish TV station would air reruns of *Psyche Getting Married*?

PSYCHE I've heard that my later work is very popular in Eastern Europe. It's a rather curious phenomenon.

HESTIA Not at all. Nothing curious about it. The Polish are a cold, ugly people. They pioneered the glory hole, for Christ's sake. The sight of you in a bikini sweetened the night of many a frostbitten man, I'm sure. And, you know, at first, I thought it was trash myself. A dirty show about a stuck-up, narcissistic little girl.

PSYCHE Gee, thanks.

HESTIA No, honey. You haven't let me finish. It took a few episodes – despite how revolted we were, we couldn't turn away, of course. But eventually I saw the humanity of it, of you. The episode that changed everything was when you walked in on your fiancé and your best friend Tyrone.

PSYCHE I remember that. They had forgotten to close the garage door.

HESTIA Yes, and your beau had Tyrone strapped across that rusty barbecue pit. I can remember it as if it happened to me. After screaming, you tore up the house, then ran frantically through the streets in your bathrobe with your makeup mingling with your tears to make you look like some sad clown. I'd never witnessed such a display of raw emotion. It was a revelation, an epiphany. Before, I thought that it was us, in the nunnery, that were pure and the world that was degraded by lies, materialism, and lust. But after seeing your breakdown, and the kindness shown to you by that handsome ice-cream-truck driver, I understood that it was I who had denied my humanity, my very womanhood. It wasn't you who had fallen, but me who had hidden. I quit the Church the next month and moved to L.A. I work at a hot-dog stand on Sunset. I always enjoyed serving the hungry.

PSYCHE That's nice. And I'm really happy for your success and self-discovery and all that. But that wasn't me who helped you, sister.

> *HESTIA places her hand on PSYCHE's knee. The two smile at one another, although PSYCHE's smile is more of an uncomfortable grimace.*

HESTIA Don't be silly, dear. Of course it was you. I'm sure as God made little green apples. Who else would it have been? You, my Psyche, are amazing. A force of nature. Never forget that. This is my stop. It was very nice to meet you!

> *HESTIA disembarks, but before she gets off the bus, she turns around.*

HESTIA By the way, my name is Hestia. And if you ever want to stop by for a free weenie, I work at Rabid Dawg on Sunset and Courtney. That's the corner where Hugh Grant picked up a prostitute back in the 90s.

HESTIA exits and PSYCHE looks on after her, dumbfounded.

PSYCHE What was that?

NED That was one ugly-as-sin nun.

Lights fade out.

Scene 4

Lunchtime the same day. PSYCHE walks into a tearoom in West Hollywood, where fashionable-looking hipsters are socializing, sipping gourmet oolong, and clacking industriously away on their laptops. PSYCHE looks around and spots ALETHEIA, a pixie-ish looking woman with a wry, sharp countenance. ALETHEIA is chatting on her cell phone when she looks up to see PSYCHE – she ends her call and shoots up to give PSYCHE an enormous hug. A woman who looks like a supermodel abruptly shoves past the two as she screams into her cell phone.

WOMAN I will cut off your balls if I find out you've been fucking her! Did you know she has the papilloma virus in her vagina? And in her mouth, if you've fucking kissed her. Call me back ASAP, you son of a bitch!

ALETHEIA Maybe when she was busy horking up lunch, she accidentally flushed her cell phone etiquette down the toilet? *(looks at PSYCHE)* Uh-oh!

PSYCHE What?

ALETHEIA You have that look.

PSYCHE What are you talking about?

ALETHEIA Don't play dumb – I've known you since college and I'm your fucking therapist. That look! You know, the one you get before you're about to launch into a litany of new complaints about Ned! What is it this time?

PSYCHE Actually, things aren't so bad in that department. Ned… is just Ned. He even came to my photo shoot today – which, by the way, was a disaster. But it was really sweet of him all the same.

ALETHEIA So he wasn't simply there to ogle the eye candy on set? Doubt it. By the way, sweetheart, you look like shit!

PSYCHE Yeah, well, I had trouble sleeping. Plus, I'm at loggerheads with Cytherea.

ALETHEIA *(contemptuously)* Again? Is the old cougar demanding another flesh offering? Or are you not appealing enough to the pre-dawn softcore porn set?

PSYCHE *(sighs)* Aletheia, you know I love you, but I do wish you'd ease up on the scorn-heaping sometimes.

ALETHEIA I don't mean to be a scold, but as your best friend and shrink, I kind of feel like your work is the giant elephant in the room. We've already deduced that all the one-night-stands, FWBs, ex-holes, and failed relationships are just a repetition of the same Freudian primal scene that dredges up your issues around childhood abandonment, blah blah blah, can I get an amen… but have you ever thought it's your work you should be doling out the big bucks to bitch about?

PSYCHE *(icily)* I don't follow.

ALETHEIA Honey, I'm no moralist. You of all people should know that. I'm not seeking to change the world one Oprah viewer at a time. I'm happy to eat the carcasses of non-grass-fed animals. I'm picky about my wine, but fuck if I care whether it's organic or biodynamic. I prefer retail therapy to power yoga. I will ecstatically drop moolah on couture from fashion houses with questionable labor standards. To everyone who kvetches about the horrors of advertising, I say fuck that – we're awash in subliminal messages that have very little to do with Gucci or Prada or *People* magazine. And far as I'm concerned, feminism as we know it had its last gasp decades ago – so you can keep rotting your neurons with *Sex and the City* and the *Twilight* movies as much as you want. But if you're swimming in that shit 24/7, you're gonna get dirty. I mean, look at you.

PSYCHE *(unimpressed)* Gee, thanks, Germaine Greer.

ALETHEIA I'm serious! Do you ever sit and watch reels of all your infomercials? That shit is just boring! It's like an echo chamber of advertisements – all of the same crap gets recycled in perpetuity.

PSYCHE Not quite in perpetuity. It's about trends. Anti-cellulite cream one day, getting rid of wrinkles by injecting the fat from your ass into your face the next. *(giggles despite herself)*

ALETHEIA This is no laughing matter! Ten years from now, you're going to wish you'd made an about-face in your career much earlier.

PSYCHE Oh, please! That's melodramatic, even for you, Aletheia.

ALETHEIA You'll wake up and you'll be just like Cytherea – padding her wallet by selling fancy lies to broads who just don't know any better. Dignity be damned!

PSYCHE *(wryly)* Actually, that sounds like me right now.

ALETHEIA Oh honey, I'm sorry. But… what about your agent? Did you get cast in that pilot about… what was it about?

PSYCHE Teenage witches in black magic rehab. *(ALETHEIA gives PSYCHE a blank look)* Vampires cornered the market last season, but witches are where it's at now.

ALETHEIA What was the part you auditioned for?

PSYCHE The sympathetic mental health counselor trying to get the rebellious coven on track.

ALETHEIA Perfect! You can study me for inspiration!

PSYCHE I don't think I got the role. They're looking for someone a little less Tori Spelling, more Zooey Deschanel. It's HBO.

ALETHEIA But you're nothing like Tori Spelling! Honestly, I think it's time to get a new agent. I don't know why you continue letting her cheat you out of better opportunities. You're highly talented, and you need to start believing in yourself a little more!

PSYCHE Thanks for trying to convince both of us, but I'm really okay with it. Honestly. Steady paychecks are preferable to the humiliation of a mid-series cancellation.

ALETHEIA I don't know why you torture yourself with that kind of pessimism.

PSYCHE This, coming from you? Can we please change the subject?

ALETHEIA All right, all right! Tell me what else is on your mind.

PSYCHE I've been having funky dreams.

ALETHEIA What about? The nightmare that Ned is cheating with the busty receptionist Cytherea's grooming to be the next you? Or is it the one about being forced to do a number two in a public restroom sans toilet stalls?

PSYCHE You're on fire today. And… ewww!

ALETHEIA Thank you. Continue.

PSYCHE I'm having dreams about… Aphrodite.

ALETHEIA As in, the goddess? What does she have to do with anything?

PSYCHE No clue, but suddenly, it's like… she's everywhere! I mean, not just in my dreams, but I think I've been seeing her on the set at work, and in random places. And she's kind of a bitch!

ALETHEIA What's her general message?

PSYCHE Hmmm, something along the lines of "I'm going to destroy you, you little ant."

ALETHEIA Dreams aren't my specialty, but from what I understand, recurring visitations from divine beings are not to be taken lightly.

PSYCHE So you think this is all real?

ALETHEIA Well, nothing's real, dear, but as a poetic complement to what's going on in your life, it's certainly interesting.

PSYCHE Well, she said she came because I'd summoned her.

ALETHEIA Even better! You were sending a help signal.

PSYCHE So you think she's here to help? I didn't invite her, though – and she's fucking scary!

ALETHEIA *(wisely)* The fact that this invitation for help wasn't conscious is part of what is making it so easy for you to discount. Just keep paying attention to those dreams and I'm sure you'll figure out why the goddess of love and venereal disease is pestering *you*.

PSYCHE You make it sound ominous!

ALETHEIA Relax, I'm just having a laugh at your expense. Seriously, this too shall pass.

PSYCHE When people say that, it feels like I'm waiting for a long-overdue bowel movement.

ALETHEIA Well, perhaps it's time to give your life an enema since you've already given it a bellyache. Anyway, are you talking to your mirror like I suggested?

PSYCHE Aletheia…

ALETHEIA What? Isn't that something TV people are already trained to do? Get the onstage rictus grin down pat? It's not like I'm asking you to tape your sex acts so I can give you a blow-by-blow analysis of why your life is so complicated. Sister, you can talk beauty trends all you want, but therapy trends are even more demented.

PSYCHE I've been doing it but I don't know if it's really helping. I'm not coming up with any deep insights. Mainly, I just feel like a giant moron.

ALETHEIA You're supposed to feel like a huge idiot. Leveling with yourself always means edging outside your comfort zone. And let's be honest. My bedside manner can leave, er, a bit to be desired, so I know there's stuff you aren't telling me. This is a way for you get in touch with your feelings instead of letting them get derailed by my pejorative remarks about how you aren't doing it right.

PSYCHE That is surprisingly insightful of you.

> *PSYCHE glances at her watch and jumps out of her seat.*

Shit, sorry. I need to bolt.

ALETHEIA Late for a very important date?

PSYCHE Yeah, plus… *(sheepishly)* I kind of wanted to get in some Pilates before I get called into the principal's office.

ALETHEIA Cytherea's raking you over the coals again because of your weight?

PSYCHE *(with faux thoughtfulness)* I think she'd prefer if I went for the quick fix, but bulimia's never done it for me and lipo just isn't in my budget this season.

ALETHEIA I can't believe you're being so nonchalant about this.

PSYCHE It's all in the line of duty. Call me!

> *PSYCHE gives ALETHEIA an air kiss and dashes out. ALETHEIA rolls her eyes and takes a huge angry bite of her Greek yogurt.*

ALETHEIA Actresses, man!

Scene 5

> *CYTHEREA'S office, a windowless room with fluorescent light fixtures and a smorgasbord of plastic trees. Images of glamorous icons – Jackie Onassis, Audrey Hepburn, Anna Wintour – spatter the stark white walls, along with random awards from the Electronic Retail Association and other script-to-screen guilds. CYTHEREA is sitting at her laptop, typing an e-mail with only her index fingers. PSYCHE bursts into the office, looking harried and just slightly sweaty. She sinks into an armchair next to CYTHEREA'S desk.*

PSYCHE Sorry I'm late! Pilates went a little long today. The instructor was intent on having me perfect my jackknife.

CYTHEREA Sit.

> *PSYCHE sits and CYTHEREA opens a drawer. She matter-of-factly pulls out a baggie of cocaine and proceeds to do a couple bumps. PSYCHE looks at her producer, in shock.*

PSYCHE Cytherea, I had no idea…

CYTHEREA For someone who made her official debut in reality television, you are astoundingly naïve!

PSYCHE I just… you seem so together!

CYTHEREA Relax, this isn't a leisure sport for me.

PSYCHE Then what is it?

CYTHEREA What do you think gets me through the day, the magic of Disney??? I need to make sure I'm on my A game at all times. That's hardly possible for the sleep-deprived.

PSYCHE Cytherea, you produce infomercials, not Hollywood blockbusters. How much sleep can you really be losing?

CYTHEREA More than you'd like to know. Infomercials constitute a multi-billion dollar industry – the only other businesses that top us are show and blow: porn or drugs – take your pick! We've cornered the market on the world's most sought-after beauty products, and believe you me, missy, there are legions of backbiting queens just like Dexter who want to see us fail.

PSYCHE But why?

CYTHEREA Why? You ask why? Because they hate women! Behind those simpering smiles and designer scarves are feminine wiles much more finely developed than ours. Thanks to every fucking fruitfly out there who places stock in the passing whims of her gay husband, fags are the ones calling the shots.

PSYCHE I don't know about that…

CYTHEREA Don't contradict me! After 20 years in this industry, I am 110 percent convinced that it's not straight men or the media's beauty standards that have done women in. Feminism got the kiss of death from queers who were quite intent on planting it with a wet one. Hit the glass ceiling in this town, and it's the gay men who'll be drop-kicking you down the rungs. And please don't tell me that I'm a homophobe – most of my friends and associates are card-carrying members of the buggery crew.

PSYCHE On that note – what did you want to talk about again?

CYTHEREA Vaginas.

PSYCHE Vaginas?

CYTHEREA Designer vaginas, to be precise.

PSYCHE *(cocks an eyebrow)* You've got to be kidding.

CYTHEREA Have you ever known me to be a kidder? Listen, I know that I ripped you a new one early this week, but this just in! We are about to hit the motherlode. We are going to go down in history as the creators of the world's first infomercial on cosmetic vaginal surgery.

PSYCHE Say what?

CYTHEREA It's… like a major rehauling of your lady parts. Also known as labia modification and vaginal rejuvenation surgery, it can include everything from tightening the vagina to building a new hymen to thinning the labia. It's supposed to make sex feel unbelievable… especially for women whose vaginal integrity has been compromised by childbirth or simple negligence.

PSYCHE I know what it is, Ms. Wikipedia. As if regular weed-whacking weren't tiresome enough, now genital landscaping's on the menu?

CYTHEREA Don't be so self-righteous. What women do with their bodies is their own business – though, in my book, a little plumping with cosmetic injectables is way preferable to going under the knife. But regardless, talking about vaginas on television is still a revolutionary act. It's like… pussy power is shifting the pop culture discourse!

PSYCHE *(dubious)* I still don't get how this is going to make us money. We sell… tangible products, not pie-in-the-sky procedures.

CYTHEREA Psyche, we are on the cutting edge of something completely unprecedented. You may not believe this, but I'm just as tired as you are of busting out my kneepads for soulless behemoths like the fuckers who shill Radiant Beauty Caviar Cream.

PSYCHE Tell me more.

CYTHEREA We have a new client. People call him Doctor Love.

PSYCHE Are you shitting me?

CYTHEREA Doctor Love is the hottest thing to hit Tinseltown since celebrity chefs! He has a clinic on Sunset, and he wants to work with us to get the word out to the masses! The Electronic Retail Association's gonna piss themselves when they see it…

PSYCHE I'm still stumbling over the Doctor Love part.

CYTHEREA Well, his real name is Eros Theotokópoulos. God, that sounds ethnic, doesn't it? Luckily, he isn't. Luckily, he's a tall glass of water with dimples and incredible onscreen presence, so his name shouldn't affect our ratings too much.

PSYCHE *(sarcastically)* As long as we're no longer the bitches of wicked beauty syndicates.

CYTHEREA *(assumes an infomercial voice)* I can see it now. "Want to keep your man but the Kegels aren't working? Is that flippy-floppy feeling getting you down? Narrow the gates of paradise and make the garden within more sumptuous! Even if you're pushing 40, your lady parts can stay forever young!"

PSYCHE Whatever happened to aging gracefully?

CYTHEREA Please, Psyche, don't get all Reviving Ophelia on me. You're in Hollywood, the land of optical illusions. See something beautiful? Well, then, you'd better fucking believe it's been hacked off, resculpted, powdered, Photoshopped, and then some.

PSYCHE But I don't want to be forever remembered as the designer vagina woman. That's so much worse than being forced to sell ugly jewelry on QVC!

CYTHEREA It may mean your ticket to an agent who believes in you, and my next Electronic Retail Association award.

PSYCHE This is ridiculous.

There is a knock on the door.

CYTHEREA Suspend disbelief until you meet Doctor Love. Here he is right now.

PSYCHE No way!

CYTHEREA Come in!

EROS enters the room. He is tall, dark, and handsome, and clad in an expensive-looking suit. Upon sight of him, PSYCHE groans inwardly, sinks into her chair self-consciously, and fusses with a few strands of sweat-drenched hair. Even as she refuses eye contact, EROS is instantly taken by her.

Darling! So glad you could make it!

EROS *(eyes on Psyche the entire time as he air-kisses CYTHEREA)* Cytherea, so nice to see you again.

CYTHEREA Likewise! Eros Theotokópoulos, this is Psyche Pendleton, our resident princess. You may recognize her from such classics as *You Go Girl* and *Hot to Trot*.

EROS Oldies but still goodies. *(shakes PSYCHE'S hand)* It's a pleasure to meet you.

PSYCHE *(winces in embarrassment and forces a smile)* So you're Doctor Love? That's... catchy.

EROS Not a nickname I normally go by, but if it's something that'll help you remember me, I will happily assume it. *(flashes a grin)*

PSYCHE I'll probably remember you less by your name than the fact that your job involves convincing women they have vaginas the size of toaster ovens.

CYTHEREA Psyche!

PSYCHE I'm sorry, Dr. Th…

EROS Just call me Eros.

PSYCHE Eros… I don't mean to be confrontational, but isn't vaginal surgery kind of like… genital mutilation?

CYTHEREA You could make the same argument for circumcision! And I don't know about you, but I'm sure human rights groups aren't beating down doors to save men's foreskins!

EROS *(amused and delighted)* Actually, there are a lot of misconceptions about the work I do that I'm happy to go into… considering that we'll likely be working in close proximity in the near future. Typically, my work isn't about creating the ideal vagina – it's about tailoring each of my procedures to what my clients are looking for. Not all cosmetic surgeons understand vaginal anatomy and physiology, but I do, and my practice is specifically geared towards allowing women to fully enjoy and be comfortable with their bodies.

PSYCHE *(skeptically)* Has this been subjected to peer review?

EROS Well, here's my thinking. Fact: there are at least 30 medications for male impotence, and it takes millions of dollars to bring just one drug into R&D. Is there anything remotely similar for women?

PSYCHE Well, yes. Persephone's Box is –

EROS I hate to burst your bubble but the jury's still out on female arousal disorder and the pills that claim to treat it. But my point is – if men had problems like… giving birth and getting their body parts stretched out as a result, they would have been looked at and solved in a petri dish ages ago.

CYTHEREA So true!

PSYCHE I'm having trouble seeing how we're going to convince our demographic that this is something they actually need.

EROS Well, the aesthetic industry is positively recession-proof so chalk it up to the appeal of the poisoned apple. *(glances at watch)* I'm so sorry, I have a 4 o'clock, but I just wanted to drop in and say hello. *(looks at*

PSYCHE) I hope we didn't get off on the wrong foot. *(fishes around in his pocket for a card)* Honestly, there's a lot more to me and my work than nipping and tucking. Give me a call if you really think you need convincing. *(turns to CYTHEREA)* Look forward to seeing you both again.

> PSYCHE, despite herself, blushes, as CYTHEREA watches in appreciation while EROS makes his exit.

CYTHEREA I'd let Dr. Love shoot me through the heart – or the vagina – any day.

PSYCHE *(under her breath)* His arrow would probably stop somewhere in the vicinity of that lump of coal.

CYTHEREA What did you say?

PSYCHE Nothing. He's got his elevator speech down to a T, no?

CYTHEREA I swear, Psyche, you'd better not fuck this up for us. I'm crossing the Rubicon, with or without you. But admittedly, I've grown somewhat fond of you over the years, so I'd prefer you be part of my success.

PSYCHE How… benevolent.

> *Lights fade out as the two women glare at each other.*

Scene 6

> *PSYCHE and NED are in their bedroom, lying in bed together, staring into the audience. They are watching a pornographic film that the audience cannot see, but the soundtrack of male and female moans fills the space. PSYCHE is visibly uncomfortable as she watches the film, her expressions ranging from befuddled to bored and impatient. NED, on the other hand, is visibly aroused.*

NED Fuck, did you just – did you just see that?

PSYCHE I must have blinked. What did I miss?

NED Are you kidding? That was a classic move – what she did with her pussy. It's like… a porn urban legend. You hear about it, but you rarely or never see it! Hold on – let me just rewind this scene.

PSYCHE Ned, how long are we gonna do this?

NED Trust me, it was amazing. It merits a second watch.

PSYCHE Can't we just make love now?

NED But you're always complaining that there's never enough foreplay. Are you seriously not enjoying it?

PSYCHE Well, I didn't realize trying something new in the bedroom was going to turn into a spectator sport.

NED But we discussed this. We had a conversation about it. We communicated our feelings to each other. I agree to be more sensitive to your feminine needs – you know, buy you tampons when you're all out… do a late-night drive-thru Starbucks run when you have that occasional craving for a 13-shot venti soy vanilla cinnamon white mocha with extra white mocha and caramel… allow myself to be trotted out like a show dog and play the part of doting arm candy when my services are required. I agree to do all that, and you just do one simple, itty-bitty thing! I even got something I thought you'd like – one of those arty erotica flicks directed by a woman, *Taming the Stallion (looks at DVD cover of movie, which has a formidable-looking horse on it)*! Won awards and everything! *(pats PSYCHE on the back)* Compromise! It's what relationships are built on. Besides, a mutual smut habit is the new couples therapy. Works like gangbusters.

PSYCHE *(insecurely)* I guess.

NED *(tickles and kisses PSYCHE)* Come here, honey. Pookie. Shmoopie. Pumpkin. Babycakes.

PSYCHE *(giggles)* Okay, okay, enough with the baby talk!

NED We're in this together, right?

PSYCHE *(despite herself)* Yeah.

NED That's what I'm talking about. So let's do this thing!

> *NED proceeds to get more intimate with PSYCHE. Both of them are underneath the sheets now, and we can see them moving together, first somewhat awkwardly and then in unison. NED periodically pops up from underneath the sheets to watch the porn.*

PSYCHE *(a little too enthusiastically)* Yes, oh God yes, right there! No. You moved! A little to the left.

NED Am I in? It doesn't feel like I'm in.

PSYCHE What are you talking about? You're definitely in.

NED Are you sure? I mean, it doesn't feel like I'm getting a whole lotta friction here.

PSYCHE Well, that's something. That's really fucking something! I don't know how you're not getting any friction, considering that I'm dry as sawdust up here.

NED Considering that Oscar-caliber performance you were just in the middle of seconds ago, it's pretty fucked up of you to tell me that.

PSYCHE Well, if your head weren't so far up your ass, you wouldn't need me to tell you. You'd be busy doing something to remedy the situation!

NED Hey, that's only half my responsibility. I can't help it if you run through bottles of lube faster than greased lightning.

PSYCHE What are you trying to say? Are you calling me frigid?

NED I'm losing my hard-on. Fantastic, just fantastic. Bye-bye, friction!

PSYCHE Maybe your dick's too small!

NED Maybe your pussy's too big!

> *PSYCHE and NED look at each other, both of them shocked.. She bursts out in tears.*

Aww, honey, I'm sorry. I didn't mean it. Shit. Fuck. Shit.

PSYCHE *(between tears)* I can't believe you went there! I just…can't… fucking… believe it!

NED You said my dick was too small. How the hell did you expect me to react? I mean, did you think about how I would feel? Here I am, trying to do something special for my girl, and all I get is a nice healthy heaping of "You have a small dick, Ned." And you wonder why I'd rather watch porn than have sex?

PSYCHE *(realizes her grave error and is instantly apologetic)* Oh my god, Ned, you're right. I'm so sorry. I just… I've had a long day, and what with that awful photo shoot…

NED It makes it easy to take a shit on the person you love. I know – you do it enough!

PSYCHE No, that isn't true! What I meant is –

NED Look, I get it. You've had a bad day. Maybe we should just talk about it another time.

PSYCHE Ned, it isn't you… I get insecure sometimes. That's all.

NED About what? You're hot, you're semi-famous, your career's going swimmingly. You're not the one renting out adult movie theatres to produce your horribly slighted one-man show.

PSYCHE I wonder… is it that you want me to watch porn with you, or do you want me to be like the women in those videos?

NED Be like the women in the videos? What the fuck does that even mean?

PSYCHE I don't know. Let's just… forget about it.

NED I am not here to stroke your ego, Psyche. I have my own neuroses to worry about. That's Therapy 101 – haven't you learned anything?? You are completely out of line. Look at you – all in a tizzy, and over what? Damn right I'm forgetting about it. I'm sleeping on the couch tonight.

> *NED huffs out of the room but not before removing his DVD from the DVD player. PSYCHE looks forlornly after him, tries to say something to change his mind, and then thinks better of it.*

PSYCHE *(to herself)* Stupid, stupid, stupid.

> *The stage lights dim as PSYCHE buries her face in a pillow. A spotlight appears over the bed. PSYCHE is still on the bed, but she is now flanked by two identical women – two APHRODITEs who stroke her hair in unison. She awakens with a jolt and jumps off the bed.*

Who are you? What the hell is going on here?

APHRODITE 1 Who we are is a difficult question.

APHRODITE 2 One left open to interpretation. Equivocations.

APHRODITE 1 Deconstructions and adaptations.

APHRODITE 2 And, we must admit, through the years, there has been a certain fracturing.

APHRODITE 1 And sometimes I am her.

APHRODITE 2 And she is me.

APHRODITE 1 And other times we are no one at all.

APHRODITE 2 Or we are everything and everywhere.

APHRODITE 1 Or something different altogether.

APHRODITE 2 But, generally, we are the things that go bump in the night.

APHRODITE 1 Or the ones who hold you tight.

APHRODITE 2 And if you see two of us, there are a dozen of you.

APHRODITE 1 Tiny, crumpled Psyches littering the landscape.

APHRODITE 2 Soldiers left behind on the battlefield.

APHRODITE 1 Victims of the war for the Psyche.

APHRODITE 2 *(nodding behind PSYCHE)* Look, there is one now.

> *PSYCHE, looking fearful, turns away from them and begins exploring*

the dark edges of the set. The backdrop gradually begins to come into focus for her and for the audience. It's a window vista, with the sun setting over a field of corn.

You must remember this.

APHRODITE 1 1989.

APHRODITE 2 The fall of communism. Twin Peaks.

APHRODITE 1 "My Prerogative" and Richard Marx.

APHRODITE 2 Your first brush with fame.

APHRODITE 1 A star-making performance on the casting couch.

APHRODITE 2 Certainly not your last.

APHRODITE 1 But this one cost you, didn't it?

APHRODITE 2 A little girl becomes a woman.

APHRODITE 1 Oh, how sweet!

The sun begins to fade over the horizon. The stage begins to darken. PSYCHE returns to her bed, befuddled, staring at the ceiling as the two APHRODITEs group in behind her.

APHRODITE 2 How the night plays tricks on the quiet.

APHRODITE 1 And everything that begins as comedy…

APHRODITE 2 Ends as a dirge to the void.

APHRODITE 1 A postmodern celebrity and media darling.

APHRODITE 2 Failed relationships and farewell kisses.

APHRODITE 1 You overcame your juvenile fear of pregnancy.

APHRODITE 2 But look at you now.

APHRODITE 1 Trying to find light in the eyes of others.

APHRODITE 2 Can't please your man so you blame him for your failures.

APHRODITE 1 Your vacant and meaningless life.

APHRODITE 2 You lash out at the world, but what for?

APHRODITE 1 It's the same as it ever was, same ball of pain and ecstasy that's been turning through the ages.

APHRODITE 2 They're not the ones who need to change.

APHRODITE 1 What the soul hates, it loves to project onto others.

APHRODITE 2 We had so much hope for you, Psyche.

APHRODITE 1 But youth's gentle dreams failed you.

APHRODITE 2 All that promise.

APHRODITE 1 The years pass, your beauty fades.

APHRODITE 2 No white picket fence or bouncy, happy babies.

APHRODITE 1 You gave that up for the other stuff.

APHRODITE 2 Commodified your womanhood.

APHRODITE 1 Sold your soul.

APHRODITE 2 Signed on the dotted line.

APHRODITE 1 Did it in Technicolor!

APHRODITE 1 and 2 *(in unison)* And what do you have to show for it?

APHRODITE 1 A thankless job.

APHRODITE 2 A man with a wandering eye.

APHRODITE 1 Time just keeps slipping away.

APHRODITE 2 What will you do?

> *By now, the background image is completely dark and the two APHRODITEs have moved into the darkness. A small blue spotlight highlights PSYCHE, who has curled into a fetal position on the bed. She suddenly pops back up and rummages through her purse, which is on the nightstand. She is fumbling frantically around for something. She finally finds it – a business card. Business card in hand, she picks up her cell phone and dials a number.*

PSYCHE Dr. Love? I mean… Eros? This is Psyche Pendleton. We met earlier today. I was hoping that you'd have time to squeeze me into your schedule…

> *The lights fade out.*

Scene 7

> *We open on a posh-looking waiting room with plush designer chairs. We are in Eros' West L.A. plastic surgery office – a commodious loft space that looks more like a high-end hair salon than a clinic. Marvin Gaye's "Sexual Healing" is piping seductively through the speakers, and several women – most of them middle-aged matrons with stately coifs and expensive-looking attire – are sitting and flipping impatiently through magazines. PSYCHE walks in and looks around*

guardedly, as if she's afraid that someone might catch her unawares. Much to her surprise and chagrin, HESTIA is also seated and doing some crochet work. She immediately spots PSYCHE and waves to her excitedly.

HESTIA Oh, hello, dear!

PSYCHE hides her face in embarrassment as the other women look up. She pretends not to recognize HESTIA.

PSYCHE Uh, hi?

HESTIA You don't remember me? Reality TV tour bus a week ago?

PSYCHE *(defeated)* Oh, right. Of course I remember you. Sorry, I just… haven't been myself lately.

HESTIA *(sympathetically)* Personal troubles?

PSYCHE *(snorts at the understatement)* Work, love, life. You name it. It's mortal combat on all sides.

HESTIA *(sympathetically)* Well, it's just like being a nun. Fifty percent of people think you're a doubting Thomas, the rest of the world thinks you're batty for giving up sex. One can never be certain where they stand, so it's good to just smile and leave it in the hands of the big man upstairs. *(smiles pleasantly)*

PSYCHE *(shakes her head and sits down next to HESTIA)* I can't believe you were a nun.

HESTIA Does it surprise you?

PSYCHE Not exactly. I mean, a little. You're more likely to meet a dragon than a nun in L.A. No offense. Speaking of which – are you in the right place?

HESTIA If these are the offices of Dr. Eros Theotokópoulos, why, yes, I believe I am.

PSYCHE Um, okay. But how do you reconcile plastic surgery with your former profession? Aren't there rules about that? Like, you don't get to heaven if you've hacked off enough flesh to make another you?

HESTIA *(laughs heartily)* Imagine! I think God would be a terrible bore if he refused to let Joan Rivers past the pearly gates!

PSYCHE So are you here for… *(whispers)* your vagina?

HESTIA *(laughs)* My vagina? Dear me, what would I do with a brand-new vagina? A man hasn't been down there since the Eisenhower administration!

PSYCHE But isn't that the doctor's specialty?

HESTIA Oh no, you have it all wrong. Dr. Eros is a highly respected plastic surgeon. The majority of his work isn't vanity jobs – it's helping people like me. *(sees the look of confusion on PSYCHE's face and explains)* I'm here for a blepharoplasty, dear – that's Greek for eyelid surgery. You see, I lost my peripheral vision decades ago because of the way my eyelids bulge down over my eyes. I had terrible difficulty doing the most simple tasks. It's quite a challenge to handle the pickpockets when I'm on the job. *(sadly)* You have no idea how many bags of Doritos have been compromised because of it.

PSYCHE But you work at a hot-dog stand! How in the world can you afford plastic surgery?

HESTIA They're dolls here. I'm on the 20-year plan!

PSYCHE scrutinizes HESTIA but quickly averts her eyes.

HESTIA Sweetheart, it's okay if you stare. I have no illusions! I know that I'm terribly ugly!

PSYCHE No, please, it isn't that. I just… feel like a superficial cow.

HESTIA Why ever for?

PSYCHE I don't have any special talents. I haven't made any major difference in the lives of the less fortunate. My looks are all I have. I guess I can't imagine what it must be like… to not be beautiful.

HESTIA Nonsense! There is nothing wrong with placing value on your beauty. Beauty is our weapon against mortality! By it we make objects, giving them limit, symmetry, proportion. Beauty halts and freezes the cruel flux of nature!

PSYCHE That's one way to look at it.

HESTIA Indeed. But I don't fret over not having it myself. I'm alive. Everything's working the way it should. Well, sometimes my legs are slower than molasses in January. But still, I get to savor the treats of God's green earth. I've lived an interesting, full life, if I do say so myself. I may be an old woman, but I couldn't be happier!

A MEDICAL ASSISTANT comes into the waiting area with a clipboard in hand.

MEDICAL ASSISTANT Psyche Pendleton?

PSYCHE Yes, that's me.

MEDICAL ASSISTANT Doctor Theotokópoulos is ready to see you. You can fill out all the necessary paperwork in his office.

PSYCHE turns to HESTIA before exiting with the medical assistant.

PSYCHE It's so strange, running into you for the second time in a week.

HESTIA Seems that it's divinely fated! Be well, dear. I'm sure we'll meet again soon enough!

PSYCHE smiles warmly at HESTIA and the lights black out.

Scene 8

EROS' office, a casual yet elegant room with low, sleek furnishings and gleaming surfaces. He and PSYCHE are sitting across from each other as he flips through a clipboard. She crosses and uncrosses her legs as they sit together in silence. The sexual tension is palpable.

PSYCHE *(attempting to break the ice)* That old woman out there had a lot of nice things to say about you.

EROS Old woman?

PSYCHE Yeah – I think her name is Hestia? She said she was here for eyelid surgery?

EROS Ah, yes. My colleague, Doctor Hyperion, is working on her. Such a nice lady. Quite different from the regular clientele. Such simple demands. *(looks down at the clipboard)* So tell me, when was your last menstrual cycle?

PSYCHE I don't know… two weeks ago? How is that relevant?

EROS Oh, it factors in. Timing and all that. In any case, Psyche, it's so nice to see you again. When we met in Cytherea's office, I feared that you'd be a tough nut to crack. But your willingness to come in lets me know that you are far more open-minded than I gave you credit for.

PSYCHE Uh, yeah, sure.

EROS Honestly, I don't blame you for being skeptical – and I always welcome a good debate. This is, as of yet, a highly controversial procedure. And I certainly don't recommend that every woman who walks into my office go through with it. It is a deeply personal decision. The vagina is, in metaphorical terms, the heart of the woman. The essence of a female. Wouldn't you agree?

PSYCHE I guess I've never really thought about it?

EROS I bet you didn't know this, but in ancient societies – matriarchal, of course; this was before the dawn of patriarchy – the queen's vagina was considered a totem, a living example of the goddess. To this day, there are tribes in Africa that consider the organ to be sacred. Of course, in our country, and particularly in this culture – this post-WASP milieu of retarded glamour and residual Judeo-Christian values – the penis reigns supreme. You see it in our monuments, and you even see it in our airplanes. But it's our charge... no, our responsibility – you, me, and our staff of dedicated surgeons – to reclaim the primacy of the vagina. To be able to stand in front of mankind, at the pulpit of society, and proclaim the beauty of womanhood.

> PSYCHE sits, hypnotized. Her arms fall by her side and her mouth is agape.

PSYCHE I must say, Doctor, this is all a bit much. I admit that before tonight I saw this as simply another gig, and a creepy one at that. I've hawked glass dildos, spas that specialize in vaginal care, and a line of sex toys that are straight out of Dick Cheney's deepest, darkest fantasies. All of which is to say, I've never shied away from sex-related sponsorships. In fact, you could say that I specialized in them. But the idea of vaginal surgery...

EROS Of course, like I said before, it's a misunderstood field. Let me ask you this, Psyche. What is your relationship with your... womanhood?

PSYCHE Well, when I was a child, it was a very natural, unspoken thing.

EROS Yes, the relationship of children to their sex is a very carefree and enjoyable one.

PSYCHE *(thoughtfully and almost surprised, as if she is making a new discovery about herself even as she speaks)* But as I grew older, it changed from the blissful naïveté of a child to the reckless abandonment of a young adult. I didn't realize the huge responsibility that came with it. At my best, I equated it with beauty and pleasure. And, at my worst, it was a source of self-loathing and doubt.

EROS Very, very interesting. Let me ask you a question that I hope isn't too personal.

PSYCHE Yes.

EROS What do you call it?

PSYCHE Excuse me?

EROS Your womanhood. What do you call it?

PSYCHE *(laughs nervously)* I believe we're referring to two different things. I was talking in more... psychological terms.

EROS So was I, my dear.

PSYCHE I wasn't talking about my vagina, per se.

EROS And you have just answered my question. Vagina. It sounds so clinical. So abstract. It has none of the beauty and poetry of *pussy*, or the power and raw, visceral strength of *cunt*.

PSYCHE Fine. Pussy. Cunt. Whatever.

EROS No, it's too late. You've revealed yourself. I guess when I found out that you would be my spokeswoman, I wasn't aware that there was this great disconnect between your body and soul. This odd, patriarchal dispossession of the self.

PSYCHE I don't…

EROS And I'm sure it's not your fault. The rigors of the modern mating rituals take their toll. And, of course, there is the burden of childbirth, the societal pressure to use your pleasure center to spit out yet another batch of babies.

PSYCHE *(uncomfortably)* Wait, who told you that I – ? I mean, I've never had a child.

EROS I imagine that the nightly entanglements that someone of your position associates with glamour and excitement have taken their toll. They've left your pussy – excuse me, your vagina – a source of shame and insecurity.

PSYCHE No…

Something in the way EROS has been behaving shifts, and he looks at PSYCHE as if he were seeing her for the first time.

EROS Wait, you are here for a consultation, aren't you?

PSYCHE Well… not exactly.

EROS Your boyfriend or husband or partner or whoever didn't put you up to this, did they?

PSYCHE No! Nobody knows I'm here, not even Cytherea.

EROS Shit, I'm so sorry! When you called, I thought you were…

He trails off, embarrassed.

PSYCHE You thought I was…? Oh, no! No, never never never! *(laughs)* So what was that a few minutes ago? Your sales pitch? *(faux flirtatious)* Is that what you tell all the ladies, Doctor Love?

EROS I don't think of it as a sale. I actually believe in the work that I do.

Isn't that obvious? *(groans)* God, you must think I'm a giant bastard.

PSYCHE No, actually – if I were here for… that purpose, I'd almost be convinced by now.

EROS At the very least, I'm glad you don't have some boyfriend who pressured you into coming. I never recommend that a woman go through this procedure at the behest of a man. Too many of you are strong-armed into needless surgeries by idiots with money to burn who've been overly influenced by porn and Hollywood. The decision should always come down to personal preference, not media hype… But that's neither here nor there. I mean, you don't have a boyfriend, do you?

PSYCHE Yes, but…

> *PSYCHE spontaneously bursts into tears, and a confused EROS grabs a box of tissues and attempts to comfort her. She grabs a tissue and loudly blows her nose.*

PSYCHE I'm sorry – I'm a blubbering mess. I'm totally ruining your couch.

EROS Don't worry – it's pleather. Is everything all right, Psyche? I'm a little confused. You say you're not here for a consultation, so… why exactly are you here?

> *PSYCHE bursts into tears again and begins to blabber as EROS strains to understand what she is saying amid her sobs and sniffles.*

PSYCHE I don't know! I mean, everything's just been weighing down on me and I guess I had a moment of desperation, so I thought – what the heck? I just get so lonely sometimes. And not in a deep metaphysical sort of way, but in a, gee it would be nice to have someone around to talk to and exchange back rubs with and understand and cook terrible casseroles for, sort of way. Things are okay with Ned, I guess – he's trying to be less abrasive, I'm trying to be more patient, and we've been working on the communication part. But mostly, a night with Ned is a cheap bottle of wine and a movie on Netflix and him talking about his bee play, and maybe a blow job if we're tipsy. Oh Jesus, this is waaaaaaaaaaay too much information, even coming from me!! I am soooo fucking mortified!

> *PSYCHE bursts into another bout of tears.*

EROS You're very upset right now. Why don't you take a few deep breaths?

> *PSYCHE does so and gradually begins to calm down.*

PSYCHE *(sheepishly)* I can't apologize enough. I'm not normally so TMI, but I haven't been to therapy yet this week.

EROS Please don't apologize. Most of the people who come in to see me are under far more stress than the world could possibly know or care about. Women in high-power positions, forced to paint on a happy face and go about their business like everything's peachy. A doomed endeavor, if there ever was one.

PSYCHE Okay, well, thanks. Can I just pay the front desk for your time?

EROS Don't be silly. Besides, considering that we're going to be working together soon, charging you for my services or performing them on you could put me in a pretty sticky situation. Think of this as a… courtesy of sorts.

PSYCHE I appreciate your kindness. Well… goodbye, Eros.

> *PSYCHE and EROS both stand at the same time. She goes to open the door, but he reaches for the doorknob first. Just as he begins to open the door, the two make intense eye contact. Impetuously, they reach for each other and join together in a heated kiss that lasts for several moments. PSYCHE is the first to break out of their embrace. She smoothes her hair and looks at EROS, shocked.*

Whoa, hold on a second, Doc. What exactly are we doing here?

EROS Sorry, it kind of felt like you needed that.

PSYCHE *(somewhat irritated)* Excuse me? That's pretty presumptuous of you!

EROS Oh no, I didn't mean… *(trails off and gazes thoughtfully into PSYCHE's eyes)* Psyche, would you have dinner with me?

PSYCHE Uh – I sort of have a boyfriend already.

EROS One that obviously makes you unhappy.

PSYCHE *(unconvincingly)* And aside from that, you and I are gonna be working together.

EROS An on-air romance – the sponsors would be thrilled!

PSYCHE No, I'm serious. Isn't this kind of unethical?

EROS On soooo many counts.

> *The two look at each other for a moment, and then they fall back into each others' arms. Blackout. End of Act 1.*

Act 2

Scene 1

We open on NED's home office. He's perched on his desk, chatting away on his cell phone between gulps of his beer. The VOICE ON RECEIVER that the audience hears is a distorted trombone, similar to that of Charlie Brown's teacher. NED is animated, gesturing wildly as he talks.

NED So close your eyes and envision a middle-aged bee smoking a cigar.

VOICE ON RECEIVER WahWahWah…

NED Jesus. Pull over to the side of the road then. Okay? Picture a bee smoking a cigar. A bumblebee. Middle-aged. His antennas have just a touch of grey, there's a few wrinkles under his eyes, and there's a half-empty glass of single malt sitting on a nearby desk. The bee is hardboiled but attractive. Middle-aged but virile. Think George Clooney. No, Clooney is a pussy. Oh, Bruce Willis. Hasta luego, motherfucker. He'd be perfect.

VOR WahWahWah!

NED Yeah, whatever. Anyway, Bruce is sitting in a small office. It's dusk, and the lights of the city – Los Angeles – are pouring in through the half-closed blinds. There's a kid sitting in front of him. A fresh, bright-eyed bee. Intelligent, sexy, young, and athletic. I could play the part.

VOR WahWah!

NED Don't laugh. I've been going to the gym.

VOR WahWahWah.

NED I don't need a couple inches, my friend. I have everything I could possibly want in that department *(chuckles while gripping his groin)*.

VOR WahWahWahWahWahWahWah!

NED Okay. No reason to be nasty. Maybe Taylor Lautner, then.

VOR WahWahWah.

NED Yeah, I'm getting there. So, anyway, the kid is Bruce's nephew. Bruce runs a dating service, and he's just gotten a phone call from the palace. The Queen Bee is looking for a new suitor. So, instead of sending him one of those sleazy douchebags who are just looking for a fuck, he calls his nephew, the crown jewel of the hive, the Luke Skywalker of the honey pot. Flash forward to the next scene. Bruce burning the midnight oil, smoking unfiltereds, waiting anxiously for word back on the date. The minutes turn to hours, the hours turn to days. No word from his nephew. He calls the palace, speaks to the secretary. Nephew wasn't even there, according to them. Bruce smells a rat. He investigates and finds out that the queen has been…

VOR WahWahWahWah!

NED Well, this is just the elevator pitch. Besides, this movie is character-driven, like my one-man shows. The beauty is in the dialogue, in the relationship between…

VOR WahWahWah!

NED No, I don't want this to be animated! Seinfield already went there, and no way can I top the King. This would be live-action, with humans in bee costumes. We can get Henson's protégés on it. It'll be sharp, edgy, groundbreaking… Sundance material. As far as the director…

VOR WahWahWahWah…

NED Look, I don't know who Warren Herzog is, and I wouldn't want to work with anyone who just smoked a gigantic crack rock.

VOR WahWahWah!

NED Interesting – I've always liked Apatow's work, but this isn't a bro comedy… it's a serious drama. I was thinking M. Night Shyamalamadingdong.

VOR WahWahWahWah?!

NED No, he's not washed up. Did you see *Airbenders*? Movie of the year, right there. I don't give a fuck what the critics…

VOR WahWahWahWahWahWah…

NED What was that? M. Night and I can do what to one another?

VOR WahWahWah!

NED How dare you… Do you know who I am?

VOR WahWahWahWahWahWah!

NED Don't call her washed up! And I'm more than just her plus-one. Much more.

VOR WahWah!

NED Fuck you. Fuck you and your… Hello? Anyone there?

> *NED hangs up the phone in frustration and swears to himself. He digs through a pile of business cards sitting on his desk, thumbs through*

them, and then excitedly dials a number on his phone.

Hey, Dex? Yo, yo – what up, man? Ned Tolliver here. Radiant Caviar Beauty Cream? I have a business proposition for you. Picture this – the breakthrough cinema hit of the summer: A plucky yet unassuming bumblebee plots the downfall of the queen bee, and with that, the collapse of the cult of matriarchy as we know it! Yeah, man, I knew you'd be into it… So close your eyes and envision a middle-aged bee smoking a cigar.

Lights fade out.

Scene 2

PSYCHE and EROS are at a fancy restaurant, sipping wine and gazing into each other's eyes. Both of them are hyperbolically overdressed; EROS is in tails and PSYCHE is wearing an ornate mermaid gown.

EROS *(glancing at menu)* I highly recommend the veal. It is absolutely mouth-watering with the Chateâu Margaux.

PSYCHE I'm a vegetarian.

EROS I should have known. You TV personalities and your kooky diets. Well, the pastas here are fantastic. And the cheese plate is to die for. You do eat cheese, right?

PSYCHE Are you kidding? I quit raw food because I couldn't give up cheese. The French have a saying: "A meal without cheese is like a beautiful woman with an eye missing."

EROS I'll have to remember that one. Tell me about yourself, Psyche. How in the world did you get stuck with that name?

PSYCHE You're asking me about my name? Eros isn't exactly in the Top 1000 Baby Names index either.

EROS Ha – true, but I'm Greek on my mother's side. I grew up in a very proud, traditional family. I was teased unrelentingly for it. Other kids got to stuff their faces with greasy cafeteria food, and I was sent off to school with souvlaki and pita bread.

PSYCHE That explains it. I don't imagine you walk around as a ten-year-old thinking you're gonna grow up to revamp aging debutantes unless you've undergone some sort of childhood trauma.

EROS Well, I wanted to become a heart surgeon but just didn't have the brains for it, I guess. Or the stomach.

PSYCHE Sucking away fat and hacking apart pieces of people's flesh is something you can stomach?

EROS Touché. Actually, I decided I wanted to be a plastic surgeon when I was in my residency at Cedars-Sinai. A young woman was rushed into the hospital one day when I was doing my rounds. She was this 22-year-old model whose entire life – career, everything – was ruined in one fell swoop. Her boyfriend had thrown a cup of sulfuric acid at her. She had third-degree burns all over her face and chest, and she was blinded in one eye. Certainly, reconstructive surgery was in its ascendancy at that time, but it didn't matter. She was permanently disfigured. I didn't understand it. This beautiful woman with her entire life ahead of her – all of those dreams, dead in moments. How could somebody do a thing like that? Jealousy? Spite? I'd seen a lot of crazy cases in my short time as a young doctor, but for some reason, this one stood out. Now, I know that well-meaning people will say: "Beauty isn't everything. It's what's on the inside that counts." But the desire for youth and beauty affects everybody in Hollywood, regardless of whether they're conscious of it or not. In my eyes, she was serving the maximum penalty for a crime she had never even committed. Inner beauty is all well and fine, but this woman was scarred – literally, figuratively – for life. I don't know that anyone can imagine the sort of damage waged to the human spirit when one is forced to go out and face the world that way. So that's how I found my calling.

PSYCHE Wow. I had no idea.

EROS I was young, overworked, and idealistic. Granted, the rules of the game changed over the years, but my clinic still has the highest concentration of burn victims and non-cosmetic plastic surgeries in this city. Healing disfigurement from the inside out – that's our motto.

PSYCHE It seems to me there are no disfigured people in Los Angeles.

EROS Ah, but you're wrong there. This is a city overflowing with self-loathing and ugliness – defects that are practically irreversible. Cynics, the walking wounded, people hungry for happiness and acceptance. They're all alike, Psyche. Misguided in many ways, but searching for love all the same. *(takes a sip of wine)* I'm well-suited to this job, because I'm a hopeless romantic.

PSYCHE The patron saint of sagging, middle-aged women!

EROS I take issue with that! My male patients comprise a growing contingent. But enough about me. What's your story, Psyche Pendleton?

PSYCHE The long and short of it? I'm 34 years old – I have no qualms about telling people my real age; I figure they'll find out online anyway. I try not to live in the past and generally expect the best of the future. I may have a very public persona, but only about two or three people truly know me. None of those people are my mother. I believe there's nothing a good glass of wine can't help. I detest small talk. I speak fluent German – don't ask where I picked it up. I'm not an animal lover but I own a parrot named Kiki who swears like a sailor. I have no demonstrable talents, but I learn quickly. Did I also mention that I hate small talk?

EROS You did.

PSYCHE I figure, we're both here because of my vagina, at least indirectly, so it's not exactly like we need to break the ice. The significant details will surface in time.

EROS You're an intriguing woman, Psyche. And I'm a very greedy man. I can't help but want to soak up all the significant details right now. I am curious... how did you get into television?

PSYCHE My story isn't that original. Ever since I was a kid, I knew I wanted to be somebody. You know, get the hell out of Dodge and eke out a place for myself in the world. I grew up idolizing Farrah Fawcett and Lynda Carter and Lindsay Wagner – kickass women who weren't afraid to get down and dirty with the bad guys. Always had dreams of starring in the first sitcom devoted to female superheroes. But gradually, I became more realistic about my prospects. I'm not a classical beauty and I've always been squeamish about doing my own stunts. So I went the next best route.

EROS Let me guess... reality TV?

PSYCHE When I was in college, I had a boyfriend who was on *The Real World Sydney*, so it kind of gave me a taste for it. The idea of airing your dirty laundry for the world to see – that was mortifying at first, but when it comes down to it, it's no different from being on a sitcom. Only slightly less orchestrated. It took a few years, but after *Princess of the Parade*, opportunity after opportunity came a-knocking.

EROS Apparently, the world couldn't get enough of you.

PSYCHE *(laughs)* Those were the golden days. When I started, there was... still mystery, still a certain dignity to the business. I don't mind all the on-air catfights and backstabbing – that's how we get you to watch. But it's the wedding ceremonies, births, deaths, falling in love, all those private moments turned into shameless publicity stunts. That's what gets to me. You didn't put it all out there, the way people do now. Plus, you can practically see the segment producers passing notes back and forth, scripting out the drama. It used to be worth something when I started out – raw and unglamorous, people you could relate to, with interesting stories. The façade is so obvious now that it's laughable. It's just a bunch of fame-hungry wannabes vying for a spinoff show. I was a phenomenon back then, but let's face it – Psyche Pendletons are a dime a dozen today.

EROS They say imitation is the sincerest form of flattery. Talking to you in person, it's hard to believe that your entrée to prime time was reality TV. You're so much smarter than those shows.

PSYCHE Well, most people don't know this about me, but I studied literature when I was off the set. Thought of becoming a schoolteacher. I figured – good to have a backup plan.

EROS I don't know how long I would have lasted. Some of those shows were truly heinous. Like *The Charitable Life*? You and your boyfriend Mike volunteered at a soup kitchen over the holidays and he dumped you for that homeless woman. You had to spend Christmas alone.

PSYCHE You actually watched my shows?

EROS I YouTubed a few of your most highly rated clips. I don't really have time to watch TV.

PSYCHE And yet you have time to take me out to dinner. Does that mean you date a lot?

EROS No – my wife wouldn't like that. *(laughs at PSYCHE's startled look)* I'm kidding. I'm married to my work these days, sadly.

PSYCHE So it's convenient to mix business with pleasure.

EROS For the record, I would never have allowed you to become my client. I would have referred you to one of my colleagues. Not that I think you need the procedure to begin with.

PSYCHE And you're not weirded out by the fact that we'll be on the set together in a couple weeks?

EROS Why should I be? We're both professionals. We can be discreet if we need to. Honestly, my time is very valuable. I wouldn't be wasting it if I didn't think you were special, Psyche. There's something about you that I can't put my finger on. You're… fiery and beautiful and world-weary. Maybe a tad on the confrontational side. And I love the way your nose wiggles and your eyebrows scrunch like caterpillars when you laugh. I find it highly endearing.

PSYCHE You're a stickler for the details.

EROS Ned's not?

PSYCHE Are we really going to talk about my boyfriend? Awkward!

EROS There's a growing population of young women not unlike you.

Settling for losers and users because you don't think you deserve better.

PSYCHE Young? Tell that to my producer!

EROS Aging is completely relative. Think about it – just 200 years ago, a woman's life expectancy was practically chopped in half. The hardships of childbirth and mere survival often resulted in early deaths. If you lived to be 50, you were considered a fossil. The science behind longevity is revolutionizing the way we look at youth!

PSYCHE Ah, the whole "40 is the new 30" argument. I'm liking you more and more, Doc.

EROS You're mocking me.

PSYCHE No, actually, I really do like you, against my better judgment. See, when I moved out here, my mother always warned me against dating a plastic surgeon. She said it'd do a number on my self-esteem. She was always so concerned about that… I'm sure there's never been a face you've seen that didn't need some work.

EROS You think I'm a complete asshole, don't you?

PSYCHE Oh, Eros, I'm just teasing.

EROS In that "about me" speech, you didn't mention your tendency to change the subject.

PSYCHE What were we talking about again?

EROS I thought we were talking about Ned.

PSYCHE There's nothing to say about that, really.

EROS Sure there is. Like… why isn't he wining and dining his gorgeous girlfriend on a Saturday night?

PSYCHE Oh, he works Saturday nights. His one-man show is going on right now, so I barely get to see him. And… let's face it… I wouldn't be here if I didn't know in my heart that things were over between us.

EROS So I take it you have time for a nightcap after dinner?

PSYCHE Possibly. But you'll have to get me home before midnight – that's when my carriage becomes a pumpkin.

EROS Midnight? Not a chance!

PSYCHE I thought your intentions were honorable, Doc.

EROS Did I say that?

PSYCHE Thankfully, you didn't.

The two reach across the table and kiss as the lights black out.

Scene 3

We open on PSYCHE and ALETHEIA, who are both walking through Griffith Park on a sunny afternoon, eating frozen yogurt. As they stroll past moms in strollers, ALETHEIA is blithely talking PSYCHE's ear off but PSYCHE is dazed and staring dreamily into the distance. Frustrated, ALETHEIA stops and scrutinizes her friend.

ALETHEIA By the way, did I mention that I met a leprechaun last week who's 50 flavors of awesome? Dumb as a box of hair, but he's charming, sweet, single, and unnaturally good in bed. We decided we're going to elope and go to Key West, where we'll be married in a ceremony officiated by William Shatner. And a choir of gay mermen will sing Air Supply songs as I walk down the aisle wearing tube socks and ruched chiffon. Wanna be my maid of honor?

PSYCHE Mmm hmmm. Sounds great, Al.

ALETHEIA Hey! I realize that listening to me bitch about spending the weekend with my non-potty-trained six-year-old nephew is pretty blah in comparison to your narcotic interior life. But come on, you're hurting my feelings here!

PSYCHE Sorry, Aletheia. I'm just going through something right now.

ALETHEIA And it took you this long to dish?

PSYCHE I kind of thought we put the kibosh on getting too heavy outside our therapy sessions.

ALETHEIA *(sarcastically)* Obviously, that's been working well for us. Come on, let's hear it.

PSYCHE I think that Ned and I are… over.

ALETHEIA Well, fuck me! Hallelujah, stop the presses! Psyche Pendleton is back on the market! That's fantastic news! When did this happen?

PSYCHE A few days ago.

ALETHEIA What???? Why was I not the first person you called when shoe number two dropped?

PSYCHE Honestly, it feels anti-climactic. Maybe because things have been bad for such a long time. I tried to be patient. When you get to know him, Ned is a very nice person. But with the porn, the flirting, the showing up to my photo shoots and schmoozing my sponsors… not to mention all those weird names and numbers on his cell phone…

ALETHEIA Don't worry – I'll take your mind off that gigolo. We're gonna have so much fun painting the town red, just us two single gals.

PSYCHE Actually, I'm seeing someone.

ALETHEIA Come again?

PSYCHE Yeah, um, that's part of the reason I think things are over between me and Ned.

ALETHEIA You bitch! What's up with all the secrets?

PSYCHE It's still pretty new... I wanted to wait until I was sure that it was going somewhere. But *(laughs giddily)* he's incredible, Aletheia. I know I just met the guy, but I feel so comfortable with him. We have great conversations. He's smart, passionate, gorgeous, sensitive. When he looks at me, it's as if I'm the only woman in the world. It's like I've stumbled upon an endangered species of man.

ALETHEIA So who is he?

PSYCHE Eros Theotokópoulos. He's a doctor.

ALETHEIA Why does that name sound so familiar?

PSYCHE Well, he's... sort of a big deal around Hollywood. He's a plastic surgeon.

ALETHEIA *(repeats his name over and over before making the connection)* Oh my god, Psyche! You're dating Doctor *Pussy*????

PSYCHE *(defensively)* Doctor Love! People call him Doctor Love.

ALETHEIA Being someone with a very well-developed sense of irony, I am definitely not amused. How in the world did you guys even meet? *(eyes PSYCHE suspiciously)* Please don't tell me you bonded over an examination table spread-eagled with your legs in stirrups! *(shudders)* That would be uber tawdry, even for you.

PSYCHE Not exactly. We met because Cytherea is featuring the... well, procedure... for an upcoming TV spot.

ALETHEIA So it's work-related?

PSYCHE Sort of. Not really. I mean, I went to his office. But not for that! A couple weeks ago, Ned and I had a fight and... well, things just kind of bottomed out. I didn't know what to do. I could feel my life as I knew it collapsing. And there was this little voice – well, maybe two – in my head: "Psyche! Psyche! Today is the first day of the rest of your life." It's like a paparazzi bulb flashed, and boom! I knew I had to call Eros.

ALETHEIA You had an epiphany and decided to call Doctor Pussy? Still not making the connection here.

PSYCHE I know. I can barely explain it myself. I don't usually go in for new-agey stuff. You know that talk of auras and crystals and energy makes me want to throw the book at Madonna. But… it's like Eros and I have this truly cosmic bond! And the sex is off the charts.

ALETHEIA Oh Jesus, Psyche! You're fucking the guy?

PSYCHE I wanted to take it slow at first. But it just felt so right. I can be myself around him.

ALETHEIA Be yourself?? His entire career is built on the premise that women need never be themselves. A little lipo here, a facelift there – saggy labia, begone!

PSYCHE (*sounding somewhat unconvinced*) No, Eros is not like that. He's kind… and wants to help women feel better about themselves. He never does a surgery on someone who's not 100% on board. It's about…

improving self-esteem.

ALETHEIA Since when did you equate high self-esteem to having a pussy like Jenna Jameson's? Christ, Psyche! You're his publicist's wet dream!

PSYCHE You're talking about him like he's some kind of sleazebag! He got his degree from an accredited institution!

ALETHEIA I don't care if he graduated from Harvard fucking College. The man fixes up vajay-jays for a living. Far as I'm concerned, he's right up there with the guys making pornos out in Canoga Park. Both of them are sitting on small fortunes because some dumb bitches decided their bodies didn't live up to the male ideal.

PSYCHE This coming from the woman who changes her hair color every few months because she's afraid of a few grays. Your argument doesn't hold water.

ALETHEIA Dyeing your hair ain't exactly the same thing as mutilating your cooter to… why do women do it again?

PSYCHE Better tone, strength, and control?

ALETHEIA He really got to you, didn't he?

PSYCHE This is insane! You're my friend! Isn't being supportive part of the job description?

ALETHEIA What do you want me to do? Burn sage and hold your hand while your vaj is being eviscerated? Friendship isn't mental masturbation – I'm not here to stroke your ego, woman! I am here to tell you the truth!

PSYCHE Your version of the truth, Aletheia. And, for your information, I am not getting the surgery. How many times do I have to tell people that?

ALETHEIA *(struggling to be patient)* I realize that silver-tongued Lotharios are your Achilles heel – that's how you ended up with Ned – but this is beyond idiotic, even for you. You're at the ass end of a shitty relationship, so it only makes sense that you believe you're… in love or something. A slab of raw meat would look appetizing next to Ned. You just aren't thinking straight right now. I get it.

PSYCHE No, Aletheia, you do not get it. I am happy, for maybe the first time in the 15 years that we have known each other. Is it possible for you to just quit diagnosing me for a second and accept that? And be happy for me?

ALETHEIA Sorry. No can do. Remember, I was there to pick up the pieces after *Psyche Getting Married*? and *The Suburban Stunner*. If we learned anything from those experiences, it's that people you think you can trust will fleece you of all you've got if you let your guard down.

PSYCHE *(exasperated)* Aletheia, that was reality TV, not my life. I was fully aware of all the plot points.

ALETHEIA I'm not talking about the on-screen bullshit, Psyche. I'm talking about the crash and burn that came after. After producers got exactly what they wanted from you and didn't need you anymore. You'd exhausted all the tabloids and girlie magazines – in their eyes, you'd outlived your novelty. You don't need to deal with that kind of humiliation anymore. Not from career opportunists like Ned, or this Eros character. I mean, you barely know the guy. People in this town are sick – I know; many of them are my clients. Eros could have his own agenda, like… finding his name splashed across *Us* magazine after breathing new life into a former reality TV star's lady parts that are well past their prime. You could be his pet project, for all you know.

PSYCHE I just realized something. Ned's never really tried to change me. Eros thinks I'm wonderful the way I am. You're the only person in my life who is constantly telling me who to be and what to think. So maybe this is your problem, not mine.

ALETHEIA Since we're talking problems, I'll tell you what yours is. You think you're special. But I have news for you – you're not. You're just as vain, insecure, spoiled, and afraid as every other woman in Hollywood. And you make the same fucking mistakes, over and over. You've convinced yourself that the loneliness, the pain and hurt and guilt will magically disappear once you find the perfect man or land a cushy job. You look for happiness and affirmation everywhere except within yourself.

PSYCHE I'm not listening to this psychobabble. Call me when you're ready to be my friend.

PSYCHE angrily tosses her frozen yogurt into a garbage can and stalks off. ALETHEIA, unfazed, shrugs and hollers after her friend.

ALETHEIA Hey, if that means you're canceling our therapy session this week, remember I have a 24-hour policy!

Lights fade out.

Scene 4

The scene opens up with a spotlight on PSYCHE and NED. They are both suspended in the air, wearing dirty bee costumes. PSYCHE has her hands at her hips and is smiling. NED seems lifeless. His arms and legs dangle beneath him. Behind them a blue screen projects a picture of the sky. Suddenly, the voice of JUDD APATOW intervenes.

JUDD APATOW Cut… Cut… Cut! Ned, can I see you over here? Guys, can we lower Ned?

NED is lowered and waddles over to JUDD APATOW.

NED What up, J-Dog?

JUDD APATOW Ned, I hate to say it. But I gotta call it like I see it. This isn't working for me. At all.

NED Why? I thought it was going good.

JUDD APATOW Yeah… but, um, no. I mean, you maybe look a little butthurt to me, like a sagging shit on the end of a crooked stick. Psyche is chewing you up out there, man.

NED Well, she is the queen and I am her dinner. She's fixing to eat me, you know. It's in the script.

JUDD APATOW Well, there's being eaten and then there's being eaten. Listen, I signed up for this because you inspired me. Yes, you, Ned whatever-the-fuck-your-last-name-is. The idea of a little tiny peon bee overturning an evil matriarchy. It's aspirational, relatable shit, man. It's for every dude who's ever deleted their Internet history because of some histrionic, sexually repressed wife. Every guy who's forced to drink rosé or watch fucking Bravo.

NED Yeah, been there, done that.

JUDD APATOW We all have, bro. And that's what makes your script so universal. Listen, I don't know if you know this, but between decades of PC bullshit and declining male attendance at the movies, girls have overtaken cinema. This is our chance to win one for the team. But we need a little more... venom. We need you to be you, the alpha-Ned.

NED Yeah, but I don't know how I feel about us buzzing and then doing the vocal overdubs later.

JUDD APATOW It'll be great. Trust me. They've been doing it with their bee movies for years in Asia. Just focus on the chemistry between you and Psyche, and let me work out the rest.

NED Yeah, well, that's the thing. Psyche and I haven't been getting along so great as of late.

JUDD APATOW So fake it! C'mon, Ned. Buck up, buddy. I need you. We need you.

> *NED waddles back over to PSYCHE and is lifted back up into the air next to her. APATOW yells through a megaphone.*

Okay, everyone. Take your places. Let's set this up.

PSYCHE What was that about?

NED He says that you're dominating me. That I should be more aggressive.

PSYCHE Well, I am trying to eat you.

NED Yeah, that's what I said. (sighs) You know, this relationship has always been about your desires, ambitions, and talents. I've always been your plus one. I try to pretend otherwise, babe, but, deep down...

PSYCHE What are you talking about, Ned? Your one-man show has been turned into a major Hollywood production directed by Judd Apatow.

NED Yeah, but this isn't real, you know that.

PSYCHE Yeah, I guess not. I kinda figured that out when I noticed all the PAs were former Playmates. But don't be so glum, Ned. Enjoy this. It's your moment. It's your dream. Hell, have sex with one of the bunnies. You have my permission.

NED Don't want to weird you out, babe, but I think this is your dream. If this was my dream, your part would be played by Megan Fox. And I would have never invited Cytherea.

> *The spotlight shines on CYTHEREA, who is standing off to the side, stage right. She rolls her eyes and puffs on a cigarette.*

PSYCHE I thought you two had a thing?

NED Hell, no. I find her overly aggressive and alienating. I am so not into the mominatrix type.

PSYCHE Oh.

NED I know about you and Eros.

PSYCHE I'm sorry, Ned. It isn't about you. It's about me and my need for personal exploration. Let's face it – you never appreciated my unique femininity. He makes me feel…like a new woman.

NED I just don't understand you, babe. I know my eyes may have drifted, and that I haven't been particularly attentive or even hygienic, but I've loved you for who you are – washed-up reality TV star and all. Maybe I didn't always understand you, and maybe, over time, the connection was frayed, but you were always the one for me.

NED flaps his arms, puckers his lips, and stretches his neck towards PSYCHE, unsuccessfully trying to fly over and kiss her.

JUDD APATOW Okay… quiet on the set.

PSYCHE frowns, realizing that if this is indeed her dream, NED isn't the bee that she'd like to be acting alongside.

PSYCHE Well, why the hell not?

In one quick movement, NED's suspension cord snaps and he falls to the ground. His surprised scream echoes in the air, cartoon-like. As quickly as NED falls away, EROS zips up on another cord. He is also clad in a bee costume, but unlike NED, he is painfully debonair.

JUDD APATOW Action!

PSYCHE I never noticed before, but one of my wings is bigger than the other.

EROS Ah, nobody's completely symmetrical, darling.

PSYCHE giggles like a schoolgirl. The tone of the ensuing conversation between EROS and PSYCHE should be surreal yet earnest, a string of lovely non-sequiturs.

PSYCHE *(thoughtfully)* I've always been cursed when it comes to love. You name it. Cheating boyfriends, latently gay fiancés with cold feet… To get a flesh and blood man to fall in love with the whole package is like pulling a train up a steep hill by one's teeth. It happens just about every time a neighboring star goes supernova.

EROS You're like a Tootsie Pop, Psyche. It takes time and patience to crunch through that unyielding husk and arrive at the chewy center. But it's certainly worth the effort.

PSYCHE That is ridiculously romantic.

Both PSYCHE and EROS grasp each other's hands and gaze softly into each other's eyes.

EROS It would be easy to fall in love with a woman like you. First of all, you're a woman, which means that you come with all the warmth and intimacy of any human being, plus an extra helping. If you have some kind of "how am I going to get someone else to love me" or "will anyone ever love the whole Psyche, the real Psyche" syndrome, you better look it dead in the eyes, and you better be ready for a throw-down.

PSYCHE Sometimes I wonder if my beauty puts men off.

EROS It is true that sometimes attractive women make men feel uncomfortable. Coincidentally, it can sometimes make the sex much less good. That's not you. I am perfectly comfortable with you. Your vulnerability puts both men and women at ease. May I kiss you?

Suddenly, as PSYCHE and EROS bumble towards each other, the blue screen behind them crackles with static, and is abruptly replaced with a flickering image of APHRODITE, who stands in a power suit with her hands on her hips.

APHRODITE Not in the script.

PSYCHE Fuck. You again? Go away! This is my dream!

APHRODITE Impossible! You're just another insignificant bit player in my dream, darling.

EROS *(glancing at his expensive watch)* Shit, I'm sorry. I have to get going. A three o'clock.

PSYCHE Wait, you're not supposed to be taking clients in my fantasy!

EROS Aww, you're right. That's so rude of me. I'll stay.

APHRODITE Stay, leave, whatever. It's all the same in the end. Real life isn't the fairy tales or movies or info-commercials. *(whispers)* Everyone's here to do someone else's bidding.

PSYCHE Ouch! Did you just…sting me?

EROS *(sheepishly)* Yeah. She's right. It's in the script.

PSYCHE What fucking script?

EROS You know, the bee movie script? "A lowly bumblebee discovers the murderous stratagems of his queen and seeks to overthrow the cult of matriarchy once and for all." Men everywhere rejoice.

PSYCHE *(sadly)* You never told me you wanted to be an actor.

EROS I never thought about it until now. I'm really excited. Ned was way too soft for this role. I want to impress Judd – show him I'm more than a pretty face.

PSYCHE *(suddenly getting into the role)* Well, I'm the queen. You think a simple sting can take me out? *(cackles maniacally)*

APHRODITE It's not a simple sting. You love Eros, so it's a poison arrow shot through the heart. Kings become slaves, paupers become gods, immortals are wrenched cruelly off their pedestals. Haven't you been getting your daily dose of *People* magazine?

PSYCHE Wait – is it because I'm too fat? Or old? I can change, you know! Fuck, what am I saying? Is that in Ned's script too? *(becomes pale and starts to sag from suspension cord)* I feel funny…

EROS For what it's worth, Psyche, I really did like you.

PSYCHE *(with wavering strength)* Why'd you have to go and be so predictable, then? Following the script…

APHRODITE Tsk tsk. Don't personalize every goddamn little thing, dear. There's only room for one queen bee.

> On the screen behind PSYCHE, we see APHRODITE smilingly don a tiara studded with bees. PSYCHE's body goes limp, and she passes out.

JUDD APATOW And that's a wrap! Now this is what I'm talking about! Fucking queen bee needs to go down! Brilliant work, everyone!

> Lights fade out until only the smiling image of APHRODITE is left. She blows a kiss to the audience and the projection blacks out.

Scene 5

> We open up on a stage, where a spotlight is focused on two chairs. PSYCHE walks onstage and sits down in one of the chairs, while the other remains empty. An applause track is cued. When it subsides, PSYCHE looks out into the audience and begins to speak conversationally.

PSYCHE I don't typically do interviews. Let's face it, I'm not the hot commodity I used to be. But between Ned's play being optioned for the big screen and this new relationship with Eros, it's quite possible the rumor mill's gonna be abuzz in the near future. It's good to be prepared before the onslaught, just in case.

I don't talk about my past much, but I grew up in Grinnell, Iowa.

Population 10,000. It's just a little speck on the map, smack in between the Iowa and Skunk rivers, but people call it the "jewel of the prairie." It was a great place to grow up. Life in the big city isn't always easy. You have traffic jams, crowded sidewalks, people constantly rushing to get somewhere even if they don't really have anywhere to get to. Back home, you could just take your sweet time sniffing the flowers, get all caught up in the beauty of doing absolutely nothing. Life was serene. A constant stream of parades, cheerleader competitions, riverboat rides. I know it's not cool to admit, but I actually liked it. I just didn't realize it at the time. I was one of those kids who always had my head in the clouds – always looking to hitch my wagon to a star. *(PSYCHE pauses to take a sip from a water bottle next to her.)*

So I did what any ambitious young girl does – I got into beauty pageants. When I was 14, I met this guy. I'm not naming any names, but he was a pretty prominent TV producer I met when he was judging the Darling Dolls of Iowa Pageant. I won Miss Congeniality but I wasn't a finalist. He still came up to me after the show. Said he was traveling through the continental U.S. to find the next big thing. An apple-pie-eating, sweet-cheeked teenage girl. America was tired of the endless cavalcade of slutty vixens and their on- and off-screen antics. It wanted something new, something fresh and untouched. In other words: me.

You might not believe it, but I wasn't easy. When I wasn't performing, I was shy and quiet, didn't even date. But I knew a good opportunity when I saw it. And I really thought he liked me. So the next afternoon he takes me out for lunch and we're talking about our mutual love for *The Wonder Years*. Oh, that show took the omniscient voiceover to glorious heights. He says he'd love to do an impromptu audition. Nothing formal, mind you, but it would give him a better idea of where I fit in the large scheme of things.

One thing leads to another, and we're making out in my mother's bed. Nobody home. It was… weird. There I was – had never even kissed a boy, and I was naked with some guy I barely knew, who had to be twice my age. I don't know why I didn't stop it. It was like… I was standing outside my body. I tried to tell myself I was doing it for a higher purpose. I mean, I might've been a kid in a small town, but I wasn't naïve. I knew about the casting couch. And if that's what it was gonna take to be a star, well, I wasn't going to pass up the chance of a lifetime.

He calls the next day, says he's leaving to judge another pageant, somewhere in Wisconsin. And I'm like, "Well, so what next? Should I come out to L.A. in a few weeks to do an audition for real?"

And he's giving me the run-around. "Oh, I have a ton of appointments."

Finally, I get him to come straight out with it. He tells me, "Look, we had a fun time, but there are millions of pretty girls just like you who would give an arm and an ass to make it. The chances of succeeding in show business are already so slim – and frankly, I don't see what makes you so special."

I get quiet, act like I get it. No sweat off my back. Even though I'm screaming inside. All he can say is, "Better luck next time, kid. And thank you for being so mature about it."

Yeah. Can you believe that smug prick? "Thank you for being so mature." I felt like a fucking idiot, but what choice did I have but to suck it up and move on? I wasn't gonna give him the satisfaction of knowing what he had taken from me.

Well, nine months later, Stella Marie was born. I mean, I didn't get to name her, but that's what I would have called her. I didn't even get to see her. My mother thought it would change my mind about giving her up. She was probably right. Besides, I was a headstrong girl. Always had my eyes on the prize. I knew that come hell or high water, I was still going to make it.

I don't think about it that much anymore. You win some, you lose some. The sacrifices and successes even out over the years. Of course, I've run into the producer once or twice since I moved out here – you know, the occasional movie premiere or party – but I don't think he really remembers me. If he does, we've never discussed it.

One thing you might've noticed: I don't do infomercials that are parenting-centered. It's too much, even for me. But I don't have any regrets. I mean – what would you have done? Given up the best years of your life, your dreams, for one stupid mistake? No way! When you know who you are, you don't let anything get in the way.

I knew who I was, who I am. I am a star.

> As PSYCHE pronounces these final words, the applause track is cued again. Amid sounds of hooting and hollering, PSYCHE blinks and shades her eyes with one hand, as if the spotlight is too strong for her. The applause reaches a fever pitch and PSYCHE stares weakly out into the audience before the lights fade to darkness.

Scene 6

> The lights come back up. Spotlights spiral across the stage as a hard rock riff blares over the loudspeakers. The audience erupts in applause and catcalls as EROS enters the stage. He has on a tuxedo that is a little too tight and he is holding a microphone.

EROS Ladies and gentlemen, welcome one and all. We have a very special evening for you. Tonight, we will offer a study of sensuality and substance.

We, of course, will be exploring that most valued and misunderstood organ, the vagina. It's long been understood through its utility, whether as a zone for pleasure or as a means of procreation. And though we don't mean to diminish those lofty purposes, we aim to reveal its aesthetic beauty, which rivals that of any of the great works of art.

To find these sterling examples of vaginal splendor, we have scoured the country, from the nightclub denizens of our great cities to the barnyard beauties of this great nation's golden countrysides. We have met with thousands of beautiful women, and have tasted all this country has to offer. Because this is not just a celebration of the vulva. It's an acknowledgement of the American dream, the ability for each of us to define our own destiny, for each of us to be our own private supermen and women. And, tonight, we will allow you to celebrate this wonderful exploration, and meet three very special ladies, one of whom will be awarded *America's Next Top Vagina*.

> *The audience breaks out into applause as the spotlights zigzag across the stage; the rock music is cued and EROS twirls the microphone cord in front of him.*

Now, let's meet the judges. First up, we have Michael Patrick King, the former lead writer for *Sex and the City* and author of the forthcoming book, *Woman, by Men* that seeks to redefine the modern female experience through the lens of a gay man.

> *MICHAEL waves at the crowd. He's a balding middle-aged man with a little purple bowtie and pink cufflinks.*

MICHAEL Thanks, Eros. I'm looking forward to a fabulous competition tonight!

EROS Our next judge hails from New York City. He is one of the world's most respected chefs and has been an avid fan of the vulva since he was 14. Ladies and gentlemen, Tom Colicchio.

TOM Thank you, Eros. Today, I expect to see a spirited, good-natured competition involving beautiful women with lovely vulvas.

EROS Me too, Chef Colicchio. Me too. And our last judge really knows what women want. International sex symbol and star of such films as the *Lethal Weapon* series, Mel Gibson.

MEL Thank you, Eros. I want to say that I am not a monster.

EROS Of course, you're not, Mel. Well, let's keep things moving. I'd like you to extend a round of applause to our first contestant, Lucy Pearl.

> *The rock music is cued and a tall, blonde girl sashays onto the stage.*

She is wearing a tight flannel shirt and Daisy Duke shorts. She has a broad smile plastered onto her face and is blowing kisses into the audience.

Welcome to the stage, Lucy. You have an interesting story. You grew up as the daughter of Pastor Bobby Pearl, who led the Full Gospel Tabernacle Church, an offshoot of Southern Baptists known for their practice of ingesting small amounts of snake venom during communion. What was the general attitude towards the female organ in those circles?

LUCY Well, they weren't very accepting of my gifts. In fact, we weren't allowed to watch television or even possess any mirrors, vanity being an attribute of the devil. In fact, I wasn't even aware of the sexual nature of the vagina until I was 14. My father was arrested for the possession of 42 copperheads, 11 timber rattlesnakes and three cottonmouth water moccasins. I was placed in foster care and eventually adopted by a pair of hyper-hygienic, existential lesbians, who convinced me that God was a fragment of the male imagination and that a woman's greatest asset was a clean vulva.

EROS Wow, that's quite a story, Lucy. It's also important to note that in our regional competition, you were named Miss Congeniality. How did you win that designation?

LUCY It never hurts to butter up the judges.

EROS Without further ado, let's take a look at those assets.

A picture of a vulva appears on the screen behind them.

MICHAEL *(turning blue)* Dear, God. Is that what one looks like? I thought it would be smaller, more streamlined... less messy.

EROS Yes, Michael, that is in fact a vagina.

TOM A fine example, I would say. Notice how the inner lips are in perfect proportion to the outer lips and very gracefully flower out from the clitoral hood, which conceals a rather plump clitoral head. There's a certain symmetry there that is appealing, and there's also possibly just a hint of arousal, a glimpse into the ripeness and power of her vestibular bulbs. The only concern I have is a rather unusually large urethral opening. I worry that when the valves close during the foreplay process, there would be excessive swelling of the capillaries and restriction of the vaginal cavity, prohibiting the intake of particularly large penises.

MEL *(chuckling and addressing LUCY)* Well, there's one way we can test out Tom's little theory, sugar-tits. I got my lethal weapon right here, if you get my drift.

EROS Yes, Mel. I believe we all get your drift. There will be time for questions during our question-and-answer session. Let's bring out our next contestant, Psyche Pendleton.

> *PSYCHE takes the stage. She is dressed conservatively and seems awkward and uncomfortable.*

EROS Psyche, why do you feel that you have America's top vagina?

PSYCHE *(looking tentatively at the ceiling)* I don't know, honestly. I've never given much thought to my vagina until I met you. I've always just thought that it was kinda ordinary.

EROS There is nothing ordinary about your beauty.

PSYCHE Yeah, that's what you keep telling me, Eros. I sometimes wonder if you want me or the image of me.

EROS Speaking of images of you, let's take a look at that vagina of yours.

> *A picture of PSYCHE's vagina flashes on the screen behind them.*

MICHAEL *(making a gagging sound)* Please Jesus, make it stop. That's the most horrific thing I've ever seen.

TOM You know, I hate to say it, but I kind of agree here. The inner lips really overwhelm the entire area, and there's a bluish hue that is hardly attractive. Also, the vaginal opening extends too far down towards the anal area. I suppose, given her age and her sexual history, this shouldn't be surprising. But, honestly, she has no business being on this stage.

MEL Yeah, it's big enough to spot from a mile away.

EROS Let's keep things classy. Tom, can you find any value in this vulva?

TOM Well, I guess if she's not too old, or hasn't completely destroyed her uterus with excessive drug use, she could still produce a child.

> *Mortified, PSYCHE storms off the stage.*

MICHAEL Look who's a little sensitive today.

TOM Yeah, if you can't take the heat –

> *The lights abruptly black out on the side of the stage that the judges are sitting on, and the other side of the stage lights up to reveal PSYCHE, who is lying in bed. She shoots up, gasping in terror.*

PSYCHE What the fuck is going on here????

> *PSYCHE glances at the clock next to her. It's 10 PM. She hurriedly gets out of bed and throws on the clothes lying on the chair next to her.*

Guess I'll sleep when I'm dead.

> *PSYCHE grabs her purse and rushes out of the room. Lights fade to black.*

Scene 7

> *The corner of Sunset and Courtney. PSYCHE is standing, awkwardly, at HESTIA's hot-dog stand, a movable cart in the shape of a giant, grinning hot dog. HESTIA is cheerfully feeding a small army of scrappy-looking cats but notices that she has a customer.*

HESTIA I'm actually closing up now. Oh, it's you! I had a feeling we'd meet again – my spidey sense's been tingling for a few days. What brings you to my neck of the woods, dear?

PSYCHE I was just in the neighborhood… Actually, I'm lying. I remembered that you worked here, so I came to see you.

HESTIA How pleasant! But would you mind waiting just a moment so I can feed my platoon of stray cats?

PSYCHE *(jokingly)* You're a crazy cat lady. On top of the whole former nun with a hot-dog stand thing, I should've figured.

HESTIA They've been such a help when it comes to warding off the occasional foul-mouthed teenager or woozy hobo. I give away at least 50 free weenies a day, without so much as a thank-you. I'm more than happy to be generous, but I'm also trying to make ends meet here, let's be frank – pun intended! *(laughs)* Speaking of which, I have a joke for you. What did the Buddhist say to the old lady at the hot-dog stand?

PSYCHE I have no idea.

HESTIA "Make me one with everything!" *(laughs)* I thought you might appreciate it – I remember reading somewhere that you're a Buddhist. *(notices PSYCHE's harried appearance and the dark circles under her eyes)* You look as hungry as a church mouse! What can I get for you? We have the Santa Fe Bird Dog – with turkey, red peppers, and cilantro; the Louisiana Hot Link; the German Bratwurst; or if you prefer, the Veggie with wheat gluten and soy protein.

PSYCHE Uh, no thanks. This might sound strange, but I just wanted to ask you – why are you so goddamn happy?

> *HESTIA looks confused and PSYCHE grimaces with embarrassment.*

PSYCHE Shit, I didn't mean for it to come out that way. It's just… whenever I see you, you're all bright-eyed and bushy-tailed, and I can't understand why! I mean, no offense, but... you're old, as far as I can tell you're alone, you work at a hot-dog stand on one of the skankiest corners of the Strip, and...

HESTIA I'm ugly – no need to hold back, dear.

PSYCHE Let's just say you're a bit of a novelty. See, I know plenty of beautiful people, but they're all cut from the same cloth: international playboys in sex addiction rehab, spoiled rich girls on suicide watch, you name it. Everything they have has been handed to them on a silver platter, but they still walk around with storm clouds over their heads. Then there's you – you have every reason in the world to hate your life, but you don't. What's your secret?

HESTIA Oh, such a large question! How much time do you have?

PSYCHE You must think I'm bonkers. You'd probably be right. I'm just having a rough week. I broke up with my boyfriend a few days ago, then I started dating a new man – Dr. *(tries to pronounce EROS' last name but thinks better of it)* Eros, from the clinic.

HESTIA That's too bad about your other gentleman, but Dr. Theotokópoulos is quite the ladykiller. You make a delightful pair!

PSYCHE Well, that's the thing. I was happy... at first. Oh, I don't know – maybe I was just caught up in the excitement. I mean, he swept me off my feet in a way no man ever has before. But shortly after I met him, I started to have these dreams.

HESTIA Dreams? What about?

PSYCHE Bees, Judd Apatow, public humiliation, vaginas... Anyway, I don't know what's happening to me, but something's amiss. I can't put my finger on it, but I feel like I've taken a tumble down the rabbit hole.

HESTIA *(sympathetically)* You feel lost.

PSYCHE I'd never be able to explain the thick and thin of it. I'm a terrible person, Hestia. You'd hate me if you knew about what I've done, just for a cheap shot at fame. All the things, the people I've sacrificed to get here...

HESTIA Dear me, the one complaint I have about the catechisms is that they don't preach the value of forgiveness. No wonder so many people are recovering Catholics. Look, I may not be a sinner but I'm not exactly a saint, so please don't expect a tongue-lashing from me, of all people.

Let me tell you something. Ever since I was a young girl, I had always been moved by the mystics, like St. Teresa of Avila or St. John of the Cross – their unadulterated, crystal-clear desire for God. But when I was a nun, my contemplative practice never ended in a big mystical revelation. I couldn't understand why my spiritual journey wasn't progressing as it should. As devout as I was, my life was flat and ordinary for years. My favorite Mother Superior, a radiant woman with snow-white hair and joy that beamed from her like daffodils shining after a long winter, told me something one day. She held my face in her hands and said, "Why not simply be yourself? That is all God wants, has ever wanted, from you." I never had any grand visions after that, but I always remembered the Mother Superior's words – they're what gave me the strength to leave the Church after 50 years of service. By simply letting myself be me – warts and all – I found the keys to my freedom.

PSYCHE "Be yourself"? Sorry, Sister, that's a cliché that's easier said than done. I don't even know who I am half the time.

HESTIA I don't believe that one bit, dear. Perhaps you were playing a role on your TV shows, but your spunk, your spirit, your willingness to reveal your soul to the world – these are all a part of you. Of course, I've heard that it's a cruel business – I know plenty of people who came here wanting to be one thing, but Hollywood turned them into another. Chewed them up and spit them out. Some of them walk these very streets, forced to do unthinkable things, hardly sentient, zapped of everything that made them lovely and vital to begin with.

PSYCHE Hell-A is the land of walking zombies.

HESTIA Chalk it up to the foolishness of an old woman, but I still believe dreams can come true here. I see random acts of kindness every day – gestures so simple they often go unseen. These ordinary moments give me hope, and I wouldn't trade them for a million dollars. What was it the Mother Superior used to tell me? "Every path has its puddle. And a weed is no more than a flower in disguise." Or something like that. You must simply learn to love yourself.

PSYCHE Love… is shit.

HESTIA Bless my bloomers, dear! That's absolutely right. Love is the most potent shit there is. All things grow because of it.

PSYCHE So what should I do now?

HESTIA Go home, draw yourself a bath. Then sit back and simply listen. I promise – the answers will make themselves apparent.

PSYCHE Thanks, I think I'll try that. I need to get going now but… *(shyly)* do you mind if I come back to talk – you know, every now and then?

HESTIA I would love that. Hopefully, you'll bring your appetite next time!

> *PSYCHE smiles and turns to leave.*

One more thing, Psyche! *(PSYCHE turns around)* There is no time like the present, so whatever you decide to do… don't put it off.

> *PSYCHE doesn't know how to respond to this, so she nods and departs, leaving HESTIA to cheerfully attend to her hungry stray cats. Lights fade to black.*

Scene 8

> *PSYCHE is in her living room, sitting on her couch and listening to doleful opera music. She is wearing a robe and her still-wet hair is piled on top of her head in a turban. Her face is scrubbed bare of makeup and her eyes are red, as if she has been crying. She picks up the phone and dials a number. We hear the phone on the other end ringing for a while, and then it goes straight to voicemail.*

PSYCHE Ned, I've been thinking about things. What I did – seeing Eros behind your back – was really terrible of me. You were also right – it was never your responsibility to make me happy. I guess I lost touch with who I was over the years. Things just got so complicated after a while, and I know I let my insecurities overshadow our relationship. I'm not defending that behavior at all. But in a place where everything is disposable, it's hard not to think of yourself the same way. I hope you understand. Anyway, I wish you all the success in the world. And even if things didn't work out between us, I will always be here for you, as your friend. Bye.

> *PSYCHE hangs up and leans back against the couch. She closes her eyes and opens them when she feels a hand on her shoulder. She turns around and sees APHRODITE standing there, wearing a simple white gown, a smile on her face. Fresh-faced and barefooted, APHRODITE looks more like a young girl than a goddess. PSYCHE smiles back at her and faces forward, reaching back to place her hand over APHRODITE's.*

Hello.

APHRODITE Hi yourself.

PSYCHE I'm not dreaming this time, am I?

APHRODITE No, not this time.

PSYCHE Thank goodness. I was beginning to question my sanity for a while there… So, I've been doing some research on you. Is it true that you're actually two different goddesses? Carnal love on one side, true love on the other?

APHRODITE Not exactly. It's more like... two sides of a coin, or a comedy/tragedy mask. But duality is for humans. Gods are complicated.

PSYCHE Really? You don't seem that complicated. In most of the myths, you're a mega-bitch.

APHRODITE Yeah, well, most of the myths were written by misogynistic prats. Female complexity wasn't something that took up much bandwidth in the olden days.

PSYCHE So why did you start visiting me in the first place?

APHRODITE I hear the cries of all my children. All the poor souls longing to discover the source of their passion, to find true love and rapture. Your call was just a wee bit louder than the rest.

PSYCHE You couldn't have sent me the message in a nicer package?

APHRODITE Kind words and a pat on the back don't make humans change. In your case, nothing less than the sky falling would have burst that bubble of complacency you've been hiding in.

PSYCHE I've been so stupid, so blind.

APHRODITE Psyche, you weren't stupid, just willful. There's a difference. And there'd be no myths and dreams without willful mortals, would there?

PSYCHE Myths? If I'm part of one, I feel like I'm in the Tartarus of the world: Hollywood, where your dreams go to die.

APHRODITE I can't believe I'm saying this, but you remind me of myself when I was young. I was selfish and immature, easily disheartened by my mistakes, and I put far too much stock in other people's opinions.

PSYCHE This is supposed to make me feel better?

APHRODITE Maybe you already know this, but back in the day I was married to the god Hephaestus. He was madly in love with me, but I found him frightfully ugly and dull. I had many lovers while we were married, but the god of war, Ares, was my favorite. Who doesn't love a bad boy? One day, when Hephaestus was out, Ares came over. Little did I know that Heffy was tired of playing the cuckold. He was a fine craftsman, and he'd been working on an invisible net made of the most delicate silver threads. While Ares and I were making love, Heffy burst into our bedroom and dropped the net over us. We were caught in flagrante delicto. It was horrible!
Heffy called all the gods and goddesses in to witness our shame. I was so humiliated! It took me centuries to even show my face on Olympus. And longer than that to realize how much I'd hurt poor Heffy.

PSYCHE *(thoughtfully)* That reminds me of when I caught Max and

Tyrone in the barbecue pit.

APHRODITE Hey, even reality TV has its unconscious source in the myths.

PSYCHE I just don't understand why love and life can't be more simple.

APHRODITE There is nothing simple about love! Ask Paris and Helen. Aeneas and Dido. My beloved Adonis. Or my ex-husband. Bottom line – even the gods have to work at love.

PSYCHE But I have worked at it! I've done nothing but work for it all my life!

APHRODITE No, you don't get it, Psyche. Neither love nor beauty are objects to be manufactured or owned or controlled. You must allow them to purify and transform you. You can't fake the real thing or find it in the arms of a handsome man or some cosmetic injectable. Most people in your world only experience the shadow sides of love and beauty, and they believe that's all there is.

PSYCHE Wow, that's deep.

APHRODITE Well, I am a divine being.

PSYCHE So what do I do?

APHRODITE You already know what you have to do.

PSYCHE My job? And Eros?

APHRODITE Only you can decide if they're worth it.

PSYCHE I thought when I met Eros that I'd finally found the real thing. But I just don't know anymore.

APHRODITE What do you want more than anything, Psyche?

PSYCHE What do I want? I guess…

APHRODITE You don't know.

PSYCHE *(somewhat irritated)* Yes I do!

APHRODITE You can fool yourself, dear, but you can't fool a goddess.

PSYCHE Well, maybe you're right. I don't know what it is I want, but I just… I just want it to be real.

APHRODITE Easy. Now, close your eyes.

> *PSYCHE closes her eyes, and APHRODITE places her hands over PSYCHE's face. Lights fade to black.*

Scene 9

> *We open on an infomercial. PSYCHE and EROS are sitting on a sterile-looking talk-show-style set as makeup assistants powder and buff their faces to ready them for the shoot. Both of them are dressed in business formal attire. PSYCHE's face is caked with makeup already, but the woman who is working on her continues to apply more and more concealer to her face. EROS looks concerned as he stares wordlessly at PSYCHE, but she is intentionally avoiding eye contact.*

EROS What's going on? If I weren't so assured of my charms, I might accuse you of avoiding me.

PSYCHE *(absent-mindedly)* Oh, I'm sorry. I've been... catching up on my z's.

MAKEUP PERSON 1 *(irritated)* Hold still, please, miss. You have a couple age spots I'm trying to cover up.

MAKEUP PERSON 2 *(sympathetic, to MAKEUP PERSON 1)* Bells and whistles ain't working, eh? You know what I say to that? Permanent makeup.

MAKEUP PERSON 1 Tell me about it. Working on mature skin is such a bear.

EROS I had tickets to the opera a couple days ago. *La Traviata.* You said it was your favorite so I thought I'd surprise you. I must have called you a dozen times, but you didn't pick up.

PSYCHE *(dreamily)* Did you know "La Traviata" literally translates to "The Fallen Woman"?

EROS What?

PSYCHE Eros, can we please talk about this later? I like my quiet time before the cameras roll. Too much conversation puts me out of my element.

EROS Um, yeah. Okay. Maybe after the –

CAMERAMAN And we're ready in 3, 2, 1.

> *The stage lights brighten and PSYCHE puts on a bright, if forced, smile. As she speaks, a montage of scenes on a monitor behind her plays out. All of the clips are of EROS – he cuts an impressive, dashing figure. The clips range from EROS chatting conversationally with hoards of smiling, grateful-looking people in third-world rural villages; to poring studiously over anatomical diagrams; to gesticulating wildly as he speaks before rapt audiences at black-tie*

awards ceremonies; to holding the hands of emotional women as they are wheeled out of operating rooms with tears of happiness pouring down their faces.

PSYCHE Ladies, I have news for you, news that will revolutionize the way we look at the female body and spirit. World-renowned plastic surgeon, Dr. Eros Theotokópoulos, is giving women from around the world – from the habitués of Tinseltown to the tribal villagers of sub-Saharan Africa – a chance at improving what Mother Nature gave them.

With his revolutionary new techniques in laser vaginal rejuvenation, you can do everything from mitigating the effects of aging and childbearing to restoring the tone of your vagina. Today, we are going to hear straight from one of the most important leaders of women's care. Stay tuned and find out how a new vagina can lead to a new you. *(turns to EROS)* Now, Doctor T., before we go into the details of vaginal surgery, tell us a little about your philosophy.

EROS I believe that optimal health is achievable only when women realize they must have an intimate relationship with themselves before they can be intimate with others. Aside from my expertise, which you've already detailed so marvelously, Psyche, I pride myself on combining Eastern spiritual principles with my Western medical education. I think it's important to gain education on all aspects of health that affect the mind-body-spirit connection, and provide services that women of all ages and races and backgrounds can benefit from. This is work that requires both skill and, because we are working with women, intuition.

PSYCHE We'll get into the nitty-gritty of this procedure and, um, some of the misconceptions people may have about vaginal surgery a little later in the segment, but in the meantime, Dr. Theotokópoulos has brought three very special guests along with him.

> *The spotlights focus on three chairs next to EROS. Sitting in them are CHLOE, an attractive and busty redhead; MONA, a prim-looking middle-aged woman; and LAYLA, a college-aged Middle Eastern woman.*

EROS All of these women have experienced firsthand how vaginal surgery can change their lives for the better. But although the procedure is steadily gaining ground, you have to be careful when it comes to finding the right doctor. Mona is a great example of that.

MONA I was 45 when I met Dr. T. and I thought I was ruined for life. I'd already gone to a surgeon who had severely damaged me, cutting off most of my labia, leaving me disfigured and with what I thought was permanent nerve damage. I must have seen well over ten doctors, and Dr. T. was the only one who was even willing to attempt the corrective surgery. I am so glad I found him. Now my labia are as pretty as a hothouse flower.

PSYCHE *(skeptical)* I don't know that I've ever heard a man say, "She's a total catch, but those labia? That's a dealbreaker!"

MONA Well, there are definitely other benefits. It's worked wonders for my constipation. And I don't have to worry about leaking urine when I laugh or sneeze.

PSYCHE All righty, then. We're also seeing a rise in the popularity of laser hymenoplasty – that is, the repair and reconstruction of the hymen for people who wish to return to a "virginal" state. Can you speak about that, Doc? The majority of your clientele in that department are Middle Eastern women, is that right?

EROS Yes. These women are coming in for hymenoplasty because they are ready to be married in their native country. A woman will usually tell me the groom's side of the family can pick whatever doctor they want to determine if she's actually a virgin, and with that, whether she's worthy of being married to their son. So there are religious and social implications, as Layla here can tell you.

LAYLA *(in a heavy Middle Eastern accent)* You can't believe how hysterical I was when I came to see Dr. Eros. Back home, if my brother or my father knew that I wasn't a virgin, I would have been killed.

EROS Now, thanks to my speedy outpatient services, Layla has a new hymen and a new lease on life.

PSYCHE *(sarcastically)* No wonder they call you the Salman Rushdie of the Islamic vagina! According to you, Doctor, the female reproductive system and orgasmic system are so intricately interconnected that you can't touch one without tickling the other. How does this affect women's enjoyment of sex after childbirth?

EROS Well, with society beginning to really embrace women's expectations of sexual satisfaction and happiness, there is a great interest in this field of medicine. Chloe is a classic case. When she came to me, she had already had three children, and her sex life with her husband was subpar. Both of them suspected this had something to do with her last episiotomy – that's the incision that enlarges the vaginal cavity during delivery.

CHLOE I couldn't feel anything during sex. And I knew if I couldn't, he couldn't.

PSYCHE How did that affect your sense of your... womanhood, Chloe?

CHLOE Really, if women knew about this procedure, it would save marriages. Men are men. If a man's going to stray from marriage, it's for sex. Now, my vagina feels like I'm a teenager again. It's, like, back to its original state. When you are giving pleasure to a man, it affects your own sense of sexual gratification. It's not necessarily about having better orgasms. I'm so glad I did it, and my husband – well, let's just say he has nothing to complain about anymore

EROS *(puts a hand on CHLOE's knee, to PSYCHE's chagrin)* Chloe was very easy to work with. She was open and honest. Many women are so embarrassed to ask their gynecologists about vaginal looseness. And I learned so much from her, because – and most people don't realize this – most doctors are uncomfortable asking their patients about those same issues. As a result, all of us suffer from our ignorance.

CHLOE The thing about Dr. T? He's so compassionate. He probably sees, like, thousands of women a year, but you really feel special, taken care of, when he's working on you – like you're the only thing on his mind.

PSYCHE *(coldly)* Is that so? I can see why you earned the nickname Doctor Love.

EROS *(flustered)* Well, I…

PSYCHE Doctor, how do you respond to the assertion that while you say you want to liberate women from the shackles of a man's world, you're selling them what could be one of the most oppressive forms of sex and beauty fascism?

> *The guests murmur to each other, and CYTHEREA gestures angrily off camera, trying to get PSYCHE's attention. EROS, thrown off, hesitates before answering.*

EROS What I have to remind people about is that this procedure is so seldom about wanting the perfect vagina. It's more like, "Doc, I ride my bike five miles a day and it hurts," or "I can't wear tight pants." Not one of those patients has been vain.

CHLOE Of course, having it be pretty down there is an added bonus. I even brought pictures to my surgery – you know, from magazines.

EROS Aesthetic needs aren't our top priority, but we aim to satisfy all our clientele.

PSYCHE Considering that the clitoris is the sexual ground zero for women, I'm surprised you don't have more clients coming in and demanding a fully functioning love button.

EROS Pardon me?

PSYCHE Forgive me, doctor, but for the last 72 hours, all I've been hearing is "vaginas this," "labias that." It's enough to drive a semi-functional, if somewhat neurotic, modern woman insane! The way all of you are talking, you'd think that women are walking around with full-size elephant ears dangling between their legs! What's next? Crafting parts that look like a plastic-fantastic replica of Barbie's flattened cooch???

EROS Um, I, uh –

CAMERAMAN *(to CYTHEREA)* Is this intentional? Like, flipping the script or something?

CYTHEREA I don't know what's gotten into her!

PSYCHE Look, it's no secret that I've always been ambivalent about your line of work, Eros, and I just thought I should come out with it before we get to the before and after photos. Honestly, I think it would be nice if your patients remembered their priorities. Is a new hoo-ha for the holidays really what we've come to? *(to LAYLA)* I don't know what to say about your situation except… it sucks and I'm sorry… but the majority of women in the world don't need to be told that we're too fat, too ugly, too disproportionate. A vulva is like a snowflake – there are no two alike, and by golly, we should be happy for it!

EROS *(at a loss)* Yes, of course, that's what I'm trying to –

PSYCHE Are we going to let other people kowtow us into submission and sameness? When are we going to stand up and tell the world, "Enough is enough"???

CYTHEREA Cut! Take ten, everybody! We'll regroup shortly.

> *The crew is now in a state of confusion. The CAMERAMAN, befuddled, looks askance at a swearing CYTHEREA. The women sitting next to EROS onstage talk impatiently among themselves.*

CHLOE Typecasting blows.

LAYLA *(all traces of Middle Eastern accent gone)* The shit I get callbacks for would make Rush Limbaugh look like a pussycat.

MONA Got a cigarette I can bum? *(glares at PSYCHE)* Looks like we're gonna be here a while.

PSYCHE *(to EROS)* These women weren't your real patients?

EROS No, of course not. I work assiduously to protect the privacy of my patients. But all of the actresses' accounts are based on true stories!

PSYCHE I should have known. I've gotta get out of here.

EROS Psyche, wait!

> *PSYCHE makes a break for the exit door, but CYTHEREA roughly grabs her arm.*

CYTHEREA Just what the hell were you playing at up there, Psyche? This is no time for reality TV improv! Our heads are on the fucking chopping block! Where do you think you're going?

PSYCHE I'm getting some fresh air.

CYTHEREA Like hell! We have some very important sponsors backing this project and there is no way I'm letting some spoiled little tart derail the gravy train!

PSYCHE No, Cytherea, this is the end of the road for me. Honestly, I never meant to disappoint you, but I just can't pretend anymore.

CYTHEREA Listen to me, you little bitch, if you walk out that door, don't expect to ever show your face in this city again. I'm fucking serious – with your lack of talent and shitty work ethic, you will be blackballed in Hollywood for good.

PSYCHE She'll forgive you, Cytherea.

> *PSYCHE kisses CYTHEREA on the lips and walks toward the door.*

CYTHEREA Have you gone mad? You are one sick fucking biscuit!

PSYCHE No, I think I finally snapped out of it.

> *PSYCHE walks out. Lights fade to black.*

Scene 10

> *We open on PSYCHE sprinting through the lobby of the production studio, heading toward the exit. She looks dazed and elated all at once. EROS comes running after her, concerned and screaming her name.*

EROS Psyche, wait, come back! What the hell was that all about? And more importantly, are you okay?

PSYCHE Actually, I'm fine, Eros. Better than fine.

EROS You were so worked up back there. Do you want to talk?

PSYCHE No, it comes with the territory. Trust me, even that outburst was calculated. I've always known television was artificial. I mean, obviously, ever since that blowout on *Psyche Getting Married*?

EROS Sorry, I didn't watch the whole series. What happened?

PSYCHE When I found my fiancé Max having sex with my best friend Tyrone, the ratings went through the roof. That's also when I decided to quit reality TV for good, turn my attention to bigger and better things. I was known as the girl who broke reality TV. I was everywhere – *Time* magazine, the *Oprah* show, you name it. Sure, bursting out of that persona impressed some people for a while, even made me a heroine of sorts. But it didn't last. I was flushed down the toilet. People shut their doors on me and it was on to the next flash in the pan. *The Hills, Jon and Kate*… it's like I was being punished for trying to be real for once in my life. But honestly, Eros? I didn't want to give up that fantasy. So I found myself peddling yet another fantasy. Out of desperation, I went from fake to faker.

EROS Psyche… I don't know about all that, but I do know that what you and I had, it didn't feel fake. Did it?

PSYCHE I don't know anymore. I don't know where the person I am on the set ends and the person I am when I'm just being me begins. It's like I've lost myself. I can't fully explain what I'm trying to say. But this, us – how could it possibly work? We're the stuff tabloid roadkill is made of. Former reality star meets Hollywood's most eligible plastic surgeon. Sparks fly, private parts get a makeover. I'm sorry, I don't want to continue being a laughingstock.

EROS But that isn't us. We don't have to be that couple.

PSYCHE You don't get it, Eros. I can't be part of that world, your world, anymore. That isn't to knock what you're doing. I mean, half the people in this town believe that all that glitters is gold. Life is hard enough as it is; maybe we need people like you to keep that dream alive. But I'm not cut out for it anymore.

EROS The lone dissenter… So what will you do now?

PSYCHE I have no idea. I built my life on a house of cards. Now that it's come tumbling down around me, I don't know what's left. But that's okay. I've always been good at reinventing myself. Maybe I'll try my hand at being normal this time.

EROS No, Psyche, you could never be normal.

PSYCHE I don't think it would be such a terrible thing. I mean, for years, the more I stood out, the more people told me I was special. It makes me think of that one girl on MTV who got 14 different plastic surgeries because she never felt pretty. Now she has Double E breasts and it hurts when she runs or hugs people. Can you imagine that? She was pretty before she became a star. She had people who cared about and loved her – God knows that's more than most of us have. But it was never good enough. If that's the price of standing out, I don't know if it's worth it anymore.

EROS You don't think there was a reason we met each other?

PSYCHE It's a sweet thought, Eros. But I don't believe in destiny.

EROS *(looks back towards the studio)* Shit, I need to get back in there. I'm sure they're wondering where I am.

PSYCHE *(smiles sadly)* Of course you do. They need you in there.

EROS Can I… can I call you sometime?

PSYCHE I don't think so, Eros. But I'll let you know if that changes.

EROS Okay. *(turns to leave but thinks better of it)* Psyche? One more thing. Please don't ever think of changing your vagina. It's kind of perfect the way it is.

PSYCHE That would be a very sweet sentiment if it weren't so creepy. Goodbye, Eros.

EROS Goodbye, Psyche.

> *He reaches for PSYCHE, presumably to embrace her. She turns away. He pauses awkwardly and exits. PSYCHE looks after him for a long moment, then picks up her phone and dials a number.*

PSYCHE Aletheia, I have had the craziest week of my life. We need to talk. By the way, I'm firing you as my shrink. I want my best friend back, judgmental bitch and all. Call me later. If I don't pick up my phone in the next 20 minutes, meet me at the corner of Sunset and Courtney. I'm heading over to Rabid Dawg to get myself a nice big weenie.

> *PSYCHE hangs up and heads towards the exit. She passes a mirrored wall, where she glances at her reflection, which gives her pause. Her hair is a mess and her makeup has cracks in it, but she still grins at her reflection – with effort at first, and gradually with genuine feeling. Slowly, the image of a smiling APHRODITE appears alongside PSYCHE's reflection. PSYCHE gazes gratefully at it, knowing that it will be last time she will see that face. PSYCHE takes one final look around her before strolling to the door and exiting. Fade to black.*

> *The end.*

Hermes

by Bennett Fisher

Hermes

For my father

Hermes was originally presented in a reading at EXIT Stage Left in San Francisco, California on July 15, 2010 as part of the San Francisco Olympians Festival. The reading was directed by Bennett Fisher with the following cast:

Hestia	Lauren Spencer
Anne	Juliana Egley
Jack	Vijay Vachani
Brian	Charles Lewis III
Gil	Carl Lucania
Hermes	Sam Leichter
Stage Directions	Catherine Lardas

Hermes premiered as a full production on March 3, 2011 at EXIT Stage Left in San Francisco, California, produced by No Nude Men Productions with the following cast and crew:

Hestia	Lauren Spencer
Anne	Juliana Egley
Jack	Geoffrey Nolan
Brian	Brian Markley
Gil	Carl Lucania
Hermes	Brian Trybom
Director	Tore Ingersoll-Thorp
Producer	Stuart Bousel
Set Design	Tanya Orellena
Lighting	Alejandro Acosta
Sound	Colin Trevor
Video	Aubrey Millen
Stage Manager	Seanan Palmero

Characters

HESTIA, goddess of the hearth. Ageless.
ANNE, a derivatives trader. 40s.
JACK, a derivatives trader. Early 20s.
BRIAN, a derivatives trader. 40s.
GIL, a derivatives trader. 50s.
HERMES, god of commerce and trickery. Ageless.

The play is inspired in part by the role American companies played in the Greek financial meltdown of the late 2000s. Any similarity to real persons or events is entirely intentional.

The set should be simple and spare: an airport waiting area and an airport bar. Scenery may shift from scene to scene, but it's not necessary. Wherever the characters are, it's more or less the same space – the anonymous space between where you are going and where you came from.

The market is the seventh character in the play and should be present physically in some way. In the original production, there were television screens onstage with graphs showing minute-to-minute changes in the stock market. The values rose and fell throughout the play in correspondence to what was happening onstage. This is not the only way to manifest the market. If television screens are not available, for example, the market may be presented using radio announcements punctuated between the scenes.

Act 1

Scene 1

Lights rise on HESTIA, alone.

HESTIA The god came back. Shortly afterwards, the world ended. It wasn't the god most people expected. It wasn't the end most people expected either. But you must know what I'm talking about. The signs of his return are everywhere.

The world is like a hearth, a crucible where fact burns into myth, where a myth fuels a misconception so powerfully that it creates a spark. In this world, in this myth, the spark set a fire that burned more violently than intended.

And, then…

HESTIA takes out a martini shaker. She takes off the lid and shows the contents to the audience. It is filled with ashes. Delicately, she pours the ashes onto the stage in a little pile.

This is all that remains…

She looks for a moment at the ashes.

The god came back and the world ended. Those are the facts. That is the myth. No one can question it.

You want to know the truth of the story, but truth has very little place in the realm of finance, and even less in the realm of the gods. Still, like all myths, there's something to search for. An explanation.

Look closely. Even in these meager ashes, there are a few telltale signs. Let's start with most identifiable, since it's one of the largest. A continent: Europe.

> As HESTIA speaks, ANNE, BRIAN, JACK, and GIL enter, dressed in business suits. They check their watches, passports, boarding passes. They do not hear her.

ANNE Do you want to know why I'm smarter than you, Brian?

BRIAN No.

ANNE Forecasting. When you wanted to cozy up to Asia and Latin America, I said no. I said we should reach out to those socialist dinosaurs in their small, dismal, drizzly little countries because, when they need us…

BRIAN and ANNE …they will really need us.

GIL And so they do.

ANNE And so they do. Passports, boarding passes?

JACK Yeah.

GIL Yup.

BRIAN Yeah. Anyone want a drink?

GIL It's 11 AM.

BRIAN It's the *airport*.

GIL It's 11 AM in the airport.

BRIAN You should not be pointing fingers after the holiday party. (*to JACK*) Were you there for the holiday party?

JACK No.

GIL I was sober in the office on Monday. You'll be a moron forever.

BRIAN Fuck you, Gil.

ANNE Stop it. (*to BRIAN*) Get a drink on the plane.

HESTIA There are other continents in the ashes as well. And then smaller things. Cities, airports, banks, office buildings, conference rooms. Look closely and you'll see a firm specializing in not-entirely-transparent derivative trading, a truly massive amount of capital, collected from a phalanx of hedge funds and other private accounts. Look even more closely and you'll see three men, one woman, a complex formula for evaluating risk, a series of market forecasts, and a growing interest in the financial stability of a small country in the Mediterranean.

GIL So, Anne, when we talk to these guys, what's the party line? "Big Bird"?

JACK "Big Bird"?

GIL Friendship pitch. Large, cuddly, safe. Sell them on character, not what's being sold.

BRIAN No. Not "Big Bird." "Chicken Little."

GIL (*to JACK*) Sky is falling.

JACK Yeah, I get it.

ANNE "*Chicklet* Little," maybe. Tone it down.

BRIAN They're already spooked, let's keep them spooked. If they're spooked, they'll sell.

ANNE I'm telling you, tone it down. We need the bailout.

BRIAN Bailout's a certainty.

ANNE Nothing is certain.

BRIAN When the EU members look at the cost of a bailout and compare it with how inflated the euro would be if they let the Greeks default on their debts, they are going to choose the cheaper option.

GIL If that's actually the case.

BRIAN It will be.

JACK Cheaper?

BRIAN Yes.

GIL No. If it's actually the case that someone is calculating relative costs. That it is a measured, rational decision informed by an intelligent market forecast.

BRIAN It will be.

GIL Wouldn't bet on it.

ANNE Well, we are betting. I want to be smart and I want us to be decisive. We have a short window, after they start to worry but before they do the math –

GIL Assuming they do.

JACK Won't they?

BRIAN They will.

ANNE Gentlemen, that really doesn't concern us. Our betters have developed the formula. Our betters have applied the formula. Our betters have given us our criteria. We're here to chat them up, talk the price down, check items off the shopping list. It's just a matter of striking the right tone. Sobering, but not alarmist.

BRIAN All we need is one person to sell. The others will see it, they'll panic, they'll sell too.

ANNE We don't want anyone to panic. We just want them a little unsettled. The line is, "It's not a lost cause, far from it, but we're here to help you *minimize your risk*. It's not "Chicken Little," it's "Slim-Fast."

JACK "Slim-Fast"?

ANNE We are helping them get healthy, drop some extra debt that they don't need. That's the line. Got me?

GIL Right.

JACK Yes ma'am.

ANNE Brian?

BRIAN Yeah, sure.

ANNE Good. (*beat*) I would like to take a moment to impress upon each of you the true scope of our little expedition. Our betters have taken great pains developing the formula, establishing these contacts, and acquiring this capital. They are expecting a significant return. Let's not disappoint them.

The four begin to leave. JACK stops GIL.

JACK Gil?

GIL Yeah?

JACK How, how exactly…

GIL Don't worry, Jack. You're not expected to say anything in the meetings.

JACK No, it's not that. I was just… How do we even have access to these people?

GIL What people?

JACK The ones we're meeting with. In Europe.

GIL Oh.

Short pause.

JACK It just seems –

GIL I know. How to put this… You have an inquiring mind, Jack. It's an admirable quality. In some instances, however, a certain level of ignorance allows one to be indemnified against possible negative consequences… (*beat*) There's a lot of money rolling around. Don't want to get smushed.

Scene 2

The noise of a plane engine. Lights shift. Time and space shift. Lights lower to focus around HESTIA and the pile of ashes as she addresses the audience. It is a secret.

HESTIA It seems appropriate that these traffickers in debt would be the harbingers of the god. Debt and gods are similar. Both are substitutes for more tangible assets. Both require absolute faith in what cannot be seen. If you looked at these ashes for long enough, you might see the myth of men first substituting something you could hold for a number. But for now, look for something else. Smaller and smaller objects.

HESTIA looks at the ashes.

An espresso spoon. A folded napkin. A sign-in ledger at a federal office complex with a name written in ballpoint pen. A business card with an amount written on the back. Evidence of meetings with undersecretaries, under-undersecretaries, mid- and low-level bureaucrats. Little people holding the keys to big money. You would not think much of the names, but you might think again if you knew how much they could sell off. And how little approval they needed.

HESTIA fades. Three spotlights rise on ANNE, GIL, and BRIAN. They are in many places at once – offices, cafes, hotel lobbies, airport lounges – all across Western Europe. A dozen or more private meetings. The three are good. Confident, charming, assertive. Each move has been rehearsed and refined. They speak in unison. They move as a chorus, perhaps in a very Greek way, with strophes and antistrophes, dance-like movement, etc. JACK stands aside, just out of the light, observing.

ANNE Mr. Thompson?

GIL Mr. Dreyfus?

BRIAN Mr. Lang?

ANNE Mr. Piret?

GIL Mr. De Vries?

BRIAN Mr. Lopez?

ANNE Mr. Azocar?

GIL Mr. Richardson?

BRIAN Mr. Furbusher?

ANNE Mr. Wilkes?

GIL Mr. Scudder?

BRIAN Am I pronouncing that right? Furbusher?

ANNE, GIL, and BRIAN (*unison*) I know you're a busy man, so I'll get to the point. As you are undoubtedly aware, the situation in Greece is rapidly worsening. In spite of the continuing discussion, the possibility of a comprehensive bailout that can effectively combat the scope of the problem is far from forthcoming. It may not be enough, and it may not get here in time to prevent all of the loss. You know how this works, and so do we. We must all be prepared for the very real possibility that the Greeks will default on their debts, or, at the very least, that payment may not come in full and on schedule. Your government has a substantial stake in a very volatile market. Holding on to it is dangerous; selling it openly might cause a crisis of confidence. You cannot risk either of these possible outcomes, but we are in a position to help minimize your risk.

> *Collective, short pause. This too is rehearsed.*

(*unison*) I understand that it is frustrating to sell the debt owed to you at a loss, but I encourage you to consider the likely alternatives. Watching your potential profits disappear as the value of the euro plummets. Endless litigation in international courts. Late payments, countless postponements, or… nothing. These problems are significant in and of themselves, to say nothing of what they might portend for the next round of elections. You don't need that kind of exposure. Let us wrestle with the uncertainty.

> *All three extend their hands.*

Scene 3

> *Lights shift. Time and space shift. A club. Low, throbbing, Euro-pop music under a perpetual rumble of conversation. A frenzy of colored lights. HESTIA is now the bartender. She prepares four glistening drinks in four shot glasses. ANNE, GIL, BRIAN, and JACK stand near the bar. They are celebrating.*

ANNE I need more shots!

BRIAN Last time I was here the dollar was so goddamn weak. Now that the euro's tanked, it's fucking awesome. I'll probably have twice as many drinks tonight, still pay less.

ANNE To Brian!

ALL To Brian!

They drink.

ANNE Who fucking killed it today with the undersecretary.

BRIAN Fish in a barrel. Bam!

ANNE That was unbelievable today, Brian. Truly unbelievable.

BRIAN Thank you.

GIL It's just too bad it's all junk.

JACK Is it?

GIL Absolutely.

ANNE Gil!

GIL No, look, I don't mean it like that. What I got last week was junk. Look, it's *all* junk, all of it, until it's not junk. (*to HESTIA*) Another.

HESTIA pours four more shots. The four raise their glasses.

ANNE To the bailout!

ALL The bailout!

They drink.

BRIAN Look, I'll take junk over whatever else you got any day of the week. Junk's cheaper. Lower cost, greater profits. Watch how much I net from today. Tomorrow, when I do it again, watch how much I net. Let's do another.

ANNE Hell yes.

GIL I don't know.

ANNE (*to GIL*) Pussy. (*to JACK*) Jack?

JACK Sure.

ANNE One more. You're doing it, Gil.

GIL Fine.

HESTIA pours another round of shots.

BRIAN Right. To junk!

ALL Junk!

They drink again. GIL starts to look sick.

ANNE Shit. Hey Gil, Gil…

BRIAN Speaking of bailout.

ANNE and GIL exit.

He is in for a long trip. I am going out like this every time I have a day like today, and I am going to have a lot more days like today. We're just getting rolling on it, man. You better believe. We haven't even seen the real money yet.

JACK Yeah?

BRIAN Hell yeah. Do you have any conception of how much capital we have at our disposal for this little enterprise? It's insane.

JACK A lot.

BRIAN "A lot"? This is it, man, this is the epitome… we are buying and selling parts of a country, with other countries, with a budget that is comparable to that of most countries. We should have a flag and a fucking national anthem.

JACK Wow.

BRIAN "Wow" is a fucking understatement. This should be chronicled. Sung in ballad form in advanced business school seminars. This happens once in a lifetime. If that. You can just feel it, can't you?

JACK I guess.

BRIAN You totally can! It feels like the nineties, you know? The best part of the nineties. Kind of in reverse with the market but, but the same sense of, I don't know, *possibility* that we had in the nineties. Man, I loved the nineties. Stocks just like… whoosh! You remember the nineties?

JACK I was ten.

BRIAN Fuck me.

JACK Well, not for the whole, you know, but –

BRIAN No, no, I get you. Still. Fuck me. Getting old.

JACK No.

BRIAN Well, this is kind of like the nineties. In reverse. (*beat*) You don't talk much, man.

JACK I thought I wasn't supposed to.

BRIAN Why not?

JACK I'm the new guy. I mean, like you said, I was ten years old in the nineties…

BRIAN You said that. I didn't say that.

JACK Well, yeah, but you know –

BRIAN I didn't know how old you were in the fucking nineties.

JACK I'm just saying I'm inexperienced.

BRIAN So, what, there's a code of silence?

JACK Maybe. I don't know this stuff like you guys.

BRIAN Like what? What don't you know?

JACK The math.

BRIAN The math?

JACK The formula. The formula they've developed.

BRIAN Oh. Well, shit. I don't know the formula.

JACK No?

BRIAN Hell no. Some nerd developed that formula. I just know how to get people to sell.

JACK Huh.

BRIAN Listen, most of the time you only need to understand what it does, not how it works. The formula lets us know what to buy, what's going to make money.

JACK If there's a bailout.

BRIAN What?

JACK If there's a bailout. Anne said if there isn't a bailout we make, won't make any money because it'll just be junk. So what's the difference between the junk the formula tells us to buy and the junk it doesn't? See, I don't understand what the formula's supposed to –

BRIAN starts to laugh.

JACK What?

BRIAN I think you've discovered a flaw in the system, Jack. I think you understand it just fine.

JACK I don't know.

BRIAN Bullshit. You do. You just have to be assertive, OK? I want you to remember that.

JACK OK.

BRIAN How do you think I rocked the negotiation today? Assertiveness. Came in, told the dude, "Listen, you're selling this, this, and this to us for this much." And he sold it. Game. Set. Match.

JACK Huh.

BRIAN You want to get somewhere? You want to impress Anne? Show initiative. Show force.

JACK OK.

BRIAN Force! We're doing another shot!

HESTIA pours another shot for them.

JACK OK!

BRIAN Force!

JACK Force!

They do another shot.

BRIAN Debt is easy. Someone borrows something, they pay it back. Or they don't. Business is easy. You got one price, they have another price, you work it out. Or you don't. Easy as shit.

JACK Yeah.

BRIAN But hard as balls! Hard as balls! Derivatives are hard as *balls*! I mean, how much is a thing worth when it's not a thing? D'you know what I mean? The economy is fucking hard as balls. Nobody gets it.

JACK Yeah.

BRIAN Which means, sonny boy, that you're not missing it either.

Short pause.

You think of something, OK? Think of something, and think to speak up about it. OK?

JACK OK.

BRIAN OK. (*beat*) I'm getting so laid tonight it's not even funny.

The music crescendos. The lights rise to a blinding white.

Scene 4

The lights begin to lower, slowly, brutally, like a hangover. An airport café. HESTIA is behind the counter again. JACK and BRIAN are sipping coffee, in mid-conversation. BRIAN is holding a woman's scarf, turning it over in his hand.

JACK Hermes?

BRIAN No, no.

JACK What then?

BRIAN Er-mezz. It's French.

JACK Greek, I thought.

BRIAN It's French or some shit. Who cares? It's an expensive scarf, and an expensive brand.

BRIAN smells the scarf.

I should mount these on my wall. Like trophy heads.

ANNE enters.

ANNE Gentlemen.

BRIAN Hey.

ANNE *(re: scarf)* What's that?

BRIAN Junk.

BRIAN folds up the scarf, puts it in his pocket.

ANNE You seen Gil?

BRIAN Maybe he's still asleep.

ANNE No, I heard him go out.

BRIAN Ooh.

ANNE Shut up. He's in the room next to mine. You can hear the door.

ANNE sits.

Anyway, I think he's playing for the other team.

BRIAN No.

ANNE Oh yeah.

JACK How'd your meeting go this morning?

ANNE Eager to sell. Wish you had been there, Brian. After what you did with the undersecretary, well…

BRIAN I was indisposed, sorry.

ANNE Forget about it. We got what we needed.

JACK Got what?

ANNE Junk.

BRIAN Hah.

> *Short pause.*

JACK I was thinking…

ANNE Yeah?

JACK I was thinking, I don't know, that maybe in the next meeting I could…

ANNE Take the lead?

JACK Well, maybe not the lead, per se, but…

ANNE We'll talk about it.

> *ANNE looks away. BRIAN mimes to JACK – first shaking his head in disapproval, then making a muscle gesture with his arm. He mouths the word "force."*

JACK I think it would be a good learning experience.

> *BRIAN hits his head with his hand.*

ANNE We'll talk about it.

> *GIL enters.*

ANNE Where have you been?

GIL We need to talk.

ANNE You're late. Where've you been?

GIL On the phone. Short guy. From yesterday. He called this morning.

ANNE Why? To back out?

BRIAN Goddamn it Gil, I told you this "Big Bird" shit –

GIL Shut up, Brian. (*beat*) He called to sell me more. A lot more. Things I don't think we knew about the first time.

> *Short pause.*

ANNE That's not good?

GIL No, it isn't. (*beat*) I tried pressing him a little, and... well... (*beat*) I think negotiations have stopped.

JACK Negotiations for what?

>   *Silence.*

The bailout?

>   *Silence. GIL takes out his BlackBerry, cues up an email, and hands it to ANNE.*

GIL And there's this. Second paragraph. I think it suggests that support is dwindling.

ANNE Dwindling?

GIL Dwindling. Perhaps even dwindled. Past tense.

ANNE Why?

GIL (*pointing to BRIAN*) Talk to him.

>   *Short pause.*

BRIAN Talk to me about what?

GIL My guy said your undersecretary called him.

BRIAN So?

GIL So it sounded like my guy thought your undersecretary's prognosis was a little grim. Which means whatever you –

BRIAN What? I cleaned up. I got a crapload for a song. That's what we wanted, right?

GIL You scared the shit out of him. It scared the shit out of my guy. Scared the shit out of a lot of people.

ANNE Goddamn it, Brian.

BRIAN What? You tell me go get it for cheap, I deliver. Not my problem –

GIL Well, it's your fucking problem now –

BRIAN Fuck you –

ANNE Stop it! What, are you going to fight one another in the food court? Grow up.

>   *Pause. GIL and BRIAN look at the floor.*

BRIAN Listen, Gil. He is not *my* undersecretary. I am not singlehandedly responsible for –

ANNE Oh, give it a rest –

BRIAN No, I'm not going to have you all blaming me. My conversations with the undersecretary don't –

GIL takes his phone from ANNE, thrusts it in BRIAN's face.

GIL Oh yeah? Read that. (*beat*) If you spent half the energy you're using to save your ass on –

BRIAN Listen, here's a thought, if it's happening because of what I'm doing – which I'm not saying it is, because that would be crazy – but *if* it is, maybe it's happening because whole thing was a fucking conceptual nightmare to begin with. Fucking schizophrenic. Scare them so they sell the debt. Don't scare them since we'll derail a bailout negotiation. We're pulling in two entirely opposite directions and you're surprised –

ANNE I told you *tightrope*, Brian. I told you not to –

BRIAN On top of which, we're using a formula which Jack pointed out last night is totally useless if there's no –

GIL Don't blame the formula. It's not because of the formula.

BRIAN You don't know that. You don't even understand the –

GIL It's not because of the formula. It's because of you. Because of you, we're fucked.

BRIAN We're not fucked. It's still early.

GIL My guy says it's over.

BRIAN It's still early. There'll be a bailout, OK? You'll see.

GIL Really? When, Brian? A month? Two months? A year? After all the junk we've accumulated isn't even junk anymore because junk at least has the *potential* to turn into something else? After it's not junk but fucking dust?

BRIAN Lovely, Gil. That's lovely. Wonderfully poetic.

ANNE's phone starts ringing.

ANNE Shit.

JACK Who is it?

ANNE Someone who didn't want to sell four days ago.

BRIAN's phone starts ringing. So does GIL's. BRIAN hands GIL's phone back to him.

Don't answer.

BRIAN I'm not.

> *Pause. The phones continue to ring. The characters do not move. After what seems like an eternity, the phones go silent.*

GIL We should have waited till after the bailout was a sure thing.

BRIAN We wouldn't have gotten anything if we waited.

GIL We also wouldn't have bought a whole shit-ton of worthless crap.

ANNE Gil –

GIL No, that's not even right, because the crap would not have been worthless if *you* hadn't –

ANNE Gil. Take a walk. Cool down.

> *GIL exits.*

We need to think. First, I just, I want to know what we're dealing with. What are we holding now? What's the risk? No bailout, what's the risk?

> *Silence.*

Brian, how much did we buy from the undersecretary?

> *Silence.*

BRIAN What do you want me to say? (*beat*) You should have checked my homework.

> *ANNE looks at BRIAN. She is about to say something. She decides against it. She exits. BRIAN exhales deeply.*

Well, Jack. It was nice knowing you.

JACK It's not your fault, Brian.

BRIAN No, of course not. It's this half-cocked plan. It's that bullshit formula. It's the *Greeks*. Dumb fucks. (*beat*) A country that small should not be allowed to have a meltdown that huge.

> *Short pause. Lights shift. Time and space shift. The warrens of human thought. A moment of inspiration for JACK. HESTIA steps forward.*

HESTIA Debt and gods are similar. Similar, but not the same. Debt is real. A god is not. Well, at least not real in the same way. The debt comes from somewhere, something that was real, tangible, and now is invisible. A god comes from somewhere more complicated.

In the breath that precedes each prayer, in the rush of air before the words of exaltation, the plea for a blessing, there is something else said, now so quietly that only the smallest, subatomic particles are aware of it anymore. It is a question: "Why?"

A man sees the orb of the sun floating in the sky, distant and untouchable, and asks "Why?" He sees the heat it gives off scorching his crops and asks "Why?" He sees his neighbor prosper while his family starves and asks "Why?" There is a desperate, burning need to answer this question, and an unshakable faith that an answer must exist. The man asks "Why?" and then, driven by this thirst, he crawls through a labyrinth of thoughts that are at once both his most brilliant and his most foolish, and he invents the answer.

JACK Shit.

BRIAN What?

HESTIA The god.

Scene 5

Lights shift. Time and space shift. An airport café. HESTIA is behind the counter again. ANNE, GIL, BRIAN, and JACK are sipping coffee. BRIAN is a little to the side, still a pariah. JACK is standing, very animated, in the middle of a presentation of sorts.

JACK What's the problem, really what's the problem?

GIL The problem is the European Union doesn't care that Greece is fucked.

JACK No, no, no really what's the problem? With the bailout.

GIL It's not happening?

ANNE Just say it, Jack.

JACK It costs too much.

Short pause.

ANNE Give the man a prize.

JACK No, no wait. It's important. They're not categorically opposed to the *idea* of a bailout, they just think that this bailout, the proposed bailout –

GIL Whatever that was.

JACK They think it is too expensive. But if it were *less* expensive, no problem.

GIL If you don't know how expensive it was in the first place –

JACK I'm not talking about an actual monetary amount, OK –

GIL This is a waste of time.

JACK It isn't, listen to me –

ANNE Jack, the negotiations are over. And even if they weren't, the EU is not going to let us –

JACK I know, know. See, that's the thing. We don't even need to deal with the EU.

ANNE Then who do we deal with?

JACK Greece.

BRIAN Greece?

JACK Right, Greece. This is what we do. We go to Greece, we meet with all the mid-level finance guys we can in their government, and we say –

Scene 6

Lights shift. Time and space shift. A dozen or more meetings, as before, but also the airport cafe where JACK is making his case.

ANNE Mr. Theodorakis?

GIL Mr. Kanellis?

BRIAN Mr. Zappas?

ANNE Mr. Georgiadis?

GIL Mr. Cosmatos?

BRIAN Mr. Panagiotopolous?

ANNE Mr. Liakos?

GIL Mr. Doukakis?

BRIAN Am I pronouncing that right? Panagiotopolous?

JACK We say to them –

JACK, ANNE, GIL, and BRIAN (*unison*) We are on your side. We've spent a great deal of time, energy, and resources acquiring a significant amount of your debt because we believe we will get a return on our investment. We believe that you will weather this crisis.

GIL (*to JACK*) But we don't believe that anymore.

JACK Doesn't matter, say it anyway.

JACK, ANNE, GIL, and BRIAN (*out and unison, again*) Furthermore, we believe it is in everyone's interest that you do, in fact, weather this crisis. It is a global marketplace, and we are all in this together. Your success is our success.

ANNE (*to JACK*) Nice touch.

JACK Very "Big Bird."

GIL "Big Bird" is good.

ANNE Then what?

JACK, ANNE, GIL, and BRIAN (*out and unison*) The bailout negotiations have been undermined, undermined almost to the point of ending altogether, by the worst kind of isolationist nationalism, by people who don't believe in the European Union or its mission, and by a few corporate vultures –

ANNE (*to JACK*) Ooh, that's good.

JACK, ANNE, GIL, and BRIAN (*out and unison*) Or diehard free-market ideologues –

GIL and BRIAN smirk.

BRIAN (*to JACK*) That is so brazen, boy, I love it.

JACK, ANNE, GIL, and BRIAN (*out and unison*) Who are either too blind to see what's happening clearly, or more interested in their own short-term personal gain than a sustainable global recovery.

GIL (*to JACK*) They'll never buy this.

ANNE No, I think they will.

JACK They will, listen to the next part –

JACK, ANNE, GIL, and BRIAN (*out and unison*) These opponents of the bailout have been very successful at casting your country's problems in a very negative light. You have an image problem. And we would like to help.

JACK Then, pause for effect.

They do.

And here's the pitch.

JACK, ANNE, GIL, and BRIAN (*out and unison*) Once the European Union commits to a bailout, of any magnitude, they are going to see it through to the end. Even if that means a playing a more substantial role in the recovery than they are inclined to take now. In order to secure your prosperity, Europe's prosperity, the global prosperity, and, of course, our small investment, we need to encourage that first gesture of assistance – a bailout modest enough to be unobjectionable. To do that, we need to make you look better.

> *Short pause.*

ANNE (*to JACK*) And how do we do that, Jack?

> *Short pause. JACK steps forward, on his own. Thespis stepping out from the chorus.*

JACK (*out*) We make you look better by turning your debt into an asset. For a modest brokerage fee, we will set up a series of investment companies, which in actuality are really just holding companies for Greek debt. The presence of these companies will allow Greece to move its debt out of the market and away from the public eye. You can pay down your other debt, when in actuality you are simply transferring that debt to us, concealing it in these holding companies, which we alone will maintain and have access to. Since the companies are not publicly traded, no one needs to know what their holdings are. As far as the market is concerned, you are selling us an asset. Soon after, your debt seems to lessen. Confidence in the market improves. Your economy strengthens. The required bailout is less expensive so it's back on the table. And Greece, Europe, and the global economy are back on the path to recovery.

> *Long pause. The other three characters are in shock.*

JACK (*out*) Then, once the bailout comes and recovery is underway, you can move that debt back out of the holding companies and into the open market, where it won't be –

GIL Are you out of your mind? Do you have any idea how illegal that is –

JACK It's just a temporary –

GIL It's *fraud*, Jack.

ANNE If anyone found out, if the Greeks reported this to –

JACK They wouldn't report it, don't you see? They have everything to gain from –

ANNE Someone else, then, could look at these companies –

JACK They won't. Nobody is going to take notice of –

GIL How do you know? What are people going to say when you start reintroducing the debt back into the market –

JACK We'll do it subtly, in small little chunks of –

GIL This is insane. This is not a workable solution. (*beat*) Anne, Brian, tell

Jack that this is not a workable –

ANNE We could get in a lot of trouble, Jack.

JACK We are in a lot of trouble.

Short pause.

GIL Brian? Care to –

BRIAN I think the kid has a point.

GIL What?

BRIAN We're just trying to help coax a bailout and, frankly, he's right: without the bailout, everything we now –

GIL I can't believe I'm hearing this. It's fraud.

ANNE Well, Gil, what we're doing now – negotiating with mid-level bureaucrats, behind closed doors – that's not exactly –

GIL Wait, you're on his side too?

ANNE No. But I think we should be honest with ourselves about the way we do business. And, maybe, consider it as an option –

GIL The way we negotiate is OK, well, maybe we are bending the rules. Fine. This is breaking them. This isn't about gaining access or brokering deals on the side, this is about a willful attempt to deceive –

JACK You deceive people all the time. Deception is a part of buying and selling, of any business transaction. "Big Bird," "Chicken Little," "Slim-Fast" – all of these tactics rely on the same fundamental principle, which is what you're telling people and what things are aren't necessarily –

GIL I'd like to see you explain that distinction in a courtroom, Jack.

JACK You were all on board with the first part of the pitch. The spin. Making us look like the good guys. You seemed fine bending the truth there. What changed?

ANNE Jack –

JACK And the thing is, we still get to be the good guys. Truly. We help the market, we help Europe, and we help Greece. And we get to help ourselves too, yes. Is that so bad? A plan where everyone benefits? Most of the time, when we help ourselves we're certainly not doing a favor for someone else, but the beautiful thing about this is, in the end, we all win. The bailout has to happen. Not just for what we're holding, it has to happen or the whole market goes right back down the tubes. How are things going to look then? Recession, depression, a whole lot more worthless junk than there is floating around now. If we just sit by and let it get to that point, they'll really need a bailout, but who'll be able to give it?

GIL You are so full of shit.

JACK Look, you don't want to believe me, OK. Think about what happens if we leave tomorrow, holding what we're holding at its current value. What kind of reception are we going to get from the people who sent us here with all that faith and all that money?

Very short pause. This is a persuasive point.

We went all in on this, all in. And now, look where we are. How much longer do you think we have left if we don't turn it into something?

Short pause.

I have an exit strategy, Gil. It's just a temporary thing. Until the bailout. Then it goes away.

Short pause.

GIL You're serious about that?

JACK Dead serious.

Pause. GIL nods.

ANNE We're going to have to be very careful, Jack.

JACK Of course.

Short pause. There are no objections.

ANNE Right, let's make some calls.

Lights focus around HESTIA and the ashes.

HESTIA Narrow your iris. Look deeper. Try to distinguish between the smallest of objects, the grains of ash and grains that are not ash. We are very close to the moment when the spark flew. The truth. The reason for the god's return.

Scene 7

Lights shift. Time and space shift. The noise of the club, as before. HESTIA is making shots, as before. The four are celebrating, as before.

ANNE I need more shots!

BRIAN Last time I was here the dollar was so goddamn weak –

GIL Yeah, you told us –

ANNE To Jack!

ALL To Jack!

They drink.

ANNE Who fucking killed it today with the undersecretary.

BRIAN Man with the plan.

GIL Good work, son.

JACK Thanks.

GIL I mean, it's a house of cards.

ANNE Gil –

GIL But what a house!

BRIAN See? This is what I am talking about. Assertiveness. Ingenuity. We were on the mat, game over, but this man said, "Fuck the game, I'm making my own rules." Fucking game changer.

ANNE I'll drink to that.

ANNE orders silently. HESTIA pours four more shots.

To changing the game!

ALL Changing the game!

They drink.

GIL It's brilliant. It really is. Just a shame it's not legal.

BRIAN You know what? Fuck legal. Seriously, fuck legal. You know who decides legal? Stupid fucks who spend a zillion fucking euros on nonsensical entitlement programs and then don't pay what they owe –

ANNE Damn right.

BRIAN They sure didn't have a problem with what we proposed. And why would they have a problem? I mean, where the hell would they be without us?

GIL Who knows?

BRIAN Well, I do. I know. We all know. Them too. (*beat*) If I ran the EU, I would have kicked them off the euro months ago. Let them inflate the, the…

GIL Drachma.

BRIAN Drachma. Whatever. Let them inflate the drachma through the roof. They got into it alone, let them face it alone.

ANNE Well, then we wouldn't have made anything.

BRIAN We'd have found a way. Business always finds a way. Things were not always as they are, they're not always going to be that way, but when it changes, we adapt, we adjust, and we succeed. Just like we did today. Business always finds a way.

GIL Business? The hell kind of business are we in now?

BRIAN (*laughing*) What are you talking about? We created assets.

GIL We created bullshit.

BRIAN Bullshit is a business. I tell you what, I'm looking forward to when the whole world is privatized. We won't be so goddamn hung up on legality, I'll tell you that much.

ANNE Worthy of Plato, Brian. Let's do another.

BRIAN I don't know.

GIL Pussy. Jack?

JACK Sure.

ANNE One more. You're doing it, Brian.

HESTIA makes another round of shots.

BRIAN Fine.

GIL Right. To… legality? Illegality?

JACK Both.

ALL Legality and illegality!

They drink. BRIAN starts to look sick.

ANNE And Brian's new world order.

GIL Shit. Hey Brian, Brian…

ANNE Oh dear.

BRIAN and GIL exit.

He's in for a long trip. We should have a lot to celebrate. (*beat*) What do you think your business school professors would say about what you're doing now, Jack?

JACK I didn't go to business school.

ANNE No?

JACK Straight out of undergrad.

ANNE Jesus. You're a puppy. (*beat*) Just as well. About the business school. They won't teach you anything new, and that's what's really important in business, you know? New thinking. New solutions.

JACK Hmm.

ANNE Not that this is completely new…

JACK Not exactly.

ANNE You're taking some pages from a few other cooked books. But still. Not like this, not on this scale. Not with the government's *cooperation*, that's for sure. Far as I know.

JACK Yeah.

ANNE So, not 100% new, but certainly… bold. Forceful.

JACK Huh.

ANNE You've made us believers, Jack. Even Gil.

> *ANNE and JACK's faces are now very close.*

JACK Thanks.

ANNE You've made me a believer, Jack.

> *Long pause. JACK smiles.*

ANNE What?

JACK I'm not sure if I should…

ANNE Risk it.

> *They kiss. Lights rise to a blinding white. Both exit.*

Scene 8

> *Lights lower, slowly, brutally, like a hangover, until they focus in a small pool around HESTIA and the ashes.*

HESTIA Look even more closely. At some point, when the objects get so small, you cannot separate them from the ash. At some point, you cannot separate fact from myth. At some point, you cannot separate the beginning of a thing from its ruinous end. That, there, is the true beginning.

> *Very short pause.*

The god came back and the world ended. Those are the facts. That is the myth. No one can question it. But the source of return isn't a source at all. It is absence. It is need. It is complacency to fill one kind of emptiness with another. It is the essence of every lie. It is at the root of pure finance, the realm of numbers and speculation where worth is untainted by a connection to material objects. It is the nothing that makes gods undeniably, indisputably real.

> *Lights shift. Time and space shift. Outside the dining room of the hotel. Mid-morning, towards the end of breakfast. HERMES appears, in a bike messenger's outfit but with winged shoes. He sits. He waits expectantly. After a while, JACK enters, having just finished breakfast. He is a little hung over.*

HERMES Hey brah.

JACK Hello…

HERMES What's crackalackin?

JACK I'm sorry… Do I know you?

HERMES Oh, I think so…

> *HERMES stands.*

And so was the son born, a being of many shifts, blandly cunning, a robber, a cattle driver, a bringer of dreams, a watcher by night, a thief at the gates, one who was soon to show forth wonderful deeds among the deathless gods to the prophets.

> *He holds up his hand for a high-five.*

Up top.

> *JACK hesitantly goes to high-five HERMES. HERMES seizes the opportunity to punch him in the balls, hard. JACK falls to the floor, moaning. HERMES giggles uncontrollably, delighted by his prank.*

Booyah!

> *Sudden blackout.*
>
> *End of Act 1.*

Act 2

Scene 9

> *Moments later. JACK on the floor, as before, moaning in pain. HERMES stands over him, delighted.*

HERMES Oh snap! The sack tap trap, sprung on the Jack.

JACK Fuck...

HERMES Hahahaha!

JACK Why the fuck did you do that?

> *GIL, BRIAN, ANNE enter, also just from breakfast, also a little hung over. They do not notice JACK at first.*

BRIAN Continental breakfast my ass.

GIL The orange juice isn't bad.

BRIAN Fuck that. I'm from Florida.

HERMES Sup brahs.

GIL Yeah, hi.

ANNE (*noticing JACK on the floor*) Jesus! Jack, what happened?

HERMES (*to the tune of "Deck the Halls"*) Wrecked his balls with fists of fury. Tra-la-la-la-la la-la la-la. (*re: GIL*) This guy knows what's up. (*to GIL*) Up top.

> *HERMES raises his hand for a high-five, as before. GIL hesitantly goes to high-five HERMES. HERMES, again, seizes the opportunity to punch him in the balls, hard. GIL doubles over.*

GIL Jesus Christ!

HERMES Booyah! Call me jelly 'cause I'm on a roll. (*to BRIAN, also raising hand*) Don't leave me hanging, brah.

BRIAN I'm good.

HERMES You are good, Bri-pod. (*to ANNE*) Not even going to try it on you, Green Gables.

BRIAN How do you know our names?

> *HERMES examines GIL and JACK, both still in agony.*

HERMES What's eating Gilbert Grape?

GIL Fuck you.

HERMES Ooh. Vulgarity. That's a no-no. Second caller. Still feeling crappy, slaphappy Jackie?

ANNE Jack, who is this guy?

JACK I don't know. He just came along and –

HERMES Oh, come on, Jack. You know who I am.

JACK I swear to god –

HERMES Yes! Swear! Swear to the gods, you insect!

> *HERMES lifts JACK off the ground. Lights shift. Time and space shift. For a moment, the world is small enough for only the two of them. For a moment, HERMES is no longer boyish and clownlike. We see the god in him.*

And so was the son born, a being of many shifts, blandly cunning, a robber, a cattle driver, a bringer of dreams, a watcher by night, a thief at the gates, one who was soon to show forth wonderful deeds among the deathless gods to the prophets. Know, Jack, that we are mighty and we are to be obeyed.

JACK What are you saying?

HERMES Do you know what you have done, boy? What thing you have created from the absence of things? The emptiness accounted for in those accounts, the absent assets, the shell, the hole, the pit, the red turned black turned green.

JACK I don't understand –

HERMES The *fraud*, Jack.

JACK The fraud?

HERMES Fraud is God. God is Fraud. And so long as it is here, so am I.

> *HERMES tosses JACK aside. Lights shift. Time and space shift. The world returns to what it was. The traders are unsettled.*

ANNE Jack, who is this?

HERMES Strange things in heaven and earth, broheim.

Scene 10

> *Lights shift. Time and space shift. The hotel lounge. JACK, ANNE, GIL, and BRIAN are in mid-conversation. HERMES is to the side, out of earshot, ripping a newspaper into increasingly smaller pieces.*

ANNE I don't understand.

GIL No one understands. I've stopped trying to understand. He just is, OK?

ANNE But *what* is he? I don't –

JACK I've told you, he's –

BRIAN Look, what he is is less important than what he wants. What does he want?

JACK I don't know.

BRIAN Well, he came for a reason.

JACK I told you why he came. Once we created the shell companies, he –

ANNE So what does he want?

GIL Jesus, Anne –

JACK He didn't tell me what he wants! I don't know what he wants! (*beat*) I think he's just here, you know. He's just here to be here.

BRIAN He wants something.

Short pause. They all look at HERMES.

ANNE We could ask him.

GIL You go ahead. I haven't recovered.

BRIAN I don't think he's going to say.

ANNE We could still ask.

BRIAN Ask then. Go ahead and ask.

Short pause. ANNE does not ask.

GIL Here's an idea: he wants to hit us in the balls and act like an asshole. Mystery solved.

BRIAN He wants something else. I know it.

GIL Who cares? I think we should just ignore him.

Short pause.

BRIAN Let's go.

ANNE What?

BRIAN Let's leave. Let's go.

ANNE Go where?

BRIAN Away. Home. On a plane. Let's go. (*beat*) Who cares what he wants? We got what we needed. It's done, let's go. Let's go and leave him here.

Short pause.

GIL Why –

BRIAN Whatever he wants, I don't want to stick around and find out. Do you want to stick around and find out?

GIL No.

ANNE Not really.

Very short pause.

BRIAN Jack?

JACK No, I guess.

BRIAN So let's go!

Short pause.

ANNE OK, well, let's book some –

HERMES Whoosh!

HERMES throws the newspaper shreds in the air like confetti. The sound of a volcanic eruption. A sudden blackout, as the world disappears in smoke.

Scene 11

Lights shift. Time and space shift. HESTIA emerges from the gloom.

HESTIA Strange things in heaven and earth indeed.

The sound of a newscast about the Icelandic volcano. Lights shift. Time and space shift. An airport café in Athens. GIL, JACK, ANNE, and BRIAN are drinking coffee, waiting. They have been waiting all morning. HERMES is lounging near them on the floor, making a paper airplane. BRIAN is looking at a TV showing departures and arrivals, now all canceled.

ANNE You can stop staring at that screen, Brian.

BRIAN How is every flight canceled? Every flight? Why aren't they, I mean, what about flights going, I don't know –

GIL The routes are all in disarray. The proper planes haven't come in, so they can't go out –

BRIAN What are you, the fucking aviation expert?

ANNE Brian –

BRIAN How hard would it be, honestly, to just redirect some of the flights away from –

ANNE They're being overly cautious.

BRIAN They're being morons.

ANNE We should go back into town. Wait and see if something opens up tomorrow.

BRIAN We should try to get on a flight to Japan or something. Go back the long way, over the Pacific.

GIL There are no flights, Brian. To anywhere. And when there are, the waiting list is going to be –

BRIAN Ugh! This is interminable!

HERMES Word up, Bri-focals.

> *Short pause.*

ANNE You don't think he – ?

HERMES Nope. Nothing to do with it. Not my department, Anne for all Seasons.

GIL What is your department?

HERMES Keeping it real.

BRIAN He's lying.

HERMES I'm not keeping it real, bro?

BRIAN He did this. We decide to go and leave him here, and all of a sudden –

GIL I still don't get why he's here.

HERMES Explain it to them again, Jack-o-Lantern.

JACK Just try to ignore him.

HERMES Hah. Not an option.

> *HERMES, now finished making the paper airplane, throws it at GIL's head.*

GIL (*swatting the airplane*) Shit!

HERMES Flight 123 to Gillinois now arriving.

GIL Screw this, I'm going back to the hotel.

BRIAN Just wait. One more hour. Something might open up.

HERMES Way to keep it optimistic, Bri-polar! Up top!

> *HERMES raises his hand for a high-five, as before. BRIAN hesitantly goes to high-five HERMES. HERMES, again, seizes the opportunity*

to punch him in the balls, hard. BRIAN doubles over.

HERMES Booyah!

BRIAN Shit!

HERMES Haha! Knew I'd get you.

BRIAN Why the fuck did I do that?

ANNE Let's go back.

BRIAN Yeah, fuck it, we're going back…

BRIAN attempts to move, but has not sufficiently recovered.

Shit. Give me a minute. I'll catch up.

JACK You OK?

BRIAN No. Fuck…

ANNE We'll meet you at the lounge.

BRIAN Yeah, yeah, OK…

The others exit.

HERMES You're right about the flight paths.

BRIAN Fuck you, man.

HERMES So many better plans to be devised, but they stick with the one they have. In spite of changing circumstances.

Short pause.

Want to know what I want, Broseph?

Short pause.

I want some answers.

BRIAN Well, that makes two of us.

HERMES But my questions are better. For instance, I want to know if you guys are really going to stop what you're doing when the bailout comes?

BRIAN Will it get rid of you?

HERMES Might.

BRIAN Yes, then.

HERMES Don't know why you're so hard hearted towards me, Richard Coeur de Brian. We've only just met.

BRIAN You ever get tired of making nicknames?

HERMES Rarely. (*beat*) I know that it was Jack's idea, but we both know you could really run with it. You know how to sell.

BRIAN How would I run with it?

HERMES Other companies have ventured into these murky waters before, and the further you go, the more challenging it is to navigate. You know the dangers and are right to be wary of it. But I've put the wind in your sails. My hand is there guiding yours on the tiller, bro. With my help, you could go into that uncharted ocean, Brian, if you wanted, and find what treasure there is on that far shore. (*beat*) Or, you can continue to dawdle in this little inlet for a while, and then come skulking back to the beach.

Short pause.

Why would you, why would anyone want to dismantle something this good?

Long pause. BRIAN is tempted, but resists.

BRIAN The current plan is fine.

HERMES Fine. *Fine*. Is that all you want to aspire to? Adequacy? Want to know what I think?

BRIAN Not anymore.

HERMES I think you need to act like you have some balls. There it is. That's it. That's what the high-fives are all about, Broledad Bro'Brien. To *remind* you.

BRIAN, now recovered, prepares to leave.

BRIAN We hold it, the bailout comes, we sell it back. That's the plan, and it's not changing. Stop hounding me.

HERMES Arf! Arf!

BRIAN I'm going.

HERMES steps in front of BRIAN.

HERMES Can't run away, Bri-antelope. I will be heard.

BRIAN I told you to stop hounding me.

HERMES You may not want me as a friend but you certainly don't want me as an enemy.

BRIAN They're waiting. I need to go.

BRIAN exits. HERMES watches him go.

Scene 12

> *Lights shift. Time and space shift. The club, as before. The four are in positions as before, but now with HERMES in tow. The mood has changed. The four are less exuberant, but HERMES more than enough so to counterbalance them. HERMES is dancing while the others are at the bar.*

ANNE (*unenthused*) I need more shots.

HERMES (*coming over*) Last time I was here, the –

BRIAN Shut up, OK?

> *HERMES raises his hand for a high-five. No one responds. HERMES smiles, then goes back to dancing. HESTIA brings the shots over.*

GIL To the volcano.

> *BRIAN, JACK, ANNE, and GIL all try to pronounce the name of the volcano a couple of times, with difficulty, ad lib as necessary. This should not go on long.*

ANNE Ay-ja-frall…

JACK (*overlapping*) Eee-jaff-err…

BRIAN (*overlapping*) Ey-ja-don't give a fuck.

GIL (*cutting them off*) Whatever. The volcano!

ALL The volcano.

> *They drink.*

GIL I don't know, a week more in Athens, might not be too bad.

BRIAN Other circumstances, maybe. Not with him. (*nods in HERMES' direction*)

ANNE What, sore that you fell for the high-five thing?

GIL Sore. Hah.

BRIAN Fuck you. I don't trust him.

GIL He's harmless. An asshole, but harmless.

BRIAN The hell he is. When you guys left, he tried to talk to me about it.

ANNE About what?

BRIAN What do you mean what? What Jack did, what we're doing, that's what. Says we weren't making as much as we could off of it.

GIL How not?

BRIAN Didn't say.

ANNE No?

BRIAN I didn't let him finish, OK? I don't trust him.

> *Short pause.*

JACK Well, maybe he's got a point.

BRIAN What?

GIL I agree. Maybe the man's got a point.

BRIAN But he's not a man.

ANNE Maybe not.

BRIAN He isn't, right, Jack?

JACK Look, let's just talk to him, listen to what he has to –

BRIAN I don't want to listen, OK? I do not trust him. Whatever he's going to propose is not in any way a viable –

JACK How do you know that? I don't understand this, Brian, you were all gung-ho for –

BRIAN He's evil? OK? Evil. Whatever he wants, whatever he suggests, I guarantee you, at the end of the day, our heads are going to be on the chopping block.

JACK (*very condescending*) Look, if you can't handle it here with him, fine. Don't stop the rest of us from –

> *BRIAN grabs JACK violently by the lapels.*

BRIAN Monstrosities! Both of you are fucking monstrosities. You know that?

ANNE Brian! I think you've had enough. OK? Go walk it off.

> *Short, tense pause.*

BRIAN Yeah, yeah, al lright. Fine. (*to JACK*) Stay here with him, then, dumb shit. You deserve one another.

> *BRIAN goes to exit, stumbling a little. HERMES sees BRIAN leave and moves to intercept.*

HERMES Packing it in for the night?

BRIAN Just taking a little walk.

HERMES Walk? You should be dancing! (*making beat noises*) Boom boom boom boom boom boom.

BRIAN Listen, man… Whatever you're offering, I don't want it.

HERMES How can you be sure?

BRIAN Trust me. I'm sure.

HERMES I think we want the same things.

BRIAN I want to stay in my job and stay out of prison. I don't think you have those concerns.

HERMES Thought you weren't so goddamn hung up on legality, bro.

> Short pause.

"I'm looking forward to when the whole world is privatized…" (*beat*) Isn't that right?

> Short pause.

Well, now I'm here. Opportunities abound.

BRIAN This conversation is over. I'm going out.

HERMES The world is shrinking, Christopher Brolumbus. Not enough space to go somewhere all on your own anymore. If you're not careful, you'll walk out of here tonight and step right off the edge. Then where will you be?

BRIAN I'll take my chances.

> *BRIAN exits. HERMES watches him go, seething. He turns back to the group, studying each of the three very closely. He considers possibilities and tactics. Eventually, he makes his way over to where they are at the bar.*

HERMES Friend's got a bad attitude.

ANNE He just needs to walk it off.

HERMES Undoubtedly. (*beat*) Well, that's a Brian shame. How about you, Karenina? Kevorkian? 'N Sullivan? Dance?

GIL No, thank you.

HERMES Fine. Drinks then.

> *HERMES orders four more shots. HESTIA pours drinks. HERMES produces a credit card and slides it across the counter.*

ANNE You're getting this?

HERMES Mmmhmm.

ANNE Do you… do you people… have money?

HERMES Nope.

ANNE Then how are you paying for it?

HERMES Credit. Duh. Ah, how limited your perception is, my little bros. You have a problem with scope. Thinking too much about the terrarium and not the open terrain.

HERMES holds up his glass.

The liquid in your shot? You see how it is in the glass and forget that it can take any number of shapes if contained in the right way.

HERMES drinks his shot down.

Or not contained at all! Wooohah!

Hesitantly, the remaining three drink their shots.

I'm telling you, friends, bromans, countrymen, I am feeling good. Could be better, though.

He looks over at JACK.

Why such a sad sack, buddy Jack? You don't seem to talk much since I got here.

JACK Nothing to say, I guess.

HERMES Well. Lucky for us, *I* have something to say. Apropos getting better, matter of fact. I have to admit it's getting better, a little better all the time. I have to admit it's getting better, a little better, since you've been mine. Get-ting so much bet-ter all the time!

ANNE Look.

HERMES It's getting better all the ti-i-ime!

ANNE Screw this.

HERMES Better! Better! Bet-ter!

ANNE I'm done.

ANNE makes to leave.

HERMES (*with the voice of a god*) I'm not done!

HERMES bangs his fist on the counter. ANNE stops. The group tenses. All three of their phones start ringing. Soon other phones start ringing in other parts of the bar.

GIL The hell…?

Chaos. On the video screens, we see the market plunge.

ANNE Jesus.

GIL (*to HERMES, panicking*) What are you doing?! Make it stop!

HERMES (*laughing*) What do you mean, make it stop, bro? I didn't do anything.

> *ANNE, GIL, and JACK reach for their phones, answer, and begin to reassure their panicked clients. HERMES wanders back to the dance floor. The music crescendos, mixing with the sounds of the ringing phones. The voices of the three are drowned out. HERMES revels in the pandemonium.*

How now Dow Jones!

> *Power failure. The screens go dark. The ringing abruptly stops. All the cell phones have gone dead. The three try redialing. No use.*

ANNE Shit, shit, shit, shit, shit –

GIL What have you done to the phones?

HERMES What are you so afraid of, Edgar Allan Bro? You should feel safe. You should feel free. What you have ensconced in those little shell companies is invulnerable to market fluctuation. Why do you care?

ANNE You're kidding, right? It's debt. It has negative value.

HERMES Only for you. For everyone else… you've told them what its value is. And, if you feel it bros, its value can be infinite. You could keep buying, buying, profiting, profiting, rising, rising…

GIL I don't get it.

HERMES No. Regrettably.

> *Short pause. HERMES studies the three, making a disapproving clicking noise as he does.*

I had such hopes. Your beginning was so promising. But now, your resistance, your general torpor has gone from amusing to irritating to infuriating. So. When you do "get it," bros, when you're finally ready, then find me. It'll be in your interest. When the end comes, you'll want to be in my camp.

> *Short pause.*

Your time is running out. If I don't get what I want, I'm moving on.

HERMES exits. Short pause.

GIL The hell was that about?

Short pause.

JACK I think it might be a good idea.

GIL What is a what?

JACK What he was just saying. That we should, you know, just keep buying, buying… We could make that money –

ANNE It isn't money. It's debt, it's futures.

JACK It's still sellable. It's still worth something if someone will pay for it. I don't see why you're so resistant to the idea of putting it to use. You wanted us to be smarter for next time, well, what's smarter, making what we have work for us, or sitting on our hands and waiting for the bailout?

ANNE What he's, what *you're* proposing – it'd be like taking out a second mortgage to buy another house.

JACK It's not a bad thing if you sell the new house at a profit to pay down the mortgage.

ANNE He'd want you to mortgage the new house to buy a –

JACK If you're making a profit, I don't see how it –

ANNE It's not prudent, Jack. Would you, in good conscience, take out another mortgage to –

JACK I would if I knew I would make it back. And then some.

ANNE Well, then you're an idiot. Jack, you don't use a mortgage to – You know what? You don't have a mortgage, so you don't understand. I can't explain this to a child.

JACK Anne, why do you think –

ANNE (*overlapping, to herself*) Poor choice of words –

JACK (*continuing*) –That I would be incapable of understanding what he's talking about if I'm the one who devised, on my own, the whole damn –

ANNE Jack, we have a plan in place. A great plan. *Your* plan. If we fuck this up by –

JACK We won't. There are ways to do it that will ensure we won't.

ANNE There are no ways to ensure we won't –

JACK There are ways to minimize the risk.

ANNE You're starting to believe the crap we use to sell this kind of thing to people, Jack.

JACK When did we become opposed to the idea of making money?

ANNE We're not opposed, we're –

ANNE and JACK – waiting for the bailout –

JACK I heard you. Well, frankly, I don't think we have to wait. Let's use our muscle a little, OK?

Short pause.

ANNE Jack, I appreciate your enthusiasm, but when you've been doing this for a little longer, you become more acutely aware of the fact that there are ways to win and there are ways to lose. And you don't get points for experimenting with something different when there is no need to experiment.

JACK I don't believe this.

ANNE Believe what?

JACK This. (*beat*) We started with nothing. Nothing. And out of it we made something that is more powerful than any kind of financial… And now that it's here, now that we have that force at our fingertips, you want to pretend like it does not exist? He, his presence, he proves that you don't need material, you don't need an asset, you can sell an idea. But still, the three of you, you're all still clinging to this notion that you have to be able to touch it for it to be real, even when every step we've taken categorically refutes that logic.

ANNE You can't make something out of nothing, Jack. This is not what you think it is.

JACK No. You're wrong. You've been at this too long, all of you. You're too old to see it.

ANNE Shut up.

Pause.

What do you think, Gil?

GIL, who has been a little out of it during this last exchange, turns to look at the other two.

GIL I think I am a long way from home and a long way from things I recognize. I think we are dealing with things beyond our control or understanding. I think the world we knew just changed. We're cockroaches and someone just turned the light on.

JACK We're not the cockroaches. We flipped the switch.

GIL You don't think we're vulnerable?

JACK I don't know. I don't think so.

GIL What do you think, then?

JACK I think he has a point.

GIL I don't know what that point *is*. What's the endgame?

ANNE Exactly.

JACK What do you mean, endgame?

GIL OK, so we go futures on futures on futures on futures. Fine. Then what?

JACK Then what? Then we profit like crazy, that's what?

GIL No, we're just postponing payment. It's not profit. You're missing part of the equation.

   Short pause.

I can't conceive of what he wants. Either it is needlessly complicated. Needlessly complicated when we've got something in place, that's more to the point. Or, we're missing something. All of us.

JACK Which is why we should do what he says. I don't think he misses anything.

   Short pause.

We can understand it. We should be able to understand it. We're smart.

GIL Not that smart.

JACK Smart enough. So he wants us to, what, to go crazy on the futures market –

GIL Like mortgaging a house only to buy –

ANNE Yeah, thank you, Gil. So, let's say we do. We open up the holding companies, we take that debt, we'll sell it off to buy…

GIL Other derivatives.

JACK Other debt.

GIL Sure. More debt. Worth more.

JACK And if it's worth more, than it's…

GIL Less secure.

ANNE Less secure. So maybe it's not worth more.

GIL OK.

JACK And then we profit.

ANNE Maybe.

GIL Or maybe not, since it's greater risk.

ANNE Right. And if we do profit, those profits go into…

JACK Buying more derivatives.

ANNE Which we use to buy more and more.

GIL As far as I can tell.

ANNE This is just a Ponzi scheme.

JACK Well…

GIL Kind of.

ANNE Pretty much. It's not sustainable. Keeps getting bigger and bigger until…

JACK Someone gets left with the bill.

ANNE Until something breaks.

GIL So what breaks?

ANNE What breaks?

JACK What breaks?

    Short pause.

ANNE We break. That's what breaks.

    Very short pause.

There's a point at which something ceases becoming unorthodox. Just starts being wrong.

JACK Who gives a shit?

ANNE I give a shit. (*beat*) We've indulged his line of thinking far enough. He's done nothing but torment us since he arrived. It's finished. Break off communication.

JACK But –

ANNE We're done with him.

    ANNE and GIL start to exit.

JACK (*quietly*) I'm not done.

Scene 13

> *Lights shift. Time and space shift. The world shrinks to the size of HERMES' palm. HESTIA steps forward.*

HESTIA The god came back and the world ended. Those are the facts. That is the myth. No one can question it. As for the rest, the truth of the rest… the possibility of knowing that for certain is complicated by a fundamental flaw in truth itself.

> *HESTIA draws a line in the ashes.*

There is a line border between two regions. This one is here, and this one beyond. Here. There. Fact. Myth. Separate and distinct. (*beat*) But when we scrutinize that concrete, irreversible distinction, when we strive for perfect truth, perfect specificity, how much is cast into doubt. Which grain of ash marks the definite border? The *true* border. If that grain is flicked beyond that point, is a different border made? There is a lingering uncertainty at the heart of things, an uncertainty with terrible potential.

> *Short pause.*

The god came back and the world ended. Those are the facts. That is the myth. No one can question it. What is also indisputable is that he challenged the others' perceptions of the truth. Of the limits, the borders, the boundaries of things. How much could be borrowed. How much could be spent. How much could be concealed. How much could be transformed. How much could be made with nothing. This is his gospel. And one, more than the others, listened and believed.

> *JACK turns and notices HESTIA, truly seeing her from the first time as a being of power. He is a little surprised.*

JACK Hi.

HESTIA Hello.

JACK Did he… Do you know where he…

HESTIA Yes. I do.

> *Short pause. JACK expects HESTIA to respond. She does not.*

JACK I need to know where he went. I need to speak with him.

HESTIA Are you sure?

JACK Am I sure what?

HESTIA Are you sure you need to?

Short pause.

He seems to think you're already decided, the lot of you. That it's not a matter of *if*, but just a matter of *when*. I hope he isn't right.

Very short pause. HESTIA relents.

Well, if you insist.

HESTIA takes the martini shaker and pours the ashes into a trail.

JACK What's this?

HESTIA A trail. From the future to the past, and the other way. Follow it, you'll find him. If that's what you want.

Scene 14

Lights shift. Time and space shift and become irrelevant. HESTIA recedes. JACK follows the circle of ashes. HERMES appears. JACK meets him in the middle of his dominion – the realm of thought, the realm of inventiveness, the de-militarized zone between myth and fact, true and untrue.

HERMES Well?

JACK I need to know what breaks.

HERMES Yes. Good.

JACK I can't see it.

HERMES Well, then. Stonewalls are still up, Jackson.

JACK Then help me tear them down.

HERMES Why?

JACK Because I want to know.

HERMES I made one of you an offer before and he spat in my face. I shake the market to teach the rest of you and you cover your eyes with fear. I empower you to speak and you lose your voice. My faith and my patience are dwindling. Perhaps even dwindled. Past tense.

JACK I want to learn. I can learn.

HERMES Hah.

JACK I can learn.

Short pause.

I believed in you. Believe in me.

HERMES You believed in me, bro? You don't know what I am.

JACK A god.

HERMES Just because you know the name doesn't mean you have any idea about the rest. Since I've arrived the lot of you have feared, resented, mistrusted, or underestimated me. What kind of knowledge is that?

> *Short pause.*

We're not meant to be known, Beanstalk. We're meant to be revered.

JACK I made you. I brought you back. I needed you then and I need you again. I need to know what breaks and I'm…

> *Short pause.*

HERMES Lost.

JACK Yeah.

HERMES Tough shit, bro.

JACK I thought you wanted to help us. I thought you wanted –

HERMES You have no idea what I *want*. You cannot even begin to approach the meaning of the word. What does an insect know of *want*? What could it possibly signify to you? An unguided thirst shuffling beneath that scrapheap of synaptic spasms that passes for conscious thought. *Want* for you is lurching in the darkness towards something you can't even define.

JACK I'm not –

HERMES Oh? You think I'm lying? Tell me different, then. Tell me what you want, other than to come out alive.

> *Short pause. JACK cannot think of an answer.*

You can't, can you? You want what an animal wants. What men want. Pathetic. I had a vision for this world that transcends your conception of desire. After centuries of unimaginativeness, something singular and magnificent. The handiwork of a god.

JACK You need me to do it.

HERMES What?

JACK I saw it when the others didn't. The shell companies, the consolidation of the… Whatever you want, you need something like me to make it real.

HERMES Something?

JACK Someone.

HERMES All right, then...

HERMES considers.

How do you make the most money?

JACK What?

HERMES How do you make the most money?

JACK What do you mean?

HERMES I mean, how do you make the most money?

JACK I... I don't know.

HERMES Why not?

JACK Because I don't know what you're asking.

HERMES I am asking the question you should always ask. How do you make the most money?

Short pause.

The variables are these: a firm specializing in not-entirely-transparent derivative trading, a truly massive amount of capital collected from a phalanx of other hedge funds and private accounts. Three men, one woman, a complex formula for evaluating risk, a series of market forecasts, and a growing interest in the financial stability of a small country in the Mediterranean. When you first came here, how did you know what to go for?

JACK They told us. We had a system.

HERMES You had a system?

JACK We had a formula.

HERMES A formula. To tell you what?

JACK Nothing. It didn't work.

HERMES Told you something.

JACK Told us nothing. Was supposed to tell us risk, but if all risk is negated by a bailout, what good is that?

HERMES How do you make the most money?

JACK I don't know!

HERMES You do! Everyone does! (*beat*) Later, you realize everything's in jeopardy, what's your solution?

JACK The shell companies.

HERMES Shell companies. A new system. To do what?

JACK To save us.

HERMES Hasn't saved you. It mitigated your risk. How do you make the most money?

JACK Stop asking me that!

HERMES I'm asking because you never did. All this time spent worrying about your miserable survival! Scurrying for safety, limiting your exposure, minimizing your loss, retreating into this fraud because you can't cut it out there. And as long as it's here, so am I. How do you make the most money?

JACK I don't know!

HERMES And so was the son born, a being of many shifts, blandly cunning –

JACK I don't –

HERMES A robber, a cattle driver, a bringer of dreams, a watcher by night, a thief at the gates –

JACK I –

HERMES One who was soon to show forth wonderful deeds among the deathless gods to the –

JACK Profits.

Short pause.

HERMES Profits. (*beat*) Change the game, Jack. Offense, not defense. (*beat*) With both systems, the flawed and the fraud, you're swimming against the current. Mitigating the risk of the riskiest market. What needs to break is the old system, the old rules, the old, tired, insect ways of doing things. And, once you break those, you break –

HERMES and JACK Greece.

JACK Greece. God.

HERMES Business always finds a way.

JACK That's it.

Scene 15

GIL and ANNE appear.

ANNE What's it?

JACK There was something Brian said.

JACK and HERMES Things were not always as they are, they're not always going to be that way, but when it changes, we adapt, we adjust, and we succeed.

GIL OK…

JACK We've been thinking about this all wrong. We don't profit from hiding the debt, we use it to break Greece. And *then* we profit.

ANNE What?

JACK What happens if it gets too bad? Unstoppably bad. If that debt, most of which we're now holding, doesn't get paid off but keeps getting borrowed against and borrowed against. If the system of spending is so irreparably broken, so entangled in an endless cycle of futures trading, that simply counteracting that deficit is not enough. What's the good of a bailout then? What happens if it gets too bad for the EU to even want to help, to tolerate their presence, to –

GIL To keep them on the euro.

JACK Exactly. To keep them on the euro. If things get unstoppably bad, Brussels will kick them back to the drachma. And then…

GIL Massive inflation.

ANNE Unimaginable.

GIL Like Germany after World War One.

JACK Well, maybe. Who knows? That's not our concern.

ANNE Still –

JACK Think how far our dollar would go.

Short pause.

We can do this. We're holding enough of their debt to make this happen. They'd be unable to protest, since they'd have to admit to the presence of the shell companies, to their collusion with us.

ANNE They'll never change the currency back to the –

JACK If they don't change the currency, then that's even better. Then it's not contained. Then we have the entire continent at our mercy to –

ANNE The continent?

JACK Yes! Look, all we need to do is move a little money around so –

GIL They'd shit a brick at the office if they knew.

ANNE No company has done something like this before. Not on this scale.

JACK But we could.

ANNE We could bankrupt the country. I mean like truly…

Short pause.

I don't know, it's…

ANNE is about to raise a moral objection. She looks to GIL and JACK to validate her reservations. They give no sign of hesitation.

I, I guess…

Short pause. The magnitude of it starts to sink in. ANNE exhales.

GIL Wow.

JACK "Wow" is a fucking understatement. This should be chronicled. Sung in ballad form in advanced business school seminars. This happens once in a lifetime. If that. You can just feel it, can't you?

Scene 16

Three spotlights rise on ANNE, GIL, and JACK, as in Act 1. They are in many places at once – offices, cafés, hotel lobbies, airport lounges all across Europe. A dozen or more private meetings. The three are good. Confident, charming, assertive. Each move has been rehearsed and refined. HERMES stands aside, just out of the light. He guides every action.

ANNE Mr. Thompson?

GIL Mr. Dreyfus?

JACK Mr. Lang?

ANNE Mr. Piret?

GIL Mr. De Vries?

JACK Mr. Lopez?

ANNE Mr. Azocar?

GIL Mr. Richardson?

JACK Mr. Furbusher?

ANNE Mr. Wilkes?

GIL Mr. Scudder?

JACK Am I pronouncing that right? Furbusher?

ANNE, GIL, and JACK (*unison*) I know you're a busy man, so I'll get to the point. As you are undoubtedly aware, the situation in Greece is rapidly worsening. Actually, worsening is a gentle way of putting it. A more accurate way to put it would be like this: the sky is falling.

Scene 17

Lights shift. Time and space shift. All spaces and all time. HERMES moves to the pile of ashes, and begins to gather it back up into the cup. HESTIA watches from a distance.

HESTIA Things were not always as they are. Once there were twelve, each with his or her own dominion, each ruling in balance. Once this place was a place of ideas and innovation, prosperity and possibility. Once there was a thing and not a memory, a ruin. Once, maybe, people and gods would have acted differently.

The values on the screens starts to fluctuate more severely. HERMES, JACK, ANNE, and GIL appear. They each hold a shot glass.

HESTIA The god came back and the world ended. Those are the facts. That is the myth. No one can question it. The signs of his return are everywhere. We see his acolytes in cities, airports, banks, office buildings, conference rooms, hotels, coffee shops. We can see the footprints in the ashes of where he's gleefully trampled on the world.

As HESTIA speaks, noise and possibly videos of riots in Greece, foreclosures, poverty, and other signifiers of the economic collapse of the late 2000s filters in.

I find him much changed from what he was, but maybe he isn't. Maybe he's just found the sort of followers he wanted but could never have back then – ravenous, capable, immune. Or maybe, now that his work is almost complete, now that his presence has left so very little unsigned, I am able to see him as something more menacing than a trickster or a messenger, a thing, like any debt, like any god, whose potential is more dangerous than its value.

There's little truth in this story, but I'm sure that you recognize its source in others. When he blazes his way to here, don't let the smoke get in your eyes.

The noise of the club music filters back in, along with the other sounds. News clips covering Greece's ongoing financial collapse through the present day. The graph jumps wildly in time with the beat, heaving dramatically between dizzying highs and lows, shaking the globe to pieces. The four raise their glasses in a silent toast and drink.

The end.

Hera
or
Juno en Victoria

by Stuart Eugene Bousel

Hera
or
Juno en Victoria

Hera, or Juno en Victoria was originally produced in a reading at EXIT Stage Left in San Francisco, California on July 30, 2010 as part of the San Francisco Olympians Festival. The play was directed by Claire Rice with the following cast:

Hera	Michelle Jasso
Hestia	Celeste Russi-Van Etten
Hebe	Katrina Bushnell
Heracles	Bryce Duzan
Ganymede	Joseph Miller
Iris	Megan Briggs
Stage Directions	Julia Heitner

Hera or Juno en Victoria premiered as a full production on June 9, 2011 at Stage Werx in San Francisco, California, produced by Wily West Productions with the following cast and crew:

Hera	Michelle Jasso
Hestia	Celeste Russi-Van Etten
Hebe	Katrina Bushnell
Heracles	Bryce Duzan
Ganymede	Travis Howse
Iris	Kalinda Wang
Director	Claire Rice
Costumes	Miriam Lewis
Sets and Lighting	Quinn Whitaker

Characters

HERA, *a provincial society matron. Mid-forties to early fifties. Beautiful, poised, gracious, powerful, sad.*
HESTIA, *her older sister, mid-fifties to early sixties, a subtle mix of spinster sternness and motherly tenderness; fiercely protective of her sister.*
HEBE, *Hera's daughter. Twenty. Truly lovely, if perhaps somewhat ridiculous.*
HERACLES, *Hebe's fiancé. Mid to late twenties. Handsome, kind, not at all bright.*
GANYMEDE, *a groomsman. Early twenties. Quite good-looking,*

sharp, rural lower-class.
IRIS, a housemaid. Late twenties. Attractive but icy. London working class, but educated.

Setting

The country estate of Hera's husband, Zeus, about a two-hour train ride from London.

1855

The year Charlotte Brontë died and Thomas Bulfinch's Age of Fable was first published.

Act 1

The sunroom. Early afternoon. It is a bright room of many windows, floor-length, the central ones opening to a garden beyond, translucent white curtains blowing in the breeze. On either side, a pair of palms in vases. There is a pair of divans as well, with a small table between them, center. An ottoman off to the right. A side table with a vase of peacock feathers on it to the left. Everything is in perfect taste, and there is a bright, golden hue over it all. Down left and right are doorways leading to the rest of the house. HESTIA and HERA are present at rise. HESTIA is knitting a stocking; HERA is reading a book. For a long moment they sit in silence and do these two separate things. A bird sings out in the garden. HERA raises her eyes from the book for a moment and listens. She smiles. She goes back to her book. Another moment of silence. A gentle breeze rustles some wind chimes out in the garden. HESTIA looks up from her knitting, listens, and smiles. She goes back to her knitting. A third moment of silence. HEBE enters, carrying a tray of tea things. She stumbles over the ottoman and sends everything flying.

HEBE FUCKING CUNT!

Wordlessly, HERA and HESTIA turn and glare at her, mortified.

HEBE *(with a roll of the eyes)* Oh come off it. I think it's perfectly understandable to swear when one has just abolished tea for the afternoon – and the tea set for life, most looks like.

HERA and HESTIA turn to one another and break into smiles. They turn to HEBE.

HERA Are you all right, dear?

HEBE I'm fine, thank you for asking.

She gets up and begins collecting the shattered tea things.

HERA Do you want any help?

HEBE No thank you, I'm quite all right.

HESTIA Tell us, darling, where did you learn to talk like that?

HERA Where do you think? From her father.

HESTIA Not really?

HERA Who else do we know uses language like that?

HESTIA Well, our father –

HERA Who do we know who is still alive, dear?

HESTIA Mother.

HERA Which is just one more reason to keep her at Parnassus End. Just think of that dirty mouth of hers left unhinged in this house. We'd never have a peaceful breakfast again.

HESTIA It's a wonder you haven't sent Zeus to Parnassus End as well.

HERA Oh I've thought of it, believe you me.

HEBE *(cutting herself on a shard of tea-cup)* Fucking cunt!

HERA Darling, are you sure you wouldn't like some help?

HEBE I'm fine. I just nicked my finger is all.

She gets up and deposits the tray of broken crockery on the side table, angrily.

There. It's all done now anyway.

IRIS enters with a tea kettle.

IRIS The tea, ma'am.

The women all look at one another.

HESTIA Tea, Hera?

HERA Shall I cup my hands or were you planning to just pour it directly into my mouth?

HESTIA Which would you prefer?

HERA Wait a moment. Hebe?

HEBE Yes, Mother.

HERA Bring me the sugar, will you? If it's still mostly intact, of course.

> *With a tremendous sigh, HEBE picks up the sugar bowl and takes it over to HERA. She selects a cube from the bowl and places it in her mouth, between her teeth.*

All right, Sister, give us a pour.

> *HERA and HESTIA burst out laughing. HEBE smirks, but doesn't join in. IRIS looks confused, and stands frozen with the tea kettle in her hand.*

IRIS I don't… pardon me, ma'am, but I'm not sure I –

HEBE It's all right, Iris, they're just having a laugh at us. Or me, rather. I've smashed all the tea-cups, you see.

IRIS Shall I ask Cook to get out the Christmas china then?

HERA Oh goodness no! What shall we use at Christmas then when she's smashed all those too!

HEBE Yes, yes, you're very clever.

HESTIA We're sorry, dear, it was just too funny.

HERA And we'd been having such a dull day.

HEBE Last time I ever try to help out around here.

HERA Oh, come now. If it had been me you'd have laughed about it too.

HEBE Not for this long.

HERA Yes, well, that's the advantage of being young and having many exciting things happening all the time. For your aunt and I this is about as adventurous as it gets these days. Iris, I think we'll just skip tea today.

HEBE It's far too hot anyway.

HERA Agreed. Bring us some lemonade, we'll use the sherry glasses from the sideboard. Oh, and a cake or two for Miss Sourpuss over here.

IRIS Very good, ma'am.

HERA And send Ganymede out to buy a new everyday set, if you would.

IRIS He's out hunting with the Master.

HERA Oh yes. I'd quite forgotten. Never mind, Iris. Just leave him a note to do it tomorrow.

IRIS Yes, ma'am.

> *IRIS exits.*

HEBE Father always goes hunting on Tuesdays.

HERA When he's at home, which used to be hardly ever. That's why I didn't remember. I'm not used to having him around the house on weekdays.

HESTIA *(with just the slightest edge in her voice)* He has been spending less time in the City, hasn't he?

HERA Has he? I barely notice sometimes.

HEBE Too busy laughing at me probably.

HERA Oh, don't sulk, dearest, you know that's hardly the case. Come sit by mother and I'll braid your hair.

HEBE I think I'd rather go help Iris with the lemonade.

HERA Use the cart this time, won't you? We have it for a reason.

HEBE I was practicing my bridal walk.

HERA Eyes open or closed?

HEBE *(stamping her foot in a tantrum)* Oh what do you think!

> *HEBE storms out. HERA watches her go. She sighs.*

HERA Oh dear. I've done it again. Nothing I say to that girl fails to infuriate her.

HESTIA She's at an age where that is normal. You were the same way once.

HERA Nonsense. When?

HESTIA The summer you were married, same as her. She's nervous and scared.

HERA Oh I was never nervous and scared.

HESTIA You were as uncertain about everything as she is.

HERA No, I just pretended to be uncertain to keep Zeus interested. As opposed to now, where I pretend to be uncertain to keep the house relatively peaceful.

HESTIA Sometimes a blind eye is better than a careful one.

HERA Precisely.

HESTIA Though someday I wish you'd hire a maid he had no interest in diddling.

HERA Oh Zeus isn't carrying on with the staff again, is he?

HESTIA I'm afraid so. I was going to say something earlier but I didn't want to ruin tea. Then when your daughter removed *that* obstacle I decided that now was as good a time as any.

HERA How disappointing! And I was having such a good day.

HESTIA No wonder Aphrodite never keeps female servants.

HERA Can you imagine this place if we filled it with men? Can you imagine Ganymede lacing you into a dress or polishing anything besides a gun?

HESTIA I could help lace you into a dress and there are many men who can polish silver.

HERA It's good to have other women around the house. Reminds one that none of us are getting any younger.

HESTIA I thought that's why one had children.

HERA Is that why you never had children?

HESTIA I would have loved children. They were the one part of not getting married I regret. Thankfully you had five. Solved that problem for me. And I don't have to worry about who is diddling the servants. Of course, Demeter never got married and she had a child. Not that it worked out for her, poor thing. All alone in that house now up in Whitby. And it's always so cold up there on the coast. Poor dear. We really should invite her down here more often.

HERA Yes, but then I'd have to worry about my husband diddling her too.

HESTIA I thought Zeus rarely struck the same tree twice.

HERA Hestia. Don't even you think that was a bit too far?

> *HERA goes back to her book. Suddenly the light goes dark, except for a spot on HESTIA, who addresses the audience.*

HESTIA My youngest sister has a tendency to think of herself as a heroine in a novel, preferably written by Jane Austen. This affliction seems to run in our family, as our middle sister fancies herself a figure of Brontëan affliction and sorrow. I myself have no illusions about my place and importance in the world. How I emerged from the same nest so sensible is a miracle, I suppose. Only I don't believe in miracles. And yet, maybe I do. Our father, who was a monster, died in a fire. He was murdered by a business partner who arranged for the explosion that destroyed our Canterbury mill, but it looked so convincingly like an accident no one was the wiser. We were all so grateful for the lack of scandal that when the arsonist confessed to Mother what he'd done she simply smiled and pretended she hadn't heard him. He was so guilt-ridden he didn't take a cut of the business when he sold it off for us. Mother built an orphanage she had named after our father and then went conveniently mad so that she could play bridge all day at the fashionable asylum we placed her in. Hera takes after her, and that worries me. Women are supposed to fight for their homes, not let the men handle it and swallow whatever they don't manage or simply don't care to settle for us. The center of the hearth is a fire, and so should the center of every woman be. Every woman should burn.

> *The action returns to normal with the lights. IRIS enters pushing a cart loaded with refreshments.*

IRIS The lemonade, ma'am.

HERA Thank you, Iris. Put it on the table, please.

HESTIA Where is Hebe? Wasn't she helping you?

IRIS Miss Hebe is in the garden with her gentleman.

HERA When did he arrive? I didn't hear the bell.

IRIS She saw him walking up the lawn.

HERA When is the Master due back, Iris?

IRIS He didn't say.

HERA He never does. Tell Cook to assume we're eating late then.

IRIS Very good, ma'am.

HERA And tell Hebe and what's-his-name to come inside for a spell or we'll die of boredom and there will be no wedding.

IRIS Yes ma'am.

> *IRIS exits. HERA watches her go, then gets up and crosses to the sideboard. She gets out four glasses.*

HESTIA Do you think she knows that we know?

HERA Do they ever?

HESTIA Well, the last one certainly didn't.

HERA The last one was a conceited cow and as stupid as a boot. This one seems to be a little bit wiser. I think I'll let her figure it out for herself.

HESTIA And then you'll sack her?

HERA Not likely. Once they figure out that I know what's going on they usually sack themselves. The only reason why I got rid of the last one is because she was terrible. Iris on the other hand is quite good. I'd hate to lose her. I've lost a lot of really excellent help thanks to my husband's appetites.

HESTIA Though ironically never your cook.

HERA Yes, well, he seems to draw the line at actual cow-sized, if not cow-eyed. Lemonade?

HESTIA Only half a glass, please, it doesn't always agree with me, as you know.

HERA Cake or biscuit?

HESTIA A sliver of the first, three of the second.

HERA I believe there's nuts in these.

HESTIA Walnuts?

HERA Almonds.

HESTIA Oh, it is a good day.

> *HERA finishes serving HESTIA and then serves herself. For a moment they savor their respective treats. HESTIA puts down her glass.*

You know, dear, I've always wondered why your husband never made an attempt at my virtue.

HERA Before or after our wedding?

HESTIA After, of course. Before hardly matters, don't you think?

HERA I don't know. I do know he was interested.

HESTIA Really?

HERA Oh yes. Why else do you think he started coming around so frequently?

HESTIA We lived in Whitby. He was summering there. It's a small town. We were fashionable, and so was he. What were his other options?

HERA There were other families.

HESTIA You and Demeter were both so pretty. Other families had a pretty daughter, maybe, but not two.

HERA Three.

HESTIA I was too old by then, and you know it.

HERA Don't be ridiculous. You are eight years older.

HESTIA Twenty-six feels quite old when your sisters are eighteen and twenty.

HERA I know for a fact he was quite taken with you at first.

HESTIA How?

HERA I met him when he was climbing a tree to peek through your bedroom window.

HESTIA Were you in the tree too?

HERA No, I was sitting in the window. My window. He'd gotten the bedroom wrong.

HESTIA That sounds just like your husband.

HERA Well, he made the best of it.

HESTIA That also sounds just like your husband.

HERA I remember looking out the window – I'd been sitting at it, you see, because it was so hot that day – just like today – but the breeze was cool and we could see, out on the water, that a storm was coming in. So I had the window open and I'd been reading... *Moll Flanders*, of all things... and I'd fallen asleep. Just sitting in the armchair – my old burgundy one that I loved so, remember? I couldn't have been out of it for more than a moment or two but it was just enough, I suppose, for me to start dreaming, for noises to become much louder, in the way they always do just as you doze off or come awake, and I heard this sound like thunder just outside the window – as if the storm was literally quite suddenly overhead, instead of hours off, brewing on the horizon as it had been. My eyes snapped open, but of course the storm hadn't hit yet, it was just Zeus, trying to keep his balance on a branch and kicking off his second boot. The first had already hit the ground. That was the sound I'd heard.

HESTIA And you weren't frightened?

HERA Not at all. Of course, we knew him by then. He'd been by a few times, with his mother, remember? When they'd taken that house down by beach proper. Oh, I was startled, of course, to see anyone out on that old oak tree, but once he heard me gasp he looked up and smiled so broadly it was like a flash of lightning that just struck me quite through the... the heart. Then he nearly lost his balance but he grabbed onto the tree limb for dear life and once we'd both stopped screaming we both started laughing and once that stopped too I called to him and said, "Well, come in then, silly cuckoo. You've ruined your waistcoat and that's not all that will be ruined if any of the neighbors see you." So I helped him into the house, during which he almost fell twice more times, and then ran down to fetch his boots for him. I didn't even ask him why he was there until I came back.

HESTIA And what did he say?

HERA "I came to visit your sister and profess my love to her."

HESTIA He probably meant Demeter.

HERA No, he meant you. And I know this because he then said, "But I think I'll have better luck with you." And when I asked him why he pointed to my bookshelf and said, "You've better taste in books."

HESTIA And what does that have to do with me?

HERA Don't you remember? The second time he came to tea with his mother?

HESTIA *(not following)* We talked about the Bible. She and I were both quite fluent in it.

HERA Exactly.

HESTIA *(now she understands)* Ah. What a charming story.

HERA Yes, isn't it?

HESTIA I had no idea.

HERA Well of course not. Do you think I could have let anyone know he spent the night in my room before we were even courting, let alone promised?

HESTIA He spent the night? How scandalous!

HERA He slept on the floor.

HESTIA It's still scandalous!

HERA It's precisely because of that attitude we've kept it a secret for years.

HESTIA Oh, I don't really care.

HERA I know. I meant society as a whole. Or at least Mother and most of Whitby – who would have never let us forget it.

HESTIA I am a little bit jealous though. How dare you not have sent him to my room once you knew he was there for me!

HERA Because you would have done what with him once I had?

HESTIA Kicked him out amidst many a scream and Scripture quote.

HERA Precisely.

HESTIA Not that either has done me much good.

HERA You hardly ever scream any more.

HESTIA Or believe in God.

HERA Hestia!

HESTIA Well, it's true. Why do you think I was so religious back in those days? I was praying for a husband, so terrified was I that my sisters would get married before I did – making me the old maid everyone knew I was going to turn out to be anyway. And look what happens! I think I, more than anyone, have good reason to doubt the Holy.

HERA I just thought you'd finally gotten bored with it all.

HESTIA Well, there was that too. And then watching what you and Demeter went through made me realize –

HERA That marriage wasn't all it was supposed to be?

HESTIA Or that my goals might have been a little bit misguided. I'm sure marriage is splendid in its own right, but I can now safely say it wasn't for me – and not just because it never happened.

HERA Well, maybe God protected you, then. Maybe you're the proof God does exist.

HESTIA I'd more readily agree to that if your marriage was more happy.

HERA My dearest sister, my marriage is happy. It's only my romance that has ended tragically. And what of that? They usually do.

HEBE and HERACLES enter. HEBE is holding a bouquet of flowers.

HEBE Are there still cakes left or has Auntie eaten them all?

HERA If she hasn't I'm sure your young man will.

HERACLES Where I come from, Madam, a healthy appetite is a sign of good manners and good constitution.

HERA Well there's still half a cake left, sir, perhaps we shan't bother to slice it and just give you the plate and a fork?

HESTIA Those are pretty flowers, Hebe. Come bring them so I can see them.

HEBE sits down next to HESTIA and HERACLES sits next to HERA.

HEBE Heracles picked them for me. Aren't they lovely?

HERACLES They come from your garden.

HESTIA Isn't he romantic? Here, let me put them in your hair.

HEBE Oh would you?

> *HESTIA proceeds to festoon HEBE with flowers. Suddenly, the lights dim to just a single spot on HEBE, who addresses the audience.*

Everyone in my family treats me like I'm ten years old. Everyone but my grandmother, that is. She knows it's a dangerous world out there. And she knows it's not all fairy puddings and chocolate crème in here. Being the pretty one, that is. Being the daughter of the house. I have sisters, of course, but they're oddly spirited and undesirable, so one has devoted her life to work and the other is always traveling. I think I should quickly find both of these pastimes tedious. My grandmother says a home is a man's castle, but a woman's kingdom, and therefore every daughter is a princess in training for her crown. I think my mother is lovelier than Queen Victoria. But I would not marry my father. He is, of course, steady as the proverbial rock, but I should like a man less brilliant, less intrepid, less proud. Which is not to say I don't love Heracles, because I do. He's funny and generous and pliable, and in an industry where there's lots of money, which means lots of security. He has already promised to build me a house even more lovely than this one. I told that to my grandmother and she said I'd chosen well. It was the first time I understood what it meant to be a grown-up.

> *The lights return to normal. HERA turns to HERACLES.*

HERA And how are the railways?

HERACLES As much of a fright as ever. I swear that between the loading and unloading, the stops and whatnot, it's still faster to just take a carriage down here, or a plain old horse if you have one.

HERA You must be tired. I didn't realize you were coming today.

HERACLES I just stopped off on my way to the pater's. Wouldn't even have come inside except that Hebe said you have fairy cakes.

HEBE Aren't I sweet enough for you?

HERACLES Sweet as honey, Ducks. Where's the Master, by the by?

HERA He's out hunting.

HERACLES Wrong season for... what is it? Deer, or something?

HERA Geese and rabbits are, I believe, the quarry. Is that a large enough slice?

HERACLES Deadly, thank you.

HERA And how is the bank?

HERACLES Well. Floating on the top, as it were.

HERA Good news, as always.

HERACLES Never any reason to expect anything less. Anything I get my name onto is safe as houses.

HERA Of course, dear. That's why we're giving you Hebe.

HEBE You're not giving me to anybody, Mother. I chose Heracles of my own free will.

HESTIA Hebe, this isn't a romance. Don't talk to your mother like that.

HERA Oh, Sister, I think it's good for girls to be a little defiant. Don't you, my boy?

HERACLES As long as they know their place, of course.

HERA Of course.

HEBE What a brutish thing to say, Heracles.

HERACLES I'm only teasing, Ducks.

HEBE Still, you'll see if I kiss you goodbye.

HERACLES What if I kiss you against your will?

HEBE You wouldn't dare!

HERA Children, fighting about who gets to kiss who when you're three weeks from the wedding is going to give your aunt and I such a headache.

HEBE Oh, Auntie knows we're just being foolish for fun.

HESTIA Yes, and with these flowers in your hair you look the part.

HEBE Now I must see.

> *She gets up and moves over to the sideboard, opens it and pulls out a hand-mirror.*

I look just like the Spring.

HERACLES By way of Ophelia.

HEBE Brute!

HERACLES What? Everyone thinks Ophelia was pretty, don't they? I don't know. I never read *King Lear*.

HEBE I want to wear my hair like this at my wedding. My cousin wore flowers in her hair at hers, didn't she?

HESTIA Yes, she did. But Persephone's was a country wedding.

HEBE Ours will be too.

HESTIA Oh this is hardly the country anymore. Not since the train arrived.

HERA How long are you down for, Heracles?

HERACLES Through the weekend, maybe Monday too. The pater has been a bit laid up since he pulled that muscle at the cricket. My mother could use a bit of help around the place, especially since my brother's new baby has him tied up in Dorset.

HERA You should all come to tea on Saturday.

HEBE And stay for supper.

HERACLES I'll ask my parents, certainly.

HERA Yes, do. It's been so long since I've seen dear Alcmene. They're so close, of course, but we do seem to rarely, if ever, leave the house these days. Isn't that so, Hestia?

HESTIA It's true, we've become quite the wallflowers.

HERACLES My mother is the same. Barely ever leaves the house now. And when she does, she just complains the whole time. Hardly worth it, really, all the bother she causes us.

HEBE My mother never complains.

HERA Hebe, don't exaggerate.

HERACLES You know that's true, Ma'am. I never do hear you complain.

HERA Well, of course not. If you did, how impolite of me that would be, don't you think? But that hardly means I don't complain. If I didn't, think what would we do with your poor auntie?

HESTIA It's true. Without my role as confidante, I'd be hard-pressed to find a way to pass these long days and nights until my death.

HEBE You see how they join forces to mock us, Heracles? It was far worse earlier, let me tell you.

HERACLES I like your mother, Hebe. She has so much wit and spirit. Your aunt too. You're both excellent ladies. And always such good hosts.

HESTIA I don't know, Hera. I suspect Master Heracles just likes the cakes. What do you think?

HERA I think it doesn't matter, Sister, so long as he pays for them in compliments – and kisses to my daughter, of course.

HERACLES Flowers are kisses of a sort, aren't they?

HEBE Not when they're plucked from one's own garden, brute.

HERACLES It's not your garden, Ducks. It's your father's.

HEBE It's mother's, actually.

HERACLES But your father's family owns the house.

HEBE But mother planted the garden.

HERA It's true. I did.

HERACLES Why, then I love your mother's garden as well as her cakes.

HERA Don't be so hasty with the praise. Hestia baked the cakes.

HERACLES Really?

HERA Of course not, Cook did. Do you think any of us actually know how to bake?

IRIS enters.

IRIS Master Heracles? Your mother has sent a driver around.

HERACLES How did she know I was here?

HERA It's a small town, Master Heracles, even in this day of trains. And you do cut such a dashing and recognizable figure.

HERACLES *(blushing)* Balderdash.

HEBE Mother, stop flirting with my fiancé.

HESTIA Shall we have Iris wrap the rest of your cake?

HERACLES I'm sure Mother's got one waiting for me at home.

HESTIA And here you've spoiled your appetite.

HERACLES Hardly.

To HEBE.

You got a kiss for me or not then?

HEBE Course I do.

They kiss goodbye. He turns to HERA, who has given them a polite distance.

HERACLES I'll be around Saturday then? With the mater and pater, I mean.

HERA That sounds lovely.

HERACLES And Zeus will be in?

HEBE Daddy's always around on weekends.

HERACLES Spending a lot more time in general around here these days, I hear.

HERA Apparently the rabbit hunting is very good. Shall we show your young man to the door, Hebe?

HEBE Yes.

IRIS Shall I stay and clear up, ma'am?

HERA Please do, Iris, thank you. Coming, Hestia?

HESTIA *(eyes on IRIS)* No, I think I'll linger a bit longer over my last biscuit. Have a good evening, Master Heracles. Wish your father better for me?

HERACLES Certainly, Ma'am. Very good to see you.

HESTIA And you!

> *HERA, HEBE and HERACLES all exit. IRIS begins to clear the dishes. The light is noticeably shifting towards late afternoon. HESTIA finishes another biscuit while she watches IRIS work. Eventually, she has cleared everything back onto the service cart except for a single small dish, sitting on HESTIA's lap. They lock eyes over the dish for a moment. There is an unsaid tenseness that creeps into the room.*

IRIS Might I… I'm sorry, ma'am, are you… are you quite finished with that plate, I mean to say.

HESTIA There appears to be nothing on it. What do you think, Iris?

IRIS Shall I take it away then?

HESTIA Have you cleared the sideboard? I believe Miss Hebe left the remains of our previous tea set collected over there.

IRIS Of course, Miss.

> *IRIS moves over to the sideboard, picks up the tray of shattered tea cups and takes them back to the service cart. She turns back when she's finished.*

IRIS Will that be all, Miss?

HESTIA Ma'am, Iris. I may be unmarried, but I am also much older than you, not to mention superior in other ways. Do remind yourself that when seeking the manner in which to address me.

IRIS Yes, ma'am.

HESTIA And no, that will not be all. Do take this plate with you before you go.

> *She holds out the plate at arm's length. After a moment of hesitation, IRIS walks over and takes the plate in her own hand, but HESTIA does not let go of it either. Their eyes lock again.*

Mistress Hera may be too polite to complain but I'm not.

IRIS Have I done something wrong, ma'am?

HESTIA Do you really think asking the question will somehow throw me off the scent of a bitch when I smell one?

IRIS Ma'am?

HESTIA Don't "ma'am" me and don't play innocent. We know all about you.

IRIS Know what – ?

HESTIA I said, don't –

IRIS Don't talk to me like a slave. I'm not one. And if you think I'm going to stand here and let you call me a bitch without knowing why just because you happen to employ me at this particular moment of my life – you are gravely mistaken. Ma'am.

> *A long moment. HESTIA releases the plate. IRIS drops it onto the service cart.*

HESTIA Well, I wasn't expecting that.

IRIS People like you never are. Now may I ask again the reason for your insulting me, for I should very much like to keep my position and it would be hard for me to do so under such conditions as have just transpired.

HESTIA You want to keep your position?

IRIS I do. I find the house beautiful, the work manageable, Mistress Hera and Miss Hebe and yourself all very agreeable – up until this moment at least.

HESTIA Do you find your master agreeable?

IRIS Master Zeus?

HESTIA He is the only master in the house, is he not?

IRIS I find him perfectly agreeable when he is home.

HESTIA How agreeable?

IRIS What are you implying?

HESTIA What do you think I'm implying?

IRIS Nothing I would admit to – were there any truth to it – which there isn't.

> *Beat.*

I am not interested in men anymore. My husband was a sailor. He died at sea three years ago. When they told me, I was pregnant. I lost the baby. I have nothing in my heart but empty, howling wind.

> *Beat.*

How twisted your mind is.

HESTIA Live as long as I have – see what I have seen – and I challenge you not to become a little bit twisted, my dear. Assuming you haven't already.

> *Beat.*

I believe you, by the way. So we can be friends again, if you like. Though we have not yet solved the problem.

IRIS Problem?

HESTIA My sister suspects you have been dallying with her husband. Which is not entirely an unnatural expectation, so don't be so quick to be offended by her suspicions. You are very pretty, my dear: you hide your iciness well. And Master Zeus has a reputation. It has happened before, with three of your predecessors. Europa. Io. Danae. And several women in the local countryside. Leto. Maia. Eurynome. Semele. Two more up in London: a Metis and a Themis. And our sister. Demeter. Once. A long long time ago now. There was an incident with his younger son's wife too but… well… he's quite a rake, actually. That's the short of it. You must be quite the paragon of virtue to have rebuffed him for so long, even considering your inner sorrow. My condolences, by the way.

IRIS Thank you.

HESTIA We're not altogether different, you and I.

> *She points to her heart.*

I'm all ashes here, when it comes to romance. But the rest of me is embers when it comes to all else. I love my sisters dearly, especially my youngest one, and I do not take kindly to the misdeeds of her husband. I have been known to burn her rivals quite enthusiastically when I can do so without her knowledge.

IRIS I had heard the mistress of this house could be cruel. I did not know which mistress they meant.

HESTIA Now you do know who – and why.

IRIS And will you now punish me, wrongfully, since your sister suspects, wrongfully, that I am one more harlot for her husband?

HESTIA Of course not. I've no interest in punishment for punishment's sake. But we must still find out who the culprit is.

IRIS Can you be so sure that there is one?

HESTIA Oh yes. For the last two months – just shortly after you began your employment – Master Zeus, who previously made a habit of frequenting London on business – and pleasure – during the week, has been making it a far more frequent habit to spend his days and nights here in the country. Hence, my sister's suspicions and my accusations.

IRIS But can you really be certain that an affair is in progress? Perhaps Master Zeus is choosing to spend more time at home because his daughter is soon to be married and he would like to cherish these last few months with his family.

HESTIA Perhaps. But then why is he so rarely at home with them, even though he now frequents, once again, the neighborhood?

IRIS This is all far too much intrigue for me, I am afraid. I am really much simpler in my wants and desires.

HESTIA And what are your wants and desires?

IRIS To be left alone. And out of this. Ma'am. It's none of my affair.

HESTIA I suppose that's true.

> *Beat.*

And you're sure you know nothing about this?

IRIS Nothing.

HESTIA No servants' gossip? No passing thoughts or suspicions?

IRIS Like I said, ma'am: my mind doesn't twist that way.

HESTIA How nice that must be for you. Why do you suppose that is?

IRIS I suppose it must be the difference, ma'am.

HESTIA Difference?

IRIS Between a young widow and an old maid.

> *A long moment.*

HESTIA You may go now, Iris.

IRIS Very good, ma'am.

> *She exits. HESTIA sits a moment in silence. The room has grown noticeably darker, almost blue-gray. There is a distant, low rumble of thunder. HESTIA stands and moves over to the windows, looking out of them at something in the distance. HERA enters.*

HERA Was that thunder I just heard?

HESTIA It was. Come look. Towards the east.

> *HERA joins her at the window.*

HERA Oh yes. Look at those clouds.

HESTIA Moving quite fast, aren't they?

HERA I do hope Zeus is back before long.

HESTIA He's been gone all day, hasn't he?

HERA These summer storms can be so sudden and dangerous.

HESTIA He's weathered many before, dear.

HERA I know. But even seasoned sailors drown.

HESTIA *(quietly struck by the oddness of the statement)* Yes, they do.

> Beat.

You still love him, don't you? Even after all these years and all you've… been through.

HERA Of course I do. But I wouldn't wish getting stuck in the rain on anybody.

HESTIA Why?

HERA Influenza, rheumatism, ruined suits, mud on the floor –

HESTIA Why do you still love him?

HERA I don't know. Because I'm supposed to. Because I would anyway. Because there is no reason. It's not something you can explain, can you? I mean… do you know why you still love me?

HESTIA You're my family.

HERA And he is mine. And we were very happy once. We're still happy now, just… differently so.

HESTIA When was the last time you slept together?

HERA Not half so long ago as you think, I imagine. And I'll ask you not to worry about that for me, thank you very much, Sister.

HESTIA Don't you ever wonder that you might be staying for a memory?

HERA I'm staying for my family, Hestia. Which includes you. Now if I were staying for a memory, that would make me Demeter, wouldn't it?

HESTIA And will you, like her, shut yourself up in the house once your daughter is gone?

HERA Well if I did at least it would be a much prettier house.

HESTIA I'm not being clever, Hera, I'm asking you in earnest.

HERA I know, dear, and I can't for the life of me imagine why.

HESTIA Because you don't seem happy to me.

HERA Then I must not be doing my best, must I?

> *Another low rumble of thunder. The wind chimes in the garden are heard clattering as the breeze picks up. IRIS enters.*

IRIS There's a storm coming, ma'am.

HERA So I can see. Run and check the windows, Iris. Make sure they're all closed.

IRIS Yes, ma'am.

> *IRIS exits deeper into the house. HERA closes the windows of the sunroom.*

HERA From stifling to chilly in a matter of moments. Oh how I do love the English summer.

> *HESTIA retrieves her knitting from the divan.*

HESTIA I think I'm going to lie down for a bit before dinner.

HERA Are you not feeling well?

HESTIA Too many biscuits, I suspect.

HERA I warned you that you were being greedy.

HESTIA Did you?

HERA *(after a moment)* No. But I thought it. I just didn't say anything.

HESTIA Well, that didn't help anyone at all, then, did it?

HERA No. How very foolish of me.

HESTIA You're never a fool, dear.

She kisses her.

Just a little too gracious for your own good.

HERA I learned to be forgiving from you.

HESTIA Yes, but in order to be forgiving you must first learn to see what it is you're meant to forgive.

HERA I don't know about that. God forgives blindly.

HESTIA Not any God I know.

HERA Well, and you are the expert.

She kisses her.

Have a good nap, Hestia.

HESTIA exits into the house. The thunder rumbles, the chimes tinkle. HEBE enters.

HEBE Father's not back yet, is he?

HERA No.

HEBE Pooh. I wanted to ask him if he'd take Heracles hunting with him on Saturday. He's been longing to try the new rifles.

HERA Your father is planning to give him a set of his own for the wedding.

HEBE Really?

HERA Don't tell him I said so.

HEBE What am I getting? Besides the wedding, of course.

HERA You're expecting something else, are you?

HEBE Well, all the others got presents. And I am the youngest and the last to go…

HERA So you assume yours will be particularly nice, don't you?

HEBE Shouldn't it be?

HERA Perhaps we shall give you a wrought iron tea set. Or something else you can't destroy.

HEBE Really? Are we really going to harp on me about that forever?

HERA I'm only teasing, darling.

Beat.

You know that, right?

HEBE What? Oh, of course, Mother. Please don't get all serious about it.

HERA Well, I wasn't sure. Sometimes you can be sensitive…

HEBE Not that sensitive.

HERA You've always been my sunniest – my most charming.

HEBE Your favorite?

HERA I love all my children the same.

HEBE Yes, but let's be honest: I am the prettiest.

HERA Your sisters each have their own appeal –

HEBE Eilithyia is so quiet, though. I think I have much more energy and charm.

HERA But she is helpful and good.

HEBE I'm helpful.

HERA And good?

HEBE I am good… some of the time.

HERA Most of the time.

HEBE See – !

HERA But when you're bad…

HEBE I'm still never as bad as Eris!

HERA Yes, well, Eris is a handful.

HEBE She's evil.

HERA Willful and high-spirited is more how I would describe her.

HEBE Well, she never almost drowned you… twice!

HERA You were four and most annoying then, Hebe. We all thought of drowning you at some point. Your brothers actually had a sack ready and everything.

HEBE Not Ares. He always protected me.

HERA Ares loathed you until you were ten. You, on the other hand, had a crush on him that Keats would have had a hard time putting into words.

HEBE That's not true!

HERA All of you girls did. But it made sense. He's always been so handsome, especially now, in his uniform.

HEBE You're very proud of him, aren't you?

HERA I'm proud of all of you.

HEBE Even Hephaestus?

HERA Your brother has a good soul and a fine trade. Why shouldn't I be proud?

HEBE He hit Daddy.

HERA *(remembering)* Yes, well… Daddy deserved it that time. And Daddy certainly hit him back.

HEBE Will he come to the wedding, do you suppose?

HERA Of course he will, darling. That was all a long time ago and they've patched things up.

HEBE Then why don't he and Aphrodite ever come for Christmas or Easter?

HERA Your brother is very busy with his work. And your sister-in-law isn't always very agreeable, is she?

HEBE I want a wedding dress as lovely as hers was.

HERA We've already picked your dress. You know what it looks like.

HEBE Yes, but I want it to look on me like it looked on her.

HERA It will look on you like it's supposed to: which will be beautiful and angelic – just like you.

HEBE Will you miss me when I'm gone, Mother?

HERA You won't be gone far.

HEBE Yes, but I won't be underfoot all the time either. Don't you think you'll notice that? I shall most certainly notice you not always hovering overhead.

HERA I shall always be hovering overhead. Be you here, or in London, or as far away as India.

HEBE And Daddy too?

HERA Of course.

HEBE hugs her mother fiercely.

HEBE Oh, I don't know why, but I'm suddenly so scared of all this.

HERA All of what, dear?

HEBE The marriage. The future.

HERA Oh, don't worry about that. It'll all turn out just fine. It always does.

HEBE Not always.

HERA Yes, always, my dove. Even when it doesn't. We just somehow can't see how it's fine. Learning to see it so that it's perfect – that's the trick. That's the magic.

> *There is another rumble of thunder overhead, this time much closer than previously, and a flash of lightning. Both women look up. The rain begins to splatter against the windowpanes, sparsely at first, then with progressive ferocity till it is a full-fledged torrent. During the course of the transition, HERA and HEBE drift apart so that each is staring out the darkening windows into the storm.*

I do wonder where your father is.

HEBE I'm sure he'll be home soon.

HERA I've never liked the rain. Your father has always been very comfortable in it but I… I am not. It's so cold. So aggressive. And thunder and lightning frighten me.

HEBE He'll be all right. And he has Ganymede with him.

HERA Yes.

> *She turns back into the room.*

Goodness, it's gotten dark. Run and find Iris, will you, and have her light the lamps?

HEBE We should make a fire too, in the parlor.

HERA Good idea.

HEBE And hot chocolate.

HERA You see? Always my little angel. Run and tell Cook to get out the melting pans.

HEBE I thought you wanted me to find Iris.

HERA I'll find Iris. You go to Cook and then see if you can get the fire started.

HEBE Auntie is always better at that then I am.

HERA True. And we don't want you to burn the house down.

HEBE Mother!

HERA Run! Fly!

> *They exit in separate directions. A moment. Thunder and lightning. The room grows quite dark. IRIS enters, carrying a lamp. She opens the sideboard and removes several candles in holders that she places around the room, then proceeds to light from the lamp. Thunder and lightning. As her back is turned to the windows, one of the doors to the garden opens and GANYMEDE, sopping wet, slips into the house carrying a gun. He places it on the floor as quietly as he can, but IRIS, hearing it, turns and gasps.*

IRIS Good Lord, you gave me a fright!

GANYMEDE Sorry. The kitchen door was locked and Cook didn't answer when I knocked.

> *He smiles.*

Did you hear: that was almost poetry.

IRIS Where's the Master?

GANYMEDE He went through the front door, like he's supposed to. The young Miss saw him coming and she's covering him with kisses, getting her frock all wet.

IRIS And my freshly mopped hall. Speaking of which – take your boots off and carry them. I'm not going to have you trailing mud from here to the kitchen.

GANYMEDE Won't matter if I carry them. My stockings are wet through.

IRIS Then go back around to the kitchen door and I'll let you in.

GANYMEDE You see what it's like out there? I'm not going back out into that.

IRIS Stop being impossible. What are you going to do, stand here and wait for the lamps to dry you out?

GANYMEDE If you're so worried about me making a mess why don't you run and fetch me some clothes?

IRIS I don't work for you.

GANYMEDE And I'm not worried about your freshly mopped floors.

> *He starts to head out in the direction of the hall.*

IRIS They're onto you, you know?

> *He turns.*

GANYMEDE Onto what?

IRIS You know what.

GANYMEDE Not unless you say it. How do you know?

IRIS The sister went after me about it this afternoon. Practically called me a whore.

GANYMEDE And what did you tell her?

IRIS That it wasn't me keeping the Master skulking around the homestead.

GANYMEDE And?

IRIS And that I didn't know who was.

GANYMEDE Which is true, because you don't know anything.

IRIS I know what you are.

GANYMEDE Yeah? But here's the thing, love. Nobody gives a fuck what you think.

IRIS You could go to prison, you know. Both of you. If anyone found out.

GANYMEDE Why would anyone find out?

IRIS The sister has her eyes peeled. And the Mistress isn't stupid. And you're not careful.

GANYMEDE Why do I need to be?

IRIS I just said –

GANYMEDE He has money, Iris. He has more money than God. That matters more than if people approve or don't approve –

IRIS The Law.

GANYMEDE Fuck the Law.

IRIS Are you drunk?

GANYMEDE Very. I mean what else do you think we do all day besides screw?

IRIS Aren't you supposed to be hunting?

> *GANYMEDE holds up two bloody dead rabbits. Thunder and lightning.*

GANYMEDE Want me to throw them and see if you can catch them with your teeth?

IRIS You disgust me.

GANYMEDE Go work somewhere else then. The Master will pay you off if you do. Just make it look like you've been carrying on with him and there's a hundred quid in it for you. It's worked out quite well for the girls who came before you. Europa. Io. Danae.

IRIS That's the second time you've offered me that arrangement, Ganymede. Offer it a third time and I'll make sure the Mistress does know exactly who to suspect.

GANYMEDE You think you're so holy and virtuous.

IRIS I think I'm virtuous – and I am. Holy doesn't concern me either way. And that's why I can live with you and him and all the rest of it. But if you try and tear me down to keep you safe don't expect me to let you do so without a fight.

GANYMEDE I like a good fight.

IRIS You won't with me.

Thunder and lightning. HERA enters, carrying a lamp.

HERA Ganymede? Is that you standing there?

GANYMEDE *(all good behavior suddenly)* Yes, Mistress.

HERA You're all wet.

GANYMEDE Your pardon, Mistress. The kitchen door was locked. Shall I go around?

HERA And go back out into that awful weather? I wouldn't think of it. Just hurry to the kitchen so you don't get mud all over the floors. Iris mopped today.

GANYMEDE Yes, ma'am.

HERA The Master is home too, of course?

GANYMEDE Yes, ma'am. He's in the parlor with Miss Hebe, I think.

HERA Excellent. Come join us there when you get dry. Both of you. We're making chocolate.

GANYMEDE Thank you, ma'am. I'd be honored.

Thunder and lightning.

HERA What do you think? Will it go all night?

GANYMEDE Seems to have come out of nowhere, don't you think?

HERA Storms like this always do. But they usually blow themselves out just as suddenly. So long as it clears up by the wedding, we'll be all right.

GANYMEDE Of course it will, ma'am. It only rains for three weeks in the Bible.

HERA Go get dry before you catch your death of cold.

GANYMEDE Yes, ma'am.

> *GANYMEDE turns and smiles at IRIS, then exits in the direction of the hall. Thunder and lightning. HERA turns to her.*

HERA Fetch some rags, won't you, Iris? We'll clean up this puddle he's left for us.

IRIS No better than a dog, that one.

HERA Oh we're all animals, in the end, aren't we? At least dogs are loyal. Some rags, please.

> *IRIS nods and goes out. HERA watches her go.*

HERA *(quietly, to herself)* Stupid bitch.

> *Thunder and lightning. Blackout.*
>
> *End of Act 1.*

Act 2

> *The same room, three weeks later. Rain continues to pour outside, and though it's the middle of the day there is a gray pallor over everything. HERACLES, in an immaculate and perfect suit, sits on the divan, polishing a large hunting rifle. He holds the gun awkwardly, but with a certain amount of love and ardor – as if it's something he aspires to, but doesn't exactly understand. A long moment of relative silence, all quiet but the sound of the rain and the wind beyond the glass doors of the room. Suddenly, there is a slamming door sound somewhere in the house, followed by a quick patter of footsteps, followed by another slamming door. HERACLES stops his polishing long enough to look up, listen, shake his head with mild exasperation, then goes back to polishing. Another long moment, and then something smashes off in another place in the house. HERACLES sighs, shakes his head in disbelief, and keeps polishing his gun. IRIS enters from the direction of the kitchen.*

IRIS Master Heracles – !

HERACLES *(jumping)* Good God!

He is so startled he accidentally fires the gun into the upper right side wall. There is a modest explosion of plaster followed by a shower of dust. IRIS screams.

IRIS Jesus save us!

HERACLES *(dropping the gun as if it were a poisonous snake)* I didn't know it was loaded, I swear!

IRIS You could have killed somebody, you giant oaf!

HERACLES Don't get cross with me – I told you I didn't know it was loaded!

GANYMEDE enters from the right.

GANYMEDE What the hell was that?

IRIS The young master shot the wall.

HERACLES Iris startled me!

IRIS Don't blame me.

HERACLES I'm not blaming anybody – it was an accident!

GANYMEDE Why was the gun loaded?

HERACLES I don't know! I didn't load it.

GANYMEDE Sir?

HERACLES All right, I did load it, but I didn't think I'd done it properly.

GANYMEDE I told the Master it was a mistake to give you that gun before the wedding.

IRIS You think giving it to him after the wedding would be any less of a mistake?

GANYMEDE At least he wouldn't have shot the walls in our house.

HERACLES It's not your house and at least it was the walls – please bear in mind.

GANYMEDE Of course, sir. Better the walls than someone's head.

IRIS *(under her breath)* Thank God for small miracles.

GANYMEDE Iris, fetch a broom.

IRIS Fetch it yourself. I'm supposed to go help Miss Hebe with her hair.

HESTIA enters.

HESTIA Miss Hebe is locked in the upstairs washroom and does not appear to be interested in coming out any time soon. Who's been shot?

HERACLES Nobody. The wall.

HESTIA The wall? Was it poised to attack?

HERACLES I misfired. Iris startled me.

IRIS I was going to tell him Master Zeus wanted him in the drawing room.

HESTIA Why aren't you in the drawing room, Master Heracles?

HERACLES It's stuffy and crowded.

HESTIA Yes, darling, with your wedding guests. Best you attend to them since they're here to honor *you* at *your* wedding.

HERACLES If there is a wedding.

HESTIA There will be a wedding.

HERACLES I don't see the rain letting up. Do you?

HESTIA This house doesn't have a ballroom just so we have somewhere to store the piano.

HERACLES Hebe wants an outdoor wedding more than anything. You know that.

HESTIA My niece is going to have to accept that her whole life can't be sunshine and butterflies.

HERACLES Not on her wedding day she isn't going to accept that.

HESTIA Really? Strikes me as the best day possible for her to learn a very valuable lesson. Now, young man, I think you'd better go shake some hands and thank everyone who braved the rain in spite of the invitations listing an afternoon of outdoor festivities. To do anything less than be gracious right now would be both unacceptable and unpardonable.

HERACLES *(getting up to go)* Yes, ma'am.

HESTIA And leave the gun, won't you? It's not doing anything to improve the situation.

HERACLES Oh come on, I won't shoot anyone, I promise!

HESTIA Young man, forgive me if I question the validity of your oaths when lives are at stake.

HERACLES So this is what you're all like on a bad day?

HESTIA No, this is what we're like on a good day that looks like it might turn bad. Now please go help turn it around.

HERACLES I think I should be angry about all this. But I'm not.

He leaves. HESTIA walks over to investigate the damaged wall.

HESTIA This is about the last thing we needed.

GANYMEDE Could have been worse. Could have been someone's head.

HESTIA Thank God for small miracles. Get rid of the gun, will you?

IRIS What's to be done about Miss Hebe?

HESTIA What's to be done with any bride who wakes up to find her wedding day rained out? Short of summoning the sun, that is.

IRIS Is the wedding to be canceled then?

HERA *(entering)* It is most certainly not to be canceled. Iris, please go and dress my daughter's hair. I have managed to persuade her to leave the powder room but I can not vouch for the duration of time she'll remain cooperative so the faster the better.

IRIS *(with a curtsy)* Yes, ma'am.

She goes out.

HERA Ganymede – is my husband – ?

GANYMEDE In the study, ma'am.

HERA And Master Heracles?

GANYMEDE With him. And the guests.

HERA How many actually made it?

GANYMEDE Forty-one, the last count.

HERA That's less than half.

HESTIA Our ballroom only holds sixty comfortably anyway. I assume we're moving the wedding there.

HERA The reception, yes. The wedding will happen in the garden, as planned.

HESTIA On what date?

HERA Today, as planned.

HESTIA But the tents weren't even set up. It's been raining for three weeks.

HERA We don't need the tents. We just need the trellis. And every umbrella we can muster. Which will be your job, Ganymede.

GANYMEDE Yes, ma'am.

HERA Why are you holding that gun? Isn't that one of the ones we gave to Master Heracles?

GANYMEDE Yes, ma'am.

HESTIA He used it to kill the wall.

HERA *(turning to look at the hole)* Well, at least we won't have to get his first success stuffed and mounted.

HESTIA I told you he was far too much of a city boy to properly use those.

HERA It's my fault for letting Zeus give them their presents ahead of time. But at least it bought us some peace during the second week of solid rain.

HESTIA The weather really has been unfortunate. Even for England.

HERA Oh this is beyond nature, I'm sure of it. This is God Himself coming down to stop me. But He shall not succeed. Ganymede – the umbrellas, please.

GANYMEDE Yes, ma'am.

HERA And hide the guns until after the wedding, will you?

GANYMEDE Of course.

HESTIA I vote for the next ten years.

GANYMEDE I second that.

HERA A closet in the servants' wing will do, please, thank you. Oh, and Ganymede: tell Master Zeus fifteen minutes, twenty at most, until we have the ceremony. We'll need him, the priest, the groom, the mother-and father-in-law, my children and yourself. Anyone else who wants to may attend, or they can wait for us inside. I doubt we'll be lingering over it long.

GANYMEDE Yes, ma'am.

HERA One more thing, my boy: if you think I'm mad please just say so.

GANYMEDE I don't think anything of the sort, ma'am.

HERA You look incredulous. There is an incredulous look on your face. Isn't there, Sister?

HESTIA Indeed. Quite incredulous.

GANYMEDE I'm not incredulous, ma'am. I'm impressed.

HERA With what?

GANYMEDE With what grace you always do your best, ma'am. That's all.

He goes out, taking the gun with him.

HESTIA All the help in this house is always so cheeky.

HERA Of course they are, the way we spoil them. But it's hard not to when they do their jobs so well. Besides, Ganymede always reminds me of Ares when he was that age.

HESTIA But he's not Ares. He's a gardener's son from Hastings.

HERA Oh Lord, sometimes I wish the servants were *my* children. They're so obedient!

HESTIA What kind of mother wishes her children servants?

HERA Oh, I wouldn't wish my children on anyone's household – imagine the disarray.

HESTIA Clever. Still, if Ganymede is impressed, I am incredulous. I can't believe you're going to continue holding the wedding outside.

HERA Promising that was the only way I could get Hebe to open the powder room door. If she was your daughter you would have done the same.

HESTIA If she was my daughter she wouldn't have grown up so obstinate and willful.

HERA She is hardly obstinate, Sister. She is simply over-excited and a bit fixated. You would be too if you had been waiting for something as long as she had only to have it thwarted by something as arbitrary as the English weather.

HESTIA Arbitrary, yes, but also out of our control. Life is full of things out of our control that we must, occasionally, give way to.

HERA I am the last person you need to explain the nature of graciousness to.

HESTIA Forgive me, I am speaking to you as if you were your daughter. And I am peevish and over-excited myself. I have not enjoyed being cooped up so long and nearly a month is too long for anyone, I imagine.

HERA As if we really leave the house all that often when the weather is nice.

HESTIA At least we have the option.

HERA We still do. We just must make certain adjustments to the original plan.

HESTIA Why can't she have the wedding in the ballroom? It's a lovely room.

HERA Every room in the house is lovely. That's not the point.

HESTIA What is the point? I thought weddings were supposed to be lovely.

HERA They are supposed to be significant. Lovely is a luxury. And while every room in this house is perfection itself, the center of Hebe's wedding, you may recall, is outside of the house.

HESTIA *(realizing)* The oak tree.

HERA Precisely. The sapling Zeus brought from Whitby and planted on our wedding day.

HESTIA Of course. Hebe wants to be married under it.

HERA I want her to be married under it. So does Zeus. It's something all three of us feel is the right thing. She is, after all, our youngest and… and our last.

HESTIA I understand. But it is just a tree.

HERA It's not just a tree: it's a symbol. And symbols are important, especially when it comes to marriages and to families.

HESTIA Interesting. I would have said "warmth." And it's cold out there, Sister.

HERA I know. So keep the fires stoked here inside. We are going through with the ceremony.

HESTIA I am already imagining the mud and am duly horrified.

HERA Don't be such a priss, Sister. They're wood floors. They mop easily. *(indicating the hole in the wall)* That, however, will be much more difficult to fix.

HESTIA It's not even in a good place to hang a painting.

HERA I'll have Ganymede re-plaster it tomorrow. He's clever and careful. It might not look so bad.

HESTIA You'll have to re-do the wallpaper in here.

HERA I wanted to anyway.

HESTIA Will nothing faze you?

HERA Oh don't say that, Sister. The day is hardly over yet.

She goes out. HESTIA watches her go. There is a sudden rumbling of thunder overhead, and a flash of lightning.

HESTIA *(looking up)* Excellent.

    IRIS enters.

IRIS Miss Hebe is almost ready, ma'am.

HESTIA Thank you, Iris.

IRIS She'll need help with the train of her gown, ma'am. Coming down the stairs.

HESTIA I'll go up to her, Iris. I think they'll need you in the hall where they're assembling the wedding party for their watery sojourn.

IRIS I'm to go with them?

HESTIA Someone's going to have to hold the bride's umbrella so that the groom can slip the ring on her finger. Important part of the ceremony, you may recall.

IRIS Our wedding was indoors.

HESTIA How sensible of you.

IRIS Necessary, ma'am. Poor Londoners don't often have the luxury of gardens.

HESTIA He was a sailor, you said. Why didn't you just marry on the ship?

IRIS Thought about it. His captain performed the ceremony after all.

HESTIA So then why didn't you?

IRIS Don't know. Thought it was bad luck.

HESTIA You don't strike me as superstitious.

IRIS Many people think that letting a woman on board a ship causes it to sink.

HESTIA But your husband's ship did sink.

IRIS Indeed.

HESTIA Was there a woman on it when it sank?

IRIS There was a woman counting on it. Maybe that was all it needed.

    Some more thunder and lightning. The light suddenly dims to a spot on IRIS.

I have always detested spinsters, but more so since my husband died. There is some kind of wicked glee they take, I have discovered, in the fact that I was happy and now I'm not. It's probably the only thing that makes them think it's perfectly justified to have never gone about forsaking whatever dusty, bloodless virtue they're still clinging to – or at least pretending to. As if it's some great feat not to indulge what you don't even know you're missing, or as if the Almighty gives a fig for whatever you've done or not done with your muff or your ring finger or any combination of the two. If I hate love now, at least I can say I've known what it's like and I've reached my side of things based on experience. But when some old bag masked up like a nun with or without the robes starts staring down her nose at me like I deserved what I got or my husband did or our marriage… well, there's no easier way to make me an enemy. Women are supposed to help one another, not gloat over each other's worst day. But oftentimes that's what we do. Maybe because it's the only way we can hurt someone else like we've been hurt – or disappoint them just as deeply as life has disappointed us.

The light returns to normal. She turns to HESTIA.

I've thought more about… about our conversation a few weeks ago. Do you remember?

HESTIA Of course I do. Most interesting conversation I've had in years.

IRIS I was wondering if you were any closer to discovering who –

HESTIA I'm afraid not. You were my only lead. And since you've established yourself as innocent, more or less, I've not many others to suspect. Cook isn't his type, and besides she's been with the family for two decades. I'm more of a suspect than she is. That leaves the scullery maid and she's what? Twelve?

IRIS Ten.

HESTIA There you go. He's not that sort of man.

IRIS What sort of man is he, do you think?

HESTIA Rather a precocious question for your betters, isn't it?

IRIS I recall you said we were friends.

HESTIA I was being glib when I said that.

IRIS I know. I choose to hold you to it anyway.

HESTIA What a forward little thing you are. No wonder you fit in around here.

IRIS Please answer the question.

HESTIA Why? Why should you care?

IRIS I like to understand the nature of those who I work for. It allows me to serve them better.

HESTIA Oh bravo, I almost believe that. And why should I tell you anything? What's in it for me?

IRIS A secret.

HESTIA A good one?

IRIS An important one. I'll let you decide what's good and what's evil on your own.

Beat.

So what kind of man is he?

HESTIA A good one, I think. Principled, hard-working, intelligent, fair. He has provided immensely for a large family, reared productive sons, and he has never laid a finger on his wife or his daughters that wasn't kind and gentle. He has a wandering eye which often leads to a wandering hand, and he suffers from restlessness and a tendency to hide things from people who love him, but these things just make him... well, typical, in my opinion. A typical man, at least.

IRIS Not all men are like that.

HESTIA No, it's true, some drown young and are easily romanticized.

IRIS And some live to be quite old and are neither weak-willed, nor over-privileged.

HESTIA You've heard me admit his failings but I won't call him an evil man or even a dishonorable one. If he were, I'd have made my sister quit him years ago. I won't lie that I'd not be unhappy to find her a new life yet, but since she insists on loving him and he insists on not being terrible enough to hate, I must content myself with punishing his conquests.

IRIS Well, ma'am, you're looking at the wrong people for this latest one.

HESTIA I know that already. She's not in the house, whoever she is. Clearly it's someone in the neighborhood, though, or he wouldn't have given up so many of his weekdays in London. Granted, the field is broader, but that doesn't mean I won't find my rabbit.

IRIS "Rabbit" is an interesting choice of words.

HESTIA I like it. Makes me feel like a fox.

IRIS Yes, but foxes can't catch wolves.

HESTIA Why should they need to? They're both hunting rabbits.

IRIS Yes. And some wolves hunt in pairs.

HESTIA I'm afraid the allegory has become a bit too convoluted for me, Iris. I'm not following.

IRIS That's a shame. Because I basically just told you everything.

HEBE *(off)* Auntie!

IRIS Excuse me, ma'am. But it sounds like the young Miss is ready, and I'll need to find my boots. And an umbrella. Such a rain we've been having lately, isn't it?

She exits before HESTIA can say anything.

HEBE *(off)* Auntie! Are you there? Is anybody? I can't come down the stairs in this thing without… help.

HESTIA *(calling)* I'm coming, darling, just a moment!

She goes out. Thunder and lightning. HERA enters. She is wearing a raincoat and carrying an umbrella.

HERA Hebe, darling, are you ready?

HESTIA *(off)* Give us a moment, Sister. We're coming down the stairs.

HEBE Don't look Mother: I want to surprise you!

HERA All right. My back is turned.

A moment. HERA waits, her back turned to the door HEBE will come through. HERA looks around the room. She sees the hole in the wall from the gunshot. Another sigh. She looks around, trying to come up with something to cover it. HESTIA and HEBE enter the room. HEBE is looking radiant, though sad and nervous, in a beautiful wedding gown with a train that HESTIA carries in and then helps her arrange on the floor. HEBE also wears a crown of white flowers and a set of small, ornate, gilded angel wings on her back. HESTIA motions to HEBE to be quiet and then moves to the center of the room. HESTIA clears her throat.

HESTIA Sister?

HERA I'm trying to think what we could possibly use to cover that ridiculous hole –

She turns and sees HEBE, and her voice dies away. Her hands fly to cover her mouth.

HEBE Is it all right? I don't feel like it fits the way it fit before.

HERA *(softly)* Well, they altered it, didn't they? Since then? Shouldn't it… fit better?

HEBE Yes, but… I can't… I can't quite breathe.

HERA That's not the dress, dearest. It's you.

HEBE Oh? I thought it was the dress.

HERA No, you just need to breathe. I can see you're not breathing from the hunch in your shoulders.

HESTIA Tell her she looks beautiful, Sister.

HERA Did I fail to say that?

HEBE I know you thought it.

HERA Yes, but I should say it too. You look beautiful, dearest dove.

HEBE Really?

HERA Really.

HEBE Absolutely?

HERA Positively.

HESTIA She looks like you did on your wedding day.

HERA But much prettier. Much much prettier. I have never seen anyone as pretty as you.

HEBE You can't hug me. If anyone should hug me right now I will fall to pieces. I will shatter like the crockery.

HERA I promise only to admire you from afar.

HEBE Is everything ready? Are we still going to hold it in the garden? I know I'm such a little fool, but the tree –

HERA The tree will be there. Don't worry. And so will I. And so will Heracles. And your brothers and your sisters.

HEBE And Daddy?

HERA Of course Daddy will be there. They're all waiting right now.

HESTIA And I'll be waiting for you all when you get back.

HEBE You're not coming with us?

HESTIA I'm old, dear. And I had that rheumatism last year, remember? If I catch cold it will carry me off, which I expect you would find most inconvenient at your reception. Besides, someone has to keep the fires lit so you can warm those toes in time for the dancing.

HEBE Did Auntie Demeter come?

HERA No, but she sent you a lovely bouquet. *(realizing)* And I've left it in the drawing room.

HESTIA I'll get it, don't worry.

HERA No, let me. Zeus will be the one to walk her out, after all. I'll send it with him. When he gets here, you know it's time to begin.

HEBE And we'll come from here?

HERA Yes. Just like we rehearsed. Though maybe a touch faster, darling. It is raining after all.

HEBE I know. I will. I'll walk like I have real wings.

HERA You do have real wings, darling. These are just so the regular people can finally see them.

She kisses her on the forehead.

Keep breathing. It will all be over and you'll be off and happy before you know it.

HERA exits. HESTIA smiles at HEBE.

HESTIA You really are angelic.

HEBE I'm so nervous.

HESTIA They say that is very typical of brides. Your mother and your aunt were both very nervous.

HEBE Auntie isn't married.

HESTIA Not traditionally, no. But she was still very nervous.

HEBE I wish she had come.

HESTIA You know she almost never leaves the house, especially since Persephone married.

HEBE Why?

HESTIA Who knows? Some women, their children grow up, leave home, get married… and their life is over. Your aunt Demeter is one of those women.

HEBE Will Mother be like that after I leave?

HESTIA I don't think so. She has far too much energy.

HEBE I worry about her, though. I worry about her being all alone here after I'm gone.

HESTIA Oh, she won't be alone. She'll have me, after all. And your father.

And all our cheeky servants.

HEBE I still worry.

HESTIA Don't worry about her, Dove. You're happy and that makes her happy, and nothing will trouble her so long as you remain untroubled.

GANYMEDE enters, carrying an umbrella, and a beautiful bouquet. He clears his throat.

GANYMEDE If I might interrupt, ladies. The Master sent me to fetch you.

Offering up the flowers.

This is for you, Miss.

HEBE Where is Daddy?

GANYMEDE Waiting under the tree, Miss. With Master Heracles and your families. Nearly half the party is out there, Miss. All waiting very gamely.

HEBE But Daddy's supposed to walk me down the rose lawn.

GANYMEDE I think he forgot that part, Miss. He was very caught up with herding the others out, you see. And encouraging some of the more, um… reluctant ones.

HEBE Was Eris causing problems?

GANYMEDE No, Miss. I'm afraid your brother's wife was a bit worried about her hair.

HESTIA Of course. As if Aphrodite was the one in the wedding dress.

GANYMEDE I made it a point to give her a broken umbrella.

HESTIA Very clever, Ganymede. Though she'll just make Hephaestus use it.

GANYMEDE Should I run and fetch the Master back here?

HEBE No. I suppose it doesn't really make a difference and I don't want to keep anyone waiting any longer.

HESTIA Oh, now you become accommodating?

HEBE DON'T TEASE ME, AUNTIE! IT IS MY WEDDING DAY! I THINK I'M BEING VERY ACCOMMODATING CONSIDERING THE FLOOD AND EVERYTHING!

All sweetness.

Ganymede, my bouquet.

He hands it to her.

I hope you don't mind carrying my train.

GANYMEDE It's an honor, Miss.

HEBE Auntie, the doors, please.

>*HESTIA opens the glass doors of the sunroom. The gray light pours through, and the sound of steady rain.*

HESTIA At least the thunder's stopped. That's a good sign.

>*A rumble of thunder; HEBE looks at HESTIA with mild irritation; she laughs.*

We're not superstitious people, darling. Remember that.

>*HESTIA kisses HEBE. The lights suddenly dim to a single light on GANYMEDE, who faces the audience.*

GANYMEDE When you're raised in this sort of life, your parents are very quick to make sure that you don't mistake being part of the family, for being part of the family. I can still hear my father saying "No matter what they say to you, or what you say to them, never forget – you're not one of them, you never will be, you never can be. The blood is different. It's as simple as that." And I know when he said that he meant it, and when my sister ran off with the second son of a minor lord we were all working for in Hastings we all prayed he was wrong, but when she turned up six months later pregnant and we were packed off two weeks after that I also knew he was right. Loyalty is expected of servants but loyalty doesn't stop people from looking out for their own over you any more than wishing keeps the rain away. It's all luck, really, in the end. What the weather's like. Who you're born to. But we all keep wishing anyway, don't we? The list of stupid things we do because of fairy tales is fucking endless.

>*The lights shift. GANYMEDE opens the umbrella and hands it to HEBE, who takes it in one hand, holding her bouquet in another.*

HEBE Won't you get wet?

GANYMEDE Doesn't bother me. I was practically raised by wolves.

HESTIA *(as if she just heard a bell ring)* Where is Iris? Wasn't she supposed to do this?

GANYMEDE *(gathering the train)* She said Cook needed her in the kitchen. Some sort of dumpling emergency.

HESTIA That's an unusually absurd excuse.

HEBE I don't know, Auntie. You of all people appreciate a good dumpling.

HESTIA This is true.

GANYMEDE Just as long as you all haven't eaten them before we get back, I'm happy. She's stewing them in with the rabbits. That's my favorite.

HEBE Are you ready, Ganymede?

GANYMEDE Ready, Miss.

HEBE Excellent. On the count of three, we run through the dahlias, past the fountain, down the atrium and out to the tree. Agreed?

GANYMEDE Sounds like a plan.

HEBE We will not trip on anything. Repeat that.

GANYMEDE We will not trip on anything.

HEBE Excellent.

> *Beat.*

One. Two. Three!

> *Thunder and lightning. They run out the doors and into the rain. HESTIA closes the doors and latches them. Another rumble of thunder and lightning. She pulls her shawl closer around her and stays, looking out the window until they are out of sight. IRIS enters.*

IRIS What kind of wolf prefers his rabbit in a dumpling?

HESTIA The domesticated kind.

IRIS I believe we call them dogs, ma'am.

HESTIA I believe we do.

> *They both turn and gaze out the windows. The light fades to black. End of Act 2.*

Act 3

> *The same. Much later in the evening. Lamps are burning. The drapes are all open, revealing a thick blackness. Rain continues to pour. Mud has been tracked all over the floors. The overdress of HEBE's wedding gown, along with HERACLES' suit jacket, have been laid out on the divan to dry. Other items of clothing are strewn about, or hang from a makeshift clothesline strung across a corner of the room. IRIS is pinning up a few more things. Distantly we hear the sound of a door opening and closing. IRIS looks up, then goes back to her work. A moment, and then a grandfather clock strikes midnight. Distant*

laughter. IRIS ignores it. GANYMEDE comes into the room.

GANYMEDE What are you being so smug about?

IRIS What are you talking about?

GANYMEDE The smug smile on your face.

IRIS This is not my smug smile.

GANYMEDE No?

IRIS No.

GANYMEDE Well, then, allow me to rephrase: what are you being such a stupid cunt about?

IRIS *(coldly civil)* I don't know what you mean, and as usual, I don't care, and I especially don't care for your tone of expression.

GANYMEDE *(with equal intensity)* And I don't give a fuck for your delicate feelings. And you know exactly what I'm talking about. All through the reception I saw you watching me. Every time I went in and out of the kitchen. Every time I stoked the fire or refilled a glass. Your eyes were always on me, and the only thing more obvious than the smirk in them was the one plastered across your face.

Beat.

You told, didn't you?

IRIS Told what?

GANYMEDE You did, didn't you?

Beat.

Who did you tell?

IRIS Who did I tell what?

GANYMEDE WHO DID YOU FUCKING TELL?

A long moment. A slow, sweet smile spreads across IRIS's face.

IRIS I suppose you'll have to wait and see.

GANYMEDE *(barely swallowing his rage)* Son of a bitch!

Turning back to her.

How could you betray your own kind?

IRIS Oh, we're not the same, you and I –

GANYMEDE We live on the same side of the house and we both eat in the kitchen. As far as *they* are concerned we are the same kind.

IRIS Right. Except I'm not the one who tracks mud on all the floors without repercussion, or gets to run down the rose lawn with the mistress on her wedding day. When he's not laying down for the master, of course.

GANYMEDE Do you think he treats me any different because of that?

> *Beat.*

Do you think I'd do it if I didn't fucking love him?

> *Beat.*

I still have to sleep in my own room. Next to yours. Alone. Like you.

> *A long moment.*

IRIS I'm sorry.

GANYMEDE Too late for that now.

IRIS Not that I told. I'm just sorry. For you.

> *She goes out.*

GANYMEDE Of all the stupid fucking bitches –

> *HESTIA enters.*

GANYMEDE *(catching himself)* Oh, excuse me, ma'am, I was just –

HESTIA Get out.

> *A long, tense moment. They hold each other's gaze. He straightens his shoulders.*

GANYMEDE Yes, ma'am.

> *He exits through the glass doors. HESTIA sits, looking quite pensive, slightly dishevelled, as if she's just finished a long and tiresome night. HERA enters, holding a cup of tea.*

HERA The last of the guests are finally gone. I know I shouldn't say this out loud, but I am so very very grateful that I will never host another wedding again. Indoors, outdoors, rain or shine, mud or no, what a to-do they are. Worth it, of course, when I see how happy Hebe is but…

> *Pause.*

Are you feeling all right?

HESTIA I have felt better.

HERA It's awfully late. You've eaten a lot of rich food. Perhaps it's time for bed?

HESTIA Don't talk to me like a child.

HERA Forgive me, I meant to do no such thing. I would have made the suggestion to anyone.

HESTIA Believe me, if I could sleep I would. I have tried, already, twice tonight. But there is no rest for me when I lie down.

HERA Perhaps the noise from the guests –

HESTIA I have always found noise in this house comforting, whatever the cause. I have fallen asleep to the sound of your children wailing in the next room. I would like to think I could do equally as well lulled by their laughter. No, what keeps me up is nothing so simple as exterior noise. I doubt I shall sleep at all this night.

HERA Would you like me to ring for some tea, then? I'm on my eleventh cup.

HESTIA I think… if I have any more tea… I shall set fire to the house and everyone in it.

> *A long pause.*

HERA Forgive me for asking, dear, but are you drunk?

HESTIA Of course not.

HERA Do you think, perhaps, it would be better if you were?

HESTIA *(standing, agitated)* Let us not choose this moment to be witty, Sister.

HERA Agreed, Sister, since you are so clearly upset about something. Will you tell me the cause if you know it?

HESTIA I would if I were not afraid.

HERA An uncommon deflection. What are you afraid of?

HESTIA Your reaction to what I have to say.

HERA I am hard-pressed to think of what you could say that would so distress me –

HESTIA You would not merely be distressed but also appalled –

HERA Well then I must know as soon as possible, Hestia. Please, tell me or I shall become distressed merely with the waiting for this appalling news.

HESTIA Don't be so glib, Hera! It's pride and you know it.

HERA And why am I not allowed to be proud? It is my daughter's wedding, I have been surrounded by my friends and family all night long, I am your sister – of much, have I, to be proud at this moment.

HESTIA Even if everything hinges on a lie?

HERA That's amusing. I assumed we were both old enough to know that lies are often relative, that things are very rarely hinged on truth and thus conversely lies can only be the root of so much and, lastly, that displays of histrionics over some scandal are really the preoccupation of women far less astute and educated than us.

HESTIA This is not histrionics, this is consideration for your sensibilities.

HERA Since I don't know what you're talking about I can't say for sure if that is true, but I would venture to say, if you were so considerate of my feelings, Sister, you simply never would have brought it up in the first place.

HESTIA Something like this cannot rest. It cannot be hidden.

HERA Oh anything can be hidden, darling. That's what we invented curtains and pictures for.

HESTIA But this should not be hidden.

HERA If it's as awful as you're making it out to be I couldn't disagree more.

HESTIA This is poisonous. This is criminal. This is rot.

HERA Well, now you do have me frightened.

HESTIA Only just now?

HERA Well it's not like you don't have a reputation for being overly serious, Hestia. Did you expect me to fail to take you in stride? Besides, I assumed this was just some nonsense about Zeus or something –

HESTIA That's exactly what this is about.

HERA Well, unless you're about to tell me he's bankrupt or dying –

HESTIA This is worse than either.

HERA Worse than poverty and death?

HESTIA Oh for the love of God, when will you take your marriage seriously?

HERA When will you cease to judge it?

HESTIA I judge your marriage?

HERA From the day our courtship began you have always been suspicious of Zeus –

HESTIA And I have always been right.

HERA And I have always told you I don't care. My values are not your values, Sister. What offends you does not always offend me.

HESTIA This shall offend you. This shall sicken you.

HERA It has not sickened me yet.

HESTIA Because you live in ignorance of it.

HERA If you have something to say, Hestia, then say it. This verbal fencing is as tedious as the weather.

HESTIA He's having an affair –

HERA Of course he is, he is my husband after all –

HESTIA He's having it with a man.

HERA What?

HESTIA With Ganymede.

A long moment. HERA sighs and sits down on one of the divans.

Now do you understand my trepidation?

HERA *(quietly)* Of course. I myself would be quite mystified how to break such news to somebody.

HESTIA I'm sorry. I did not wish to tell you so harshly, or on such an important day.

HERA You did as you felt best. I'm more concerned with how you found out.

HESTIA Iris told me.

HERA Iris?

HESTIA As you know, I thought she was Zeus' new conquest and when I accused her –

HERA Do you make a habit of accusing the staff of sleeping with my husband?

HESTIA Only when I suspect or know it to be true.

HERA Ah. And here I thought it was their own guilty conscience that sent them packing. I can be so naive sometimes. As you know.

HESTIA You're taking this very well.

HERA Well, Sister, naiveté and ignorance are not the same thing.

HESTIA Meaning?

HERA Meaning I knew about Ganymede. I did not know, however, that you had appointed yourself protector of my marriage. That is an enormous surprise.

HESTIA I am protecting you, not your marriage.

HERA But I am my marriage, dearest.

HESTIA If you knew of Ganymede, why have you done nothing about him?

HERA Because as long as I alone knew of Ganymede my marriage was perfectly safe. And so was I.

> *HEBE and HERACLES come running in, half-dressed. HEBE still has her wings on. They are clearly wasted.*

HEBE Mother!

HERACLES Hebe's mother!

HEBE She's your mother too now, brute!

HERACLES My mother too now! Does that mean you get mine?

HEBE Of course that's what it means.

HERACLES And all your brothers and sisters? Are they also mine?

HEBE Only Eris. The rest I'm keeping for myself.

HERACLES But I don't want Eris.

HEBE I don't either.

HERACLES I knew we should have sabotaged her carriage while there was still time.

HERA *(very bright, as if nothing has been happening)* What are you two doing?

HEBE All the guests are gone.

HERA I know. Shouldn't you be on your way too?

HERACLES Hebe hasn't packed yet.

HERA Really, darling? That was silly of you.

HEBE Well, I wasn't sure there was going to be a wedding until today.

HERACLES I don't know how you could have possibly doubted your mother would make it all happen, some way or another.

HEBE I don't either. I can be viciously small-minded sometimes.

HERACLES But so beautiful!

HEBE Just like a real angel!

HERACLES Can angels be small-minded?

HERA *(pointedly looking at Hestia)* Oh, most definitely.

HEBE The Bible is full of small-minded angels.

HERACLES Just because I go to church doesn't mean I've read the Bible.

HEBE Have you read anything?

HERACLES Not since University. Not if I can help it.

HEBE Oh! We're going to have such fun together.

They kiss.

HERA Hebe, darling, you should go pack. It's nearly three in the morning.

HEBE The train doesn't leave until nine.

HERA Yes, but your father and I didn't arrange a bridal suite for you in the village so that you cannot take advantage of it.

HEBE It's my wedding day, Mother, you can't order me around.

HERACLES Actually, the wedding's over. So go pack, Ducks!

HEBE Every day is going to be my wedding. Just you wait and see.

They kiss again and she exits. HERACLES turns to the others.

HERACLES You ladies must be exhausted.

HERA It has been a decidedly long day.

HERACLES A memorable one, though. How many weddings do you think feature the bride and groom in their skivvies at the reception?

HERA Certainly it shall be talked about for quite some time.

HERACLES I give my mother till Christmas before she'll admit how horrified she was.

HERA I think you're selling your mother short. As most children do.

HERACLES I've always been an ardent defender of my mother.

HERA Yes. May you have children as good to you as you are to her.

HERACLES Well, and if they're not, guess which grandmamma we'll be sure to bring them to for straightening out?

HESTIA *(pointedly cutting in)* Master Heracles? Shouldn't you be seeing to the bridal carriage?

HERACLES The what? Oh… that horse-drawn antique with sanitary paper all over it?

HERA You are always so charming, Heracles.

HESTIA And clever.

HERACLES All right, all right. No need to make fun of me. I'll go check on the relic and make sure it's not going to fall apart en route to my matrimonial bliss.

HERA Do, dear. I'm sure Hebe will only be a few moments.

HERACLES I don't know. Probably takes a while to pack your entire wardrobe.

HESTIA I'm sure she isn't bringing everything.

HERACLES Really? Wish I was sure about that.

> *He starts to go, when the lights suddenly shift and HERACLES finds himself in a light of his own. He looks at the audience.*

All said and done: we had a really top-notch cake at our wedding. I'm happy about that.

> *The lights shift. He exits. HESTIA picks up the conversation as if they were never interrupted.*

HESTIA How can you be safe with such a snake in the house?

HERA Ganymede is hardly a snake. If anything he is possibly the most attentive lover my husband has ever had. Far better than any of the maids, or that horrid Leto woman. Frankly, I feel quite blessed.

HESTIA And does the stableboy know you are aware of what's going on?

HERA No. But Zeus knows. I've been enormously discreet and so have they. Up until now, of course. How do you think Iris figured it out?

HESTIA Who cares?

HERA I do. The last thing my family needs is a scandal like this circulating the neighborhood.

HESTIA What about what you need?

HERA I would think that's abundantly clear.

HESTIA You must divorce Zeus.

HERA Nonsense, Sister. On what grounds?

HESTIA On the grounds of him indulging in an indecent act while married to you.

HERA What he does with his own life is his own business so long as it doesn't affect ours.

HESTIA How does this not affect your life?

HERA The house is still standing, is it not?

Beat.

Our financial fortunes and investments thrive. My children are all happy – not counting Hephaestus, which is his own bloody fault – and amply provided for. I am equally as well maintained and in return all Zeus has asked is for me to return the grace.

HESTIA And so you tolerate him –

HERA I do not tolerate him, Hestia, I support him. It is a marriage we have together, not a business; it is a family, not a government. I not only support him, I accept him, and I have from the beginning. It's why he ended up with me and not you or Demeter. He knew you would not be able to accept his various indiscretions with either sex – or you yourself.

HESTIA So your marriage has always been a sham then?

HERA No, nor is it now. It's just simply encompassed things about which you did not know – as all marriages do and should. I love you dearly but you are not invited into my bedroom.

HESTIA You mean as Demeter once was?

HERA What happened between Zeus and Demeter was unfortunate and hard on all of us. You are welcome to hate Zeus for that and I would understand it if you do. But you are not welcome to hate Zeus for that on my behalf. How he and I have resolved that moment in our lives is our concern alone.

HESTIA And that he is a sodomite is also yours and his concern alone?

HERA *(coldly)* Dearest, I don't know what that word means, but it is the first and only thing you have said that actually offends my sensibility.

HESTIA And do you now expect me to retract it?

HERA I expect you to do nothing, Hestia. If there is one thing I could say, after decades of knowing and adoring you, it is that you will always do exactly whatever it is you want.

HESTIA One could say the same thing about you.

HERA I should hope so. I am your sister after all.

   Beat.

Remember Leto? Remember how she would strut up and down the village green fat with my husband's illegitimate twins, happy as could be that the local squire had gotten her with child and everybody knew about it? Do you remember… how… painful… that was for me?

HESTIA You laughed about it at the time.

HERA That's how you should have known I was dying over it. But maybe you're not as adept at reading me as either of us think you are.

HESTIA This isn't about you and I.

HERA No, Sister, it is *only* about you and I.

   HEBE enters in a long coat, carrying bags.

HEBE What are the two of you arguing about?

HERA *(all brightness)* Arguing, dove? What makes you think we were arguing?

HEBE I can hear your voices rising and falling all the way up in my room.

HESTIA Your mother and I were having a disagreement, is all. I've decided to go back to Whitby and she doesn't want me to go.

   To HERA.

Or do you, dearest?

HERA *(slightly taken aback)* Well… I… think a visit is certainly a decision you're in perfectly good mind to make yourself –

HESTIA Oh, I thought I had made it clear I was planning to return there indefinitely.

HERA Made it clear when?

HESTIA I suppose not. Well, I am making it clear now: I am thinking of going back to Whitby.

HEBE You mean not come back?

HESTIA Not for a long time. One should never say never, I suppose.

HEBE But Auntie –

HESTIA Oh darling, don't look so glum. You forget you no longer live here either. It shall hardly affect you if I'm not around the house. And we'll see each other when you come up for Christmas as you always do.

HEBE But… who will take care of Mother?

HESTIA *(pointedly)* Who indeed? All alone in this big, fancy house. I guess I hadn't thought of that.

HEBE Well, Father will, of course, I suppose… but he is very often gone.

HERA Not as much as he used to be, dearest dove, not ever nearly so much. And when he is gone, well… then Mother will take care of Mother. As she always has.

HEBE But, Auntie, why go to Whitby? Is something wrong with Auntie Demeter?

HESTIA Nothing more than the usual. I'm going for me, dove. Change of scenery.

HEBE But… it's so cold up there.

HESTIA Well, and that's a reason to go then, isn't it? Help warm it up some.

HEBE I suppose. Auntie does seem to be so lonely.

HESTIA Yes. Doesn't she? Of course, it could be even warmer if your mother joined me, don't you think?

HEBE For a visit?

HESTIA Yes, or longer. Now that you've married such a nice young man and all your brothers and sisters are gone, she really doesn't have much to do around here, does she? We could all three of us move in together, and just be sisters again. It would be like a second childhood. Hestia, Demeter and Hera: reunited under one roof. Bright and happy and pure. What do you think, Hebe? Doesn't that sound better than your mother here all by herself? I think it does. I think it sounds warm. Like a nightlight, or a chair by the fire. Shall we convince her together?

HEBE But… Mother can't go live with you at Whitby.

HESTIA What? Why can't she?

HERA Yes, dearest dove, why can't I?

HEBE Because… Mother belongs… here, naturally. This is her home. Here where we all grew up. Here where so many things have happened. Here with Daddy.

HERA I couldn't have said it better, darling.

HERACLES enters, dressed to depart.

HERACLES Are you ready then, Ducks?

HEBE I just threw on a coat over my underthings. Do you think it's indecent?

HERACLES Don't see why it matters. We're just going from the house to the junk pile on wheels to the inn. And it's three in the bloody morning. The only people up right now are going to be of the indecent sort anyway.

HEBE Oh good. I couldn't pick what to wear, so it just seemed more practical –

HERACLES It's all going to just come off anyway –

HEBE HERACLES! MY FAMILY!

HERA It's all right, Hebe. I know what sex is. And your aunt has read about it.

> *HESTIA reacts as if punched; HERA ignores her and moves to hug HEBE.*

Have a wonderful trip. Bring us something lovely from Greece.

HEBE Not Italy?

HERA Italy too.

> *HESTIA, excluded from the circle now, moves away, wandering over towards the windows, staring out of them into the night.*

HERACLES We'll see you when we get back?

HERA As soon as you're settled, and not before. It's important to start building your home before you let your relatives in to interfere.

HERACLES Oh, you're not the interfering type, I know that, ma'am.

HERA We're all the interfering type, young man, when someone we love is at stake.

HERACLES *(taking her hands, suddenly quite serious)* You know I'll take good care of her, ma'am. Don't you? I didn't just promise that under the tree, I've been promising that every day of my life since I've known her, and I've meant it every time I've said it, aloud or otherwise.

HERA I know, Heracles. Thank you for that.

> *Beat.*

Now get out of here, both of you. Another minute and I might cry. For the fifth time today. Which will make it two times too many.

HEBE *(to HERACLES)* Brute, did you bring an umbrella for me?

HERACLES You won't need one, Ducks. The rain has stopped.

HERA Has it?

HERACLES Indeed, ma'am. Step outside and see for yourself. Not a cloud in the sky. Should have a lovely morning, in a few hours.

HERA Wonderful. I do so love sunrises after long storms.

> *A long moment. They all look at one another awkwardly. HEBE finally breaks it.*

HEBE All right then. We're off.

HERA Goodbye, dear!

HEBE Goodbye!

HERACLES Goodbye.

> *HEBE and HERACLES start to bustle out when HESTIA calls to them, from the window.*

HESTIA Hebe!

> *They stop, HESTIA turns to them.*

Be safe, won't you, dear?

> *A long, heavy moment. HEBE suddenly smiles, laughing.*

HEBE Oh, Auntie. Sometimes you are so very serious!

> *She exits, followed by HERACLES. The two sisters are alone.*

HERA So are you really returning to Whitby?

HESTIA You cannot ask me to continue living here knowing what I know.

HERA Why not?

HESTIA *(dryly)* It offends my sensibilities.

HERA Enough so to abandon your sister?

HESTIA Ask Demeter what it takes to abandon a sister – she might find my reasons comparatively dire. Besides, you hardly need me to take care of you – as you have amply demonstrated and attested to.

HERA And she does need you?

HESTIA We'll be two old maids living in the past together. And when you're finally ready you'll come to your senses and join us.

HERA Let us hope that's not for a very long time.

HESTIA You can hope that. I won't.

She starts to exit, then turns.

He could be arrested, you know? Put in prison.

HERA I am aware. It's why I hope you won't go telling people.

HESTIA And who would I tell? The one person I would have told I have – and she doesn't care.

HERA Oh, I care, Hestia. I just care differently than you.

HESTIA I suppose we shall have to see which of us comes to be haunted more for it then.

Beat.

You don't need to worry about me, but I'd watch that maid of yours. She's got a quick temper and a quicker tongue.

HERA I'll speak to Iris.

HESTIA Don't fire her, mind you. I'm depending on her to keep an eye on you for me. She's got a good head on her shoulders. And no interest in your husband.

HERA My favorite kind of woman. Just like you.

HESTIA Ha.

She exits. A long moment of silence, HERA alone. Slowly, gratefully, she exhales, and then all at once she starts to cry. For a few moments she lets herself do so and then all at once she stops, swallowing it down, dabbing her eyes and then smoothing down her hair. She takes a deep breath. Then she moves to the laundry line and starts taking down the various clothing bits and folds them, making a pile on the divan. GANYMEDE enters, crossing the room, but when he sees HERA he turns, suddenly, as if about to leave. He is carrying the gun from Act 2, which he makes a vain, almost comical attempt to hide behind his body.

HERA I thought you'd be in bed by now.

GANYMEDE *(hurriedly)* Um, excuse me, ma'am. Sorry.

HERA *(looking up)* Do you normally wander around the house with a gun?

GANYMEDE Ah, no, ma'am. This is just… I was moving it back to… I had to help Master Heracles hitch the horses and then there was a lot more shutting down to do in the stables. They were a bit of a mess, I'm afraid, what with all today's traffic and the rain.

HERA Yes. But it's stopped raining, at least.

GANYMEDE Indeed it has, ma'am. Should be a nice morning, in a couple of hours.

HERA It is late, isn't it?

GANYMEDE Beg your pardon, ma'am, but it's early, rather.

HERA It's both at the same time, isn't it?

GANYMEDE Yes, of course. I suppose that's it.

HERA Did you need something, by the by?

GANYMEDE Sorry?

HERA When you came in, were you looking for me?

GANYMEDE Ah... no, ma'am. I just saw the light in here, and thought –

HERA My husband was still up?

GANYMEDE *(awkwardly)* Or that a light was left unattended. I was going to put it out. Don't want the house burning down, do we?

HERA No, we certainly don't.

GANYMEDE *(not sure what she knows)* But, ah... is, um... your husband... still up?

HERA No. I don't believe so. Unless he's wandering around without my knowledge. Which wouldn't be the first time. But I helped him undress so if you're going to go looking for him keep your eyes peeled for a tall man in a nightshirt wondering just how much this wedding really cost him.

GANYMEDE Very good, ma'am.

HERA You can laugh at that, Ganymede, it was a joke.

GANYMEDE What? Oh, of course.

> *He gives her a quick bow and starts to exit, but she calls after him again.*

HERA *(very even)* Ganymede. I don't need an explanation for the rifle. But I'd rather not see it again, if you please. We hunt outside. Not in the home. Understand?

> *For a long moment they look at one another. A message is silently communicated. At last they both take a breath at the same time. GANYMEDE sets down the gun.*

GANYMEDE Will you be going to bed soon?

HERA No, I think not. I've passed the point where I would be able to fall asleep, and I think sometimes it's good to stay up all night.

GANYMEDE I like that too, sometimes.

HERA Do you?

GANYMEDE Yeah. It's a nice time to think, if one has things to think about. No one interrupts.

HERA True, but can't that lead to brooding?

GANYMEDE I don't think brooding is so bad, now and then.

HERA Neither do I. Though I worry I shall do too much of it, now that the children are all gone.

GANYMEDE Well, if you ever need to be interrupted, ma'am, I'm sure I or any of the other servants are happy to do so.

HERA Thank you, Ganymede, I'll keep that in mind.

> *Beat.*

You like working here, don't you?

GANYMEDE We all do, ma'am. You run a good home.

HERA If you're angling for a bonus, Ganymede, you know we only give them at Christmas.

GANYMEDE No, ma'am. I'm just saying that because it's true.

> *IRIS enters, in a nightgown.*

IRIS Is everything all right in here?

GANYMEDE What are you doing up?

IRIS I saw the light when I was passing through the kitchen. I was worried someone had left the candles burning.

HERA Only so that we could see by them. Ganymede, are you going to bed?

GANYMEDE I suspect not, ma'am.

HERA Go make us some very strong tea then. And bring any chunks of wedding cake my sons didn't devour.

GANYMEDE Of course, ma'am.

HERA Ask Iris if she wants some.

GANYMEDE You want a cup, Iris?

IRIS Oh, no, please –

HERA Of course she does. Hurry along now.

GANYMEDE Yes, ma'am.

>*He goes out. IRIS stands, watching HERA as she finishes folding the laundry.*

HERA Never turn down tea with your employer, Iris. It's usually the perfect time to back them into a corner and see what you can get out of them.

>*IRIS just stares at her, not knowing at all what to say to this.*

Help me take down this line, will you?

IRIS *(rattled)* Of course.

>*They take down the clothesline and begin to wind it up.*

HERA These floors are an atrocious mess.

IRIS I can run and fetch a mop, ma'am.

HERA Oh, it can wait until morning. It's not like anyone's coming to call. Hopefully for the next month or so.

IRIS Weddings are an enormous bother in some ways, aren't they?

HERA Completely. But anything worth doing usually is, isn't it?

IRIS I suppose.

>*A pause; they look at one another.*

HERA Sit down a moment, Iris. If you would.

IRIS Yes, ma'am.

>*She moves to one of the divans and sits. HERA sits opposite her.*

HERA We haven't talked much, have we?

IRIS Ah, no, ma'am.

HERA But my sister and you, you have become friends, have you not?

IRIS I suppose so… yes, ma'am.

HERA I'm afraid to tell you she is going to be leaving us soon. She's going to our family home in Whitby.

IRIS To visit?

HERA To stay. Our other sister is lonely and she…

IRIS Of course, ma'am. I understand.

HERA You do?

IRIS Of course.

> *Pause.*

I'm sure you'll miss her.

HERA I will indeed. It will be very lonely and quiet around here sometimes.

> *Pause.*

How good are you at keeping secrets, Iris?

IRIS Um… very good, I should think. When asked.

HERA And if I ask you to…

IRIS Then you can rest assured…

HERA Excellent. That's good to know. Because I'd like us to be friends, Iris. Like you've been to my sister. Only better, perhaps. I've never had a confidante who wasn't related to me by blood. So I suppose we'll both be finding our way on this… which shouldn't be so hard, once we've found a way to begin. If you were willing to begin, of course.

IRIS And how do we begin, ma'am?

HERA Hera, please. And I think…

> *She stands.*

…we'll start here.

> *She looks around.*

This room, I'd like to redo it. I'd like to redo the whole house but… one room at a time. In the beginning.

> *She sees the hole in the wall.*

And of course, that must be covered up. How do you think we should do it?

IRIS Ah… I don't know, ma'am. But I'm sure there's a way.

HERA Oh well, of course there is a way. There's a way to do everything. Don't you think?

> *GANYMEDE enters, with the tea tray.*

GANYMEDE The tea, ma'am.

HERA Set it down on the table and have a seat.

> *GANYMEDE does as he's told. HERA returns to her seat on the divan.*

IRIS Shall I pour?

HERA I shall. Hostess's duties.

> *HERA pours a cup of tea for IRIS, GANYMEDE and herself.*

HERA *(she raises her cup)* To a clear morning.

> *The lights cut to black except for a single spot on HERA, who puts down her cup, and stands, moving to address the audience.*

Our mother was a lovely woman – and by that I mean it was her calling. Her position in life. She knew how to handle any situation with grace and tact, whether it was our father, who was a monster, or our sister's rather socially unorthodox pregnancy, or dining with people who complimented our flatware frequently enough to make it apparent that they wanted – and expected – money from us. My sisters have both since claimed my mother was a fool or a puppet but I still very fondly look back and admire her. I loved my childhood and my maiden years – particularly after the mill fire. We were well taken care of and well respected and if she could sometimes be a bit distant and passive – well, that's where I have improved over the model God chose for me. My mother and I haven't spoken in almost a decade. It's not that we don't see each other – I visit her at Parnassus End every other Sunday afternoon – but there just hasn't been anything to say. We already know about one another everything that there is to know. And it's lovely. It's lovely to be somewhere and with someone and not have to talk. But then sometimes when I sleep, especially if Zeus is away, I'll have these dreams where my mother is screaming at me, "Run, Hera! Run if you can't fly! But go while you can, no matter how you go, and don't look back!" And of course it frightens me, as it would frighten anyone to dream such a thing. But then… then I think to myself, "No. That's not my mother. My mother would never be so weak." And my mother understands the value of silence. My mother realizes that not saying anything isn't the same as not knowing anything. And my mother holds her place in the world with all the implacable power of a statue.

> *A moment, and then the light fades out.*
>
> *The end.*

Demeter's Daughter
A One-Act Play

by Claire Rice

DEMETER'S DAUGHTER
A One Act Play

Demeter's Daughter was originally produced in a reading on July 22, 2010 at EXIT Stage Left in San Francisco, California as part of the San Francisco Olympians Festival. The play was directed by Liz Anderson with the following cast:

Louisa	Michelle Jasso
Hestia	Brianna Calabrese
Hera	Theresa Ireland
Demeter	Julia Heitner
Persephone	Gloria McDonald
Stage Directions	Chris Quintos

Characters

LOUISA A young woman in her early twenties from the United States.
DEMETER The Goddess of Grain and Children and Ritual.
HERA The Goddess of Marriage and the phases of Womanhood.
HESTIA The Goddess of the Hearth and Home.
PERSEPHONE The Goddess of the Dead and the Underworld.

Setting

Winter, Greece, 1949

A landscape of desolation. It was a farm. It was a home. It was an island. It was a place. Now it is consecrated with the bodies of men who have sacrificed for what they believed. HERA moves among the mounds where bodies lie and she prays. She lays coins atop where their eyes are. She says some words and moves on. She wears black and is very, very old. HESTIA appears from behind HERA. She is at HERA's skirts like a child or a sprite. She takes the coins from the ground and puts them in her mouth. She is unrecognizable as the solemn god she is. A hemp rope lays on the ground among the mounds. It spans the width of the stage.

HERA Stop that.

HESTIA's mouth is full and she cannot speak clearly.

HESTIA Bov shev hisint anna heed em. *(But he isn't going to need them.)*

HERA Hestia! Spit them out!

HESTIA OH! *(No!)*

HERA Yes.

HESTIA OH! AHM UNRY! *(No! I'm hungry!)*

>*HERA tries to force her hands into HESTIA's mouth to take out the coins.*

HERA Out! OUT!

>*She retrieves the coins; they are covered in spit.*

HESTIA I'm hungry!

HERA These are not for you.

HESTIA You're just putting them on the ground!

HERA The dead have to pay their way.

HESTIA The ferryman's pockets are full. He takes them over gratis now.

HERA He always asks a price.

HESTIA What price do you think he'd ask of me?

HERA Why don't you ask him and find out?

HESTIA I am your shadow now, sister Hera. I come before you in the morning, and after you in the evening. It is cold as your shadow. When can we go home?

HERA You can return to any home that will have you any time you want.

HESTIA The Bacchanal have taken my place.

HERA You made your bed, now lie in it.

HESTIA As they do?

>*She points to the mounds.*

HERA These were brave warriors. They have earned their peace.

HESTIA Such as it is.

>*HESTIA picks up a coin.*

I like them better when they are chocolate.

>*She puts the coin in her mouth.*

HERA I said stop that!

HESTIA I am hungry!

HERA Then go find some food!

HESTIA There isn't any!

HERA Then stop complaining!

HESTIA But I don't belong here!

HERA Oh, Good Zeus! If you have any love in your heart, save me from this crazed, annoying wretch! Surely, Hestia, there must be a hearth or a home or someone somewhere who still believes and prays and sacrifices for you! Somewhere there must be one who still follows the rites. Must you plague me so with your incessant whining?

HESTIA The Bacchanal have taken my place.

HERA Do you think you suffer alone? Where are my believers? Where are my temples and festivals? Where are the sacrifices made in my name? Where is the Cult of Hera? Gone. Gone! Do you think you are the only one who has been replaced? Look around you at this battlefield. These men died without a thought to our names. My temples are now armories and bomb shelters, if they are still standing. The rain, black with the soot of their machines, rips at my foundations. When did humans become so self-serving?

HESTIA The Bacchanal have taken my place.

HERA You cannot know what I suffer. You chose to remain on earth long ago. You have no husband and no children. Go or stay. Do as you choose. But I, Hera the Crone, I am in my winter and I will wander the earth caring for the fallen heroes with no mothers or wives to tend to them until my virginity is restored. Which may be until the end of time itself and beyond. And if you plague me every step of the way, Hestia, so help me I'll… well, I don't know what.

> *HESTIA picks up a coin and shoves it in her mouth, then spits it out again. The hemp rope becomes taut and rises.*

HESTIA Grave dirt.

HERA Shhhh. Someone is coming.

> *LOUISA enters. She is dressed all in black. She carries with her a suitcase and a map. She's having a hard time balancing the two. The rope is connected to LOUISA's waist and it seems to direct her movements. She does not see HESTIA or HERA. As LOUISA comes to the top of a mound she puts down the suitcase and consults the map. She cannot read it, but it doesn't matter because it is wrong now, anyway. The rope pulls LOUISA, who falls down the mound*

and lands ungracefully at the bottom. When she stands, the rope is slack. She tugs at it. Then LOUISA looks around her and seems to be waking up, as if from a very long dream. She can't get her bearings. As if a cold bucket of water has been thrown on her, she feels a realization coming on.

LOUISA I'm here! I'm finally here!! Alex! I'm here!

LOUISA begins to sob with unexpected joy and fear. Her sobbing is comically American. She wants to cry, rend her hair, tear out her eyes, but she tries to hide her grief. She vacillates uncontrollably.

HESTIA What is this?

HERA A widow, no doubt. She's come looking for the body of her husband.

HESTIA Oh, I hate widows. Why doesn't Zeus just kill them off and rid us all of their weeping?

HERA I think she's American.

HESTIA Is that a better kind of widow?

LOUISA Come on, Louisa! Come on! If this is Eleusína, then I have to pray. Come on, Louisa. Pull yourself together. Come on.

HESTIA No. Same as ever. I'm bored.

With some effort, LOUISA begins a comical attempt at prayer. She's never tried before. Not to any god other than the Christian God. Unused to any other prayer than that which is quiet and self-reflective, LOUISA has assumed that the Greek gods need more. She starts with the familiar and moves to the extraordinary, perhaps first bowing low and then finally ending in an erratic dance. HESTIA and HERA watch her. HERA smiles knowingly, cruelly. HESTIA starts to giggle, slowly at first, then with increasing speed and joy.

HESTIA Oh, sister. There is sport here.

HERA How should I approach her?

HESTIA OH! Everyone likes horses. Be a great, black stallion.

HERA I don't want to have sex with her.

HESTIA Then should I?

HERA No.

HESTIA But the orgasm is the most powerful of supplications. The little death, impaled upon your personal God, sacrifice of the self. To allow grace to completely compel you. And everyone likes a horse.

HERA Says the virgin among us.

HESTIA Says the crone rubbed to numbness.

> *HERA smacks HESTIA as hard as she can. Repeatedly. HESTIA alternates between pain and joy. She cries in terror, and laughs with insanity. DEMETER reveals herself from behind a mound.*

DEMETER Stop. Stop. STOP!

> *HERA smacks HESTIA once more. HESTIA, in the midst of her lunatic laughter, runs to DEMETER and throws herself around DEMETER's legs like a child. Her breath comes hard and fast.*

HESTIA Demeter! Sweet sister Demeter! Settle our bet! How shall Hera appear before our pilgrim? I say as a stallion. You have experience with the equine pleasures, tell her how such a rape would be.

> *HESTIA waits for an answer, then she realizes that none will be forthcoming. Though HESTIA's barb hit the mark, DEMETER will not play. HESTIA picks a coin off the ground and shoves it into her mouth, then goes to sulk on a mound.*

DEMETER Leave the poor little widow alone, Hera. She's come here looking for death, and please Zeus, she'll find it. Our time of interfering has long since come to an end.

HERA It is well for you. You are content with your watch. Maybe you don't care to take your place in Olympus, but I do.

DEMETER While you are the crone, it is your duty to give the last rites to the dead when no others will. Do you refuse your station?

HERA None of us can.

DEMETER And so I wait. So we must all wait.

HERA Persephone will not rise again. Just as no one will perform my rites, none shall perform hers, either. You may as well return to your throne and let her have her marriage.

DEMETER This is my duty as her mother.

HERA What of my children? Don't I have duties to them? Have you no pity?

DEMETER No.

HERA Bitch!

DEMETER Oh, shut up, Hera!

> *HESTIA has made her way unseen to LOUISA, who is now doing a dance as if to call the rain. When HESTIA speaks to LOUISA, HERA*

and DEMETER's argument is no longer heard, though their lips continue moving.

HESTIA Grave dirt.

LOUISA What did you say?

HESTIA The coins... they taste like grave dirt.

LOUISA looks around her, then she steps away from the mound, or off of it.

LOUISA These are graves?

HESTIA Oh, yes. There was a war.

LOUISA I know.

HESTIA Lots and lots and lots died of all kinds of terrible things. Did you bring any chocolate?

LOUISA No. You speak English like an American.

HESTIA And you make conversation like one. Why are you here?

LOUISA You won't believe me.

HESTIA You cannot know that.

LOUISA I'm looking for the goddess Demeter.

HESTIA I don't believe you.

LOUISA I know it's silly –

HESTIA I think you have some chocolate in your bag from Italy.

LOUISA Oh. Well, yes. I do. I forgot.

HESTIA You are a liar and must pay up.

She holds out her hand. LOUISA opens her suitcase and takes out chocolate coins and hands them to HESTIA, reluctantly. HESTIA kisses both coins and places them on the mound over the dead man's eyes, taking the real coins and licking them like lollipops.

LOUISA Is this a graveyard?

HESTIA It is where the dead are, that is all. Where better to meet the gods? But, really, you should have come seeking me. The goddess Hestia.

LOUISA Are you a god?

HESTIA Perhaps I should have come to you as a horse. But, I can't help that now. I am as I am, as you are as you are, as my sisters are as my sisters are.

> HESTIA *spits one of her coins onto the field before her, and DEMETER and HERA become visible to LOUISA.*

DEMETER Always your children. When I cried to you to plead with Hades –

HERA Is he not also your brother?

DEMETER You are Queen –

HERA That little cunt ran off with our brother of her own free will, what was I supposed to do?

> *LOUISA gasps loudly. HERA and DEMETER turn, both feel suddenly naked and exposed.*

DEMETER Damn it all, Hestia, what have you done?

LOUISA Who are they?

HESTIA Sssshhhh. There is a reason that things are called mysteries. Don't spoil the fun before it's been had.

> *HESTIA stuffs a coin into LOUISA's mouth.*

You have called and we have answered.

> *There is a long pause.*

DEMETER Have her, Hera. Say hello to our brothers and sisters for me.

HESTIA No, I am first and last always in all things. Louisa will love me first and last.

DEMETER Fine. I care not.

HERA I am Queen here, and I shall be the first and best to answer her prayers. After all, she comes seeking her husband and who but the Goddess of Marriage to answer her call?

HESTIA She comes seeking a child, not a husband.

HERA How do you know?

HESTIA How could I not?

HERA And what would you, Goddess of the Hearth, do about it?

HESTIA I could turn into a great black stallion and could give her a child!

> *HERA laughs excessively.*

HERA What? You? And ruin your perfect chastity?

HESTIA Jealous?

HERA Oh, for the love of Zeus!

HESTIA Yes, and where is that man? One should ask, shouldn't one? How odd there is a Goddess of Wifery, but no God of Husbandry? Oh, wait. There is. But that husbandry is the breeding of animals and wifery is nothing.

HERA You dare say I am the goddess of nothing?

HESTIA Not I, but the lonely moths that fly from you every time you open your legs!

LOUISA Am I really in the presence of goddesses?

HERA Do you really doubt it, Louisa?

LOUISA I just… didn't expect…

HERA We have chosen to appear to you in a state that would frighten you the least.

HESTIA I voted for horses.

> *Pause.*

LOUISA And are you the goddess Demeter?

DEMETER Do you seek the goddess Demeter?

LOUISA Are you she?

DEMETER Do you seek her?

LOUISA Yes. With all my heart.

DEMETER You are a fool.

> *LOUISA begins to cry. She tugs at the rope on the ground for guidance, but it lays flaccid in her hands.*

LOUISA But… will no one hear my prayer?

HERA Louisa. I will hear your prayer.

HESTIA No. Louisa, I will hear your prayer and I will do all that I can, once I have heard your words.

> *HESTIA claps her hands over her ears.*

DEMETER Preserve us, great Atlas. Louisa, I will hear your prayer if it will give you comfort to be heard, but I mean not to answer it, as no one's woes can be greater than mine.

ALL THREE Why have you come, Louisa?

LOUISA To pray.

DEMETER You are not Greek.

LOUISA No, but my husband was.

HERA You follow the martyred godling.

LOUISA I reject that God.

HESTIA You like raspberry jam. I like raspberry jam.

HERA Pay her no attention. She has lost her mind.

HESTIA The Bacchanal have taken my place.

LOUISA Who?

HERA It is a long and stupid story.

HESTIA But you do like raspberry jam, don't you, Louisa?

LOUISA I do.

HESTIA See?

She blows a raspberry at HERA, who rolls her eyes.

HERA Why have you come, Louisa?

LOUISA My husband was Greek. He came here and fought with his brothers in the war. If they were going to die, he wanted to die by their side. And they did. And he did. Here. Somewhere.

DEMETER No one can come back across the river once they have paid their way.

HESTIA He takes them over gratis now.

HERA But I can soothe you. I can make your widowhood pleasant.

LOUISA No, you don't understand, we have a daughter. She was born just after he left. I couldn't name her without him.

HERA I can go to my brother in the underworld and get her a name from your husband.

HESTIA Name her Yellow Bile!

DEMETER Hush. Your humor is lost on everyone.

HESTIA I am lost on everyone.

DEMETER It does not matter what name you give her. Now go, and leave us to our troubles.

LOUISA Please, listen. She is ill. Very, very ill. The doctors won't even let me see her. I came here, to you, to save her life.

HESTIA Then I grant you leave to name her after me. It would be a shame if she died without a name.

LOUISA I do not want her to die at all. I come to you as a mother. This is why I seek Demeter. When we were little, we used to tell Greek myths to each other. Demeter is the Goddess of Motherhood, isn't she? She has a daughter in the underworld… and… I… I hoped she would listen… that she would understand…

DEMETER Do not get your hopes up, sisters. This is no supplicant, it is a beggar going house to house. If she can reject one god so easily, she could reject us all.

LOUISA That god has rejected me! My husband, dead after only a few months of marriage. My daughter, the only piece of him that I have, and the best part of myself, dying slowly, and I can't comfort her. That god has ripped them from me. He could never know what it's like to shelter life in your body and then send it out into the world. He could never know what it is to give up all of yourself, even your name, to a man, only to have him die and leave you with nothing but the shell of his memory hanging on you like a rope. I have come looking for sisterly love from a goddess I have chosen, not from a god who likes my suffering. I have come for compassion.

They stand for a moment and stare at her. HESTIA breaks out laughing. HERA shoves HESTIA.

HESTIA OW!

HERA Stop laughing! Can't you see her pain?

HESTIA No. But if it is anything like mine, it was brought on by you.

HESTIA goes to DEMETER. DEMETER puts her arm around her.

HERA Louisa. I am Hera, Goddess of Marriage. I have heard your prayer, and I will answer it.

LOUISA Can you cure her?

HERA Your tears have turned me. I am a mother. I know our pain. And I will help you.

LOUISA Thank God. I mean, thank you. The goddess, I mean. You. Thank you.

HESTIA No!

HERA Don't be a sore loser.

DEMETER Hush your disappointments. Come. Cuddle with me.

HESTIA I deserve supplicants, too.

DEMETER Yes. Yes, my love.

HESTIA No one prays to me anymore. I hate the Bacchanal. They have taken my place!

DEMETER Come, come. Leave them to their games. Louisa will not be satisfied and she will come to you, eventually.

HESTIA But I am first and last.

DEMETER I know, dear one. I know.

> *They retreat to a mound and turn their backs to LOUISA and HERA.*

HERA It is just us two now, as it should be. Are you ready?

LOUISA Yes. But, if they are gods –

HERA They are useless creatures. I am the Queen of All. Zeus is my husband. I know you have not come seeking me, but I forgive you for that. You are as my child. Do you accept me as your Patron Goddess?

LOUISA Yes.

HERA Good. Good, my dear child. First, you must prove yourself worthy. I cannot just wave my fingers and cure your daughter.

LOUISA Of course. Anything.

HERA Good.

> *Pause.*

LOUISA What must I do?

HERA You must perform the rites of the cult of Hera. I embody the three states of womanhood. The virgin, the mother, and the crone. I am the crone, as you see, but I must be the virgin. I can do nothing for you as the crone, whose duties are to the dead. Do you understand?

LOUISA Yes.

HERA Good. Then begin.

> *HESTIA breaks away from DEMETER and she watches as the tide turns her way, again.*

Louisa, I said begin.

LOUISA I don't know how.

HERA What do you mean?

LOUISA You have to tell me.

HERA Who ever heard of such a thing? Who ever heard of a god telling her people how to pray? These are earthly rituals. Your kind made them for me. Why haven't you come here prepared? What are you saying? That you don't know the rites?

HESTIA No one does. Everyone who knew is dead.

LOUISA Is that true?

> There is a very long pause. HESTIA starts to laugh, HERA gets angry, DEMETER lies down.

Can't you just tell me? I'll do anything.

HERA No, I can't just tell you.

LOUISA But what will I do if you won't tell me?

HESTIA Go on, Hera. Tell her.

HERA Shut up, shut up, shut up!

LOUISA Do you know them?

HESTIA Why should I?

LOUISA Do you?

DEMETER Leave me alone.

LOUISA What should I do? What about my daughter? Hera! Please!

HERA Good Zeus, Louisa, I haven't forgotten you.

LOUISA What will I do?

HERA I don't know. For the love of me, I don't know the rites.

HESTIA There are reasons things are called mysteries.

LOUISA But, they are your rites.

HERA They are not my rites. They are rites for me. In my name. To me. I didn't invent them. I don't know what they are! None of us know.

LOUISA This was it. This was all I had.

HESTIA It wasn't much.

HERA That's why the three of us are here on this forsaken plain. All of our brothers and sisters can rule from on high and they long ago ascended to their thrones, never to return, unless humans learned their place and called to them again. But I am locked on this stupid rock to suffer the dead as they pass into the next world. And then Hestia. Hestia has long since lost her mind. Humanity uses fire for entertainment now, not warmth or food or out of need. The hearth has been given over to a lesser god, and so her mind has fled from her. And then, there is Demeter.

LOUISA That is Demeter?

HERA Yes. The goddess you traveled the world to see. She wanders now in an everlasting winter, waiting for one of you to perform the rites that will return her daughter to her arms. And we all wait. Wait for the rabble to remember us and give us the rites that will free us. Rites that are mysteries even to us. But go on. Pray to her now if you wish. I don't care. Demeter. The Goddess of Motherhood, of grain, of the seasons... and...

> *HESTIA laughs. LOUISA pulls on the rope, trying to get herself somewhere else. More and more rope comes onstage, gathering at her feet. It would seem to be never-ending. Suddenly, quite suddenly, she is at the end of her rope. She looks at it in horror. HESTIA pauses in her laughter, then redoubles her efforts.*

LOUISA How can you laugh?

HESTIA Don't you know anything? All the tragedy has already happened! Your husband died, your daughter is lost to you, and there isn't a god in Heaven or on Earth who cares!

> *HERA suddenly remembers.*

HERA Demeter!

DEMETER No.

HERA Yes.

DEMETER No.

HERA Yes.

DEMETER No.

> *A pause. A change of tactics.*

HERA How could I have been so stupid. The Goddess of Motherhood, and grain... and rituals. Of course. It is not my place to remember these things... you... you are their secret keeper.

DEMETER I will not speak of the mysteries, Hera.

HERA It's been so long since we've had a supplicant, I'd forgotten.

DEMETER I keep them, but I will not lay them at your feet, so you may do what you will.

HERA Sweet sister –

DEMETER You cannot con me into telling you.

HERA Did I never tell you that it was I who convinced Zeus to let Persephone come back from the underworld?

DEMETER What will you try next? Bribery? Blackmail?

HERA When I am once again in his presence, I will work my words and my love on Zeus once more and perhaps I can convince him to free her forever.

HESTIA Goddess of Wifery.

She mimes giving a blow job.

DEMETER You can make no such promise.

HERA Who the hell do you think you are? So self-righteous! You would withhold the key to all my happiness just because you, yourself, are incapable of feeling!

HESTIA Where have you been, Hera? Are you just catching up?

HERA Oh, I am aware! Louisa, look around you. These dead men died not just of war, but of starvation. And who do you think brought that on?

HESTIA When one suffers, we suffer as one.

HERA You would come and pray to her? The great goddess Demeter? You would ask compassion of her? Look around you. These men died fighting over rock and sand. They said they were fighting over their rights to believe, to walk as free men, to do as they would, to vote or whatever. Sure. Maybe some even believed it. But they were all fighting over the same thing. Food. Look around you. This land is dead. I may be stuck as the crone, but only I suffer for it.

HESTIA You, too, have your ways of making others suffer.

HERA But she. Look to her. The goddess of the grain. What little grows out of this soil grows in spite of her. If she would but show pity on your poor souls, she could make this world flourish. Every fight, every war, is over not having enough. Enough of what? Ask her. Ask the goddess of grain. Ask her if she has pity! Ask her who makes the food grow, yet does not need to eat it. Ask her, who mourns for a daughter who is not even dead! She lives! She lives happily with a husband and child even!

Happily and of her own free will. Ask her for pity! For compassion! For understanding! She has none. If she had none for all these men, she certainly has none for you.

> *LOUISA pulls the end of the rope, she drags it behind her as she walks away from the scene, dejected.*

DEMETER My daughter is supposed to come back. Everything will grow again when she returns to me.

HERA And when shall that be?

> *DEMETER cries aloud in anguish. HERA goes to her like a good sister and holds her hard, rocking her back and forth.*

Someone must perform the rites. And do you know them? Do you know the mysteries that could bring her back to you? It is not in the power of every mother to bring her child to her suffering arms. Look. Look at Louisa.

> *HESTIA runs up to LOUISA.*

HESTIA Do you have any more chocolate?

LOUISA No.

> *Pause.*

Did Hera tell the truth? Have you gone mad?

> *Pause.*

HESTIA You and I are pieces of each other. Is the world mad because we are lost to the world? Or are we mad because the world is lost to us?

LOUISA Shall I pray to you, mad one?

HESTIA Yes. Me first. Always.

LOUISA How shall I pray to you?

> *Pause. HESTIA has tears in her eyes.*

HESTIA I cannot remember. Never mind. The Bacchanal have taken my place. Perhaps you should pray to them.

LOUISA I would, if I knew how.

HESTIA What is it like? Being a mother?

LOUISA Painful. I held her for only a moment. There was so much pain. And in the worst of it, I wanted to live forever in that pain. And I knew I would. How can you give birth and not carry that pain and fear and love with you wherever you go? If she dies, this pain will have no reason and no outlet.

> *HESTIA has started to play some game with herself and does not listen any more.*

I thought if I chose my gods, they would listen better.

HESTIA Will you go back to Rome for more chocolates when you are done here?

> *Pause.*

LOUISA No. I didn't go there for chocolate. I went looking for God. The God.

HESTIA Your God?

LOUISA No. I wasn't really brought up with any particular god. My mother went to revivals…

HESTIA Mysteries… mysteries.

LOUISA And my father was an Episcopalian. Alex, he was Orthodox. When this all happened… I went everywhere, to everyone I could think of. I always felt like a stranger in someone else's house.

HESTIA What do we ever know of our gods but glimpses and hearsay?

LOUISA So, I went to Rome. To the Vatican.

> *She goes to her suitcase and takes out vial after vial of holy water. HESTIA looks at them and laughs. She takes them out and sets them up as toy soldiers.*

HESTIA Mysteries. Mysteries.

LOUISA I am to bathe her in this. If the doctors will let me near her. But, it's just water. Isn't it?

HESTIA Mysteries. Mysteries.

> *HESTIA laughs again to herself, but keeps playing.*

HERA You know her pain.

DEMETER Yes.

HERA She wishes only to feel the hand of a goddess guide her. A word would turn her to you. You know the rites that could bring back your daughter. And before you is one who is willing to perform them.

DEMETER She will perform them today, but who will perform them tomorrow?

HERA What does tomorrow matter today?

DEMETER When she has what she wants, she will be gone again. Shall we wait here forever, wait for her prayers with bated breath? No. I have done. Leave me to my misfortune.

HERA And no misfortune is greater than yours. Even as you have the power to turn it right. We must all suffer with you.

DEMETER And to which god shall I pray to bring an end to my suffering? Even as she would supplicate before me, so must I bring myself down low before her. Why must my god be a mortal, stupid, selfish, uncaring, unfeeling, and unknowing one?

HERA Maybe if you choose this god, she will listen better.

Pause.

DEMETER Go away.

HERA leaves DEMETER.

LOUISA Is it true that is Demeter?

HERA Do you think I lied?

LOUISA Can she… could she… tell me how to pray… so that I could… Is there nothing to be done?

HESTIA We could hopscotch.

HERA She is obstinate, but she will come around. We just need to give her time.

LOUISA I don't have time. My daughter could die. I can't sit here and wait for her mood to shift.

DEMETER My mood will not shift.

Pause.

LOUISA Hera's right. This war was your fault.

DEMETER What?

LOUISA All the wars are your fault.

DEMETER Is this how you would supplicate to me?

LOUISA I've felt the starvation that has been brought on by your apathy.

DEMETER Is this how you would talk to a god?

LOUISA Yes! Yes! Finally! Yes! This is how I would choose to talk to a god if I were to ever meet one. Show me, when I come upon one, so that I may yell and scream, because I am done! I can have no sympathy for you, at all! If you really were a god, you could bring an end to the suffering and pain and horror. Yes, horror! I've seen such terrible things that men do to each other when they are starving. The Great Depression. The War. And here I am. I want to give you whatever it is you want. But you won't have it. You love your suffering more than you love your daughter.

> DEMETER *stands up and, surprisingly swiftly, slaps LOUISA across the face.*

DEMETER It was you who were speaking of pain before, wasn't it? Living forever in the pain of childbirth? I live with mine; shall I live with yours, too? Every person is the child of a woman. Look around you. All these bodies. Shall I cry for all their mothers, too? Shall I ease your suffering simply because you have found me? Because you make promises? You will die one day, Louisa. And your daughter will die, either before you or after. Either way, you shall join each other in the afterlife and learn the futility of it all. I will never have such grace or comfort.

> DEMETER *takes a long look at the rope.*

You want the rites to restore Hera's virginity? So that she can answer your prayers to the best of her ability? Fine. I'll tell you, and you will suffer for it.

> DEMETER *smiles.* HESTIA *jumps up and down, clapping her hands, laughing.*

Come, Hestia, you know this story well. You play the part of Zeus.

> HESTIA *stands at attention.*

HESTIA Where are we, dear sister?

DEMETER We are at the waters of Eleutherion.

HESTIA The river has gone dry.

DEMETER Yes, we shall have a dry river.

> HESTIA *sets about and makes the rope into the river.*

DEMETER Louisa, you shall be Hera.

HERA If it is my virginity –

DEMETER That isn't how it works, dear sister. And for once, stand over there and watch with your mouth shut.

> HERA *would argue, but then she sees she has won. She takes her place atop one of the mounds and stands, happily waiting. They all watch* HESTIA *make the waters from the rope.*

Good. Now, my dear, here.

> *DEMETER takes LOUISA and puts her among the rope.*

Now, we shall need some water of some sort. We can't have a completely dry baptism.

HESTIA No. Our first time, we are so moist and ready. Blooming in spring dew.

DEMETER Yes. The first call of the spring, Hera reclaiming her virginity before being wedded and seeded.

HESTIA Wifery and husbandry.

LOUISA I have the holy water.

DEMETER That will do fine.

LOUISA Does it matter that it's blessed by the Pope?

DEMETER Who is he but a man? Now, undress.

LOUISA You want me –

DEMETER I am the keeper of ritual. Of cycles. And this one is about cleansing. And where I come from we take off our clothes to wash ourselves.

LOUISA All right.

> *LOUISA takes off all her clothes and stands naked on stage. DEMETER hands her two bottles of holy water.*

DEMETER Wash.

LOUISA Is that all? Should I sing? Or dance?

DEMETER Wash.

> *LOUISA does so as DEMETER talks.*

Wash. Wash away the years since you first broke the skin between your childhood and your womanhood. Wash away the blood it brought. Wash away the pain of first love. Wash away the pain of… childbirth.

> *LOUISA screams in pain and agony. A sudden rush of water floods the stage. Everything is washed away. The bodies in their graves. The rags off the goddesses. When the water recedes the rope is no longer a river, but looks like rows set for planting. LOUISA's suitcase sits just where it did. LOUISA is dressed in a white spring dress. HESTIA and DEMETER are also dressed for spring, but still look homely. HERA is in the bloom and crisis of youth. She will never look more radiant.*

She is the picture of a woman who could win the heart of the King of Gods. LOUISA looks around her and feels utterly empty. HERA calls out in jubilation.

HERA Demeter! Demeter! You have done it.

DEMETER Don't thank me, Hera, you must thank your supplicant, who supplicates even now.

HERA turns to LOUISA, all goddess and grace.

HERA You have done a wonderful thing, child. You have returned me to myself.

LOUISA What have I done?

HERA You have sacrificed your motherhood for my maidenhead. Isn't it splendid?

HERA laughs.

But, don't you see? Your plight is over. You need not feel any pain at your daughter's death. For you, she doesn't exist. Well, she does exist, but she is motherless. What an odd position for a human to be in. But, anyway, for you, it is as if she never lived. Isn't it wonderful?

LOUISA I feel so empty.

HERA It will pass.

LOUISA This isn't what I wanted.

HERA No. But I can't restore her health. I never could. This is all I could have done for you.

LOUISA Demeter?

DEMETER I have answered your prayers once today, isn't that enough? Now leave me alone.

DEMETER sits down far upstage, away from the action. HESTIA goes to her, but is shoved away. She wrings her hands. HERA approaches LOUISA.

HERA Goodbye, dear one.

LOUISA You can do nothing for my daughter?

HERA No. I never could. Right now, you are mourning the loss of your maternal feelings; your virginity is restored. The sadness will pass. You will go from here and rebuild your life. Find a new husband, one who will not die in a war. I can see to that, if you wish. And you can have more children. Better children who don't die.

LOUISA Can you make me mother of my child again?

HERA No. Goodbye. Thanks.

> *HERA runs offstage in a gleeful and girlish dance. There is a great silence at her exit. HESTIA approaches LOUISA.*

LOUISA Leave me alone.

HESTIA Demeter just told me I would play a part so I would shut up. But there was no part for me. There is never a part for me. In the old days, you couldn't do a thing without me.

LOUISA I don't care! I don't care! What does it matter if you had a part or not?

HESTIA It is the most important thing. I come first and last.

LOUISA Leave me alone.

HESTIA I am your shadow, now.

LOUISA I don't need a shadow. I need my daughter and if you can't give her back to me, if you can't ease my suffering, then I have no wish to ease your boredom.

HESTIA I think that was the most honest prayer I've ever heard in all my existence.

LOUISA Then I pray you heed it and leave me be.

> *LOUISA goes to a far part of the stage and turns her back to the goddesses. HESTIA looks around, bored and lost. She moves like a child about the stage. No one pays attention. She begins as an entertainment to herself, but slowly LOUISA listens.*

HESTIA Some say Hera tricked Zeus into wedding her. He would only bed a virgin, and so she washed away her indiscretions in a beautiful spring deep in the wood, a place she knew he would see her. And he did. He saw her, naked and beautiful, and made himself a bird to watch her. But, she knew he would, for he always loved being birds and things. She had laid a snare for him. When he had become trapped, he called out and she quickly came and rescued him. All in her nakedness, she pressed him to her breast, the waters of the spring that dripped off her body gave him back his godly form and he took her there. Little knowing that this was the marriage rite and they would be forever joined. But, as you know, Zeus would find his pleasures anywhere. And she goes yearly to the spring to trap him once more. Or, that is, her supplicants do in her stead, as you did, Louisa. But, dear Louisa, it is not an act of entrapment, it is the first and best act of spring.

LOUISA Why are you telling me this?

HESTIA Spring has sprung.

> *HESTIA abandons herself to joyful dancing.*

LOUISA What does that mean?

> *HESTIA does not answer.*

DEMETER Who can know? Hestia's mind is gone.

LOUISA Who is Hestia?

DEMETER She is the Goddess of the Hearth and Home. She is the first god you would pray to in the morning, and the last you would pray to before you went to bed. You would thank Hestia for giving you warmth and light and protection. For comfort. The home fire is where you would cook your food, tell tales to your children, give offerings to other gods.

LOUISA What are her stories?

HESTIA The Bacchanal have taken my place.

DEMETER She only has two stories. The one I've told you. In the other, she left Olympus forever. She felt she could better serve the people on earth, among them. She gave up her throne to the child god Dionysus. Now, she is locked here.

LOUISA But people burn things all the time. Lots of people have fireplaces.

DEMETER Do you?

LOUISA No. I have a furnace, now. It runs on gas. I don't even have to touch it.

DEMETER Where there used to be fireplaces, people now turn on radios and television sets.

LOUISA We can't afford those things. I don't know many who can.

DEMETER Yet. Yet. There will come a time. The tide has changed and it can't be reversed. The followers of Dionysus, the Bacchanal, have taken her place on earth. She is trapped here, empty, reasonless. She is the thing that Hera feared becoming.

LOUISA Do you?

DEMETER Fear becoming Hestia? No. I fear that Persephone wants to return to me, and cannot. I hold my hand to the earth and I dream that she is holding her hand to the ceiling of Hell, and yet I cannot dig into the ground and pull her out.

LOUISA Can I bring her back? The way that I gave Hera back her youth?

    Pause.

Please, Demeter. My daughter –

DEMETER Why do you stay, Louisa? Why are you still here?

LOUISA I need –

DEMETER She is dead, Louisa. Your daughter is dead. Now, it no longer matters if she has a name or not. Go. Leave us.

    Pause.

LOUISA Don't say that. You don't know!

DEMETER Oh, but I do know.

LOUISA No. You don't!

DEMETER But Louisa, I do! I am a god, am I not? Louisa, when you come to me demanding the life of your child and I tell you she is dead, you must believe it because you have made it so! If you give me the power to give her life, why, too, can I not give her death?

    Pause.

Answer me, Louisa!

HESTIA Be kind to her, Demeter. Her child has died.

DEMETER She's not a mother anymore, anyway. Go home, Louisa. Go home.

LOUISA No. No, it's not true.

HESTIA Do not cry, Louisa. Some women look pretty when they cry. You are not one of those women. Your tears are useless.

LOUISA But, I've come so far.

DEMETER And would you not have gone farther? Would her death have been a fine thing if you had only gone around the corner to beg against it?

    Pause.

Now will you pray to me, Louisa? Now that you have nothing to pray for? Now that your object has gone? Now will you believe in me and supplicate and sing of my graces? Will you praise me and my daughter and our works? Now will you give the world its summer?

LOUISA You've killed my daughter.

DEMETER I've done nothing.

LOUISA Your inaction killed her.

DEMETER HA! Her death began at the moment of her conception. Would you blame me for that, as well? Don't answer that. I know you do. I am truly sorry you've found your chosen deity so disappointing. Now, go home.

>*Pause. LOUISA starts to leave. HESTIA is all misery and anxiety.*

HESTIA No, Demeter. Don't let her go.

DEMETER It is my fondest wish to have her plague me no longer.

HESTIA But… but…

DEMETER No. I will not tell her how to pray to you, either. If she hasn't guessed it already, she is too dumb to be taught. And even if I did, she is like all the others. She will leave you, my love. She will abandon you for lesser, easier gods, who love nothing more than to please and give pleasure. And you, having felt a glimmer of your former self, will despair when your mind is gone once more. What will you do then?

HESTIA I am your shadow, sister.

>*Pause.*

DEMETER Fine. I will not stop you more. Just leave me be.

HESTIA Louisa! Louisa!

LOUISA What?

HESTIA I've always wanted to see a boat.

LOUISA I do not think you should come with me.

HESTIA Well, then, there is nothing for it. We will tea here.

>*HESTIA sits down and begins to mime tea.*

LOUISA I wish I could understand you.

HESTIA Sit. It's rude to stand and drink tea.

LOUISA There is no tea to drink.

HESTIA You know what I love more than tea? Gossip. I've got a good bit if you do.

LOUISA I think maybe I should leave.

HESTIA I think you'll like it. It's about vegetables.

>*LOUISA looks sad and dubious. She does not want to linger anymore. She looks to DEMETER, who is watching silently. She waves as if to*

give LOUISA permission. LOUISA sits and pretends to hold tea.

HESTIA You first.

LOUISA Oh. Gossip. I don't know. My neighbor, Emily, she's a war bride. Rick met her in England, where he was stationed, and brought her back. I think sometimes she doesn't like him much at all, as if maybe she just married him to come to the States. He seems nice enough, though.

HESTIA Do they consummate?

LOUISA I suppose. I don't know.

HESTIA Does Emily from England sing when she comes?

LOUISA Hestia. I don't think I can say –

HESTIA Or does she sound more like a hamster? Little hamstery chirps and squeaks?

LOUISA smiles in spite of herself.

LOUISA I hadn't really thought about it before.

HESTIA You are very bad at gossip.

LOUISA, wanting to please, gives in.

LOUISA Well, I can hear them having sex through the wall, sometimes. I can't really hear her…

HESTIA Except when…

LOUISA Except when he brings home meat from the butcher's. On those nights, she – oh, I can't say it!

HESTIA Say it! Say it!

LOUISA On those nights, she giggles the whole time and calls him "Big John" when she comes.

LOUISA laughs very hard. HESTIA does her best cartoonish impression of English bemusement and then continues drinking.

And sometimes –

HESTIA All right, I've heard enough. It's my turn.

LOUISA Sorry.

HESTIA I knew this woman named Louisa. Don't speak, Louisa, she is not you. She is a different Louisa you've never met and wouldn't know in a million billion years. She was an idiot. Not like you, mind you, but still. She went knocking on the door of every god she could think of. She didn't know many, but she figured sooner or later one would help her. Now. The God of Martyrdom and Carpenters asked her for gold; in return, he gave her water. The Goddess of Wifery asked for a sacrifice, then gave her the shaft. The Goddess of Gossip asked for a story, but getting nothing good, she gave her a bad story in return. The Goddess of Daughters asked for Louisa's daughter, and so they traded daughters. Now the idiot Louisa had a goddess for a daughter and the goddess had a mortal. This was very distressing for everyone. Everyone had become someone's daughter, and no one knew who was immortal and who was dead. Then, they all sat down for tea. The end.

LOUISA Are you the Goddess of Gossip?

HESTIA It's your turn to tell a story, now.

LOUISA What do you want to know?

HESTIA Tell me about Alex.

LOUISA He was tall with olive skin and smelled like the ocean and cigarette ashes. He would drink too much and laugh too loudly. He loved too much. He came to the States to make enough money to bring his brothers to live with him. But then, the civil war here. I got pregnant. He left to save his brothers. None of them made it.

HESTIA His soul was here.

LOUISA It is here.

HESTIA He loved too much.

LOUISA What did you mean, they traded daughters?

HESTIA My turn! What story shall I tell now? About a woman who turned into a spider? About a woman who turned into an echo? About a woman who turned into an olive tree? About a woman who turned into a monster? About a woman who turned into a bird? About a woman who turned into a cow? About a woman who turned into a stone?

LOUISA We used to tell those stories around a campfire when I was little.

Pause.

I'm such an idiot.

HESTIA We already heard that story.

LOUISA Where's some wood? What will burn?

HESTIA Don't you want any more tea?

LOUISA There's nothing around.

HESTIA You are very rude, Louisa. Very rude.

LOUISA I want to build you a fire. What can I burn?

Pause.

HESTIA Me? For me?

LOUISA Here.

She takes some of the rope and lays it on top of itself.

Now fire. I need fire.

HESTIA He already gave you that gift.

LOUISA Here. Here.

She goes into her suitcase and pulls out a book of matches. She quickly lights a fire.

How do I start?

HESTIA A rape? Many good stories start with a rape.

LOUISA Hestia, Goddess of the Hearth, who came first and last. Keep us as we go through our day. Protect this home and all those in it.

HESTIA What home? Is this a home? Is this your home?

LOUISA takes more rope and makes a square around herself and the fire and HESTIA. She shapes a little space for a door.

LOUISA Yes. This is my home. This is my home, and I ask you to give it, and all who are inside, comfort and protection

There is a great silence. The fire crackles.

HESTIA I cannot save your child.

LOUISA I know.

HESTIA Why did you do it?

LOUISA So I could understand you.

HESTIA The gods cannot be fully understood.

LOUISA No. But, maybe, to ease your suffering.

HESTIA And for that, Louisa, I give you comfort.

LOUISA shudders and collapses. She cries softly to herself. It is the type of quiet, honest weeping we do when we are with our mothers.

LOUISA Then she really is dead.

HESTIA She's been dead for some time. She died as you left for Greece.

LOUISA Why didn't you tell me?

HESTIA You did not want to know.

LOUISA What should I do now?

HESTIA I will bring comfort to all who enter your home, Louisa. All.

> *HESTIA points outside the little house to DEMETER, who still lies upon the ground. LOUISA looks out of her little home.*

LOUISA She does not want anything I can offer.

HESTIA You have offered to save her daughter, but you are not a god. Give her what you have.

LOUISA She hates me.

HESTIA Demeter hates no one.

> *Pause. LOUISA leaves her house and goes to the goddess, touching her lightly.*

LOUISA Hestia tells me it is Spring.

DEMETER Does she? Then you have no further need of me, at all.

LOUISA Demeter? You look cold out here, all alone. Come in and warm yourself by my fire.

DEMETER So. You have discovered her secret, and you've come to work your will upon me.

LOUISA I will ask you for nothing, anymore. I know you don't want to give it.

DEMETER And it doesn't matter any more.

LOUISA But I feel, now, more alone than I've ever felt. I am in a foreign country where I am unwelcome and don't speak the language. I've lost all that I love in the world. If I would pray, it would be only… if only not to feel so much alone. Come, Demeter. Please. You look cold. You are welcome in my home. Please. Find comfort here.

> *Pause. DEMETER slowly gets up from her place and walks toward the little house. She smiles despite herself when she sees her sister well and clasps HESTIA's hands in hers as she sits by the fire.*

DEMETER It is good to see you again, Hestia.

HESTIA It is good to see you, sister Demeter. Do you feel comforted?

DEMETER I have always found comfort by your good fire.

HESTIA It is not my fire. It is Louisa's.

Pause.

She's not so dumb after all.

DEMETER laughs deeply and loudly.

DEMETER No. No, I would say she is not.

Pause.

Louisa, those who have given me comfort in my time of wandering sadness have always been given a gift by me. I will give you a gift.

She pulls out a small pouch from her pocket and gives it to LOUISA.

LOUISA Thank you.

DEMETER Take it outside and give it to the soil.

LOUISA does so. Within the pouch, she finds a pomegranate. She plants it. It takes time.

HESTIA We have been cruel to her.

DEMETER Everything has happened as it should, in the course of events.

HESTIA It is a sudden turn.

DEMETER It is as it should be.

HESTIA Maybe we should have just told her.

DEMETER You would have if you could. But, dear Hestia, I fear, still, the outcome of this event. The rush of happiness, the glee, the wonder of life, the joy. The supreme joy. I will forget that it can all be undone. And it will be undone. And she will be ripped from my arms again as if it was the first time. I fear that moment the most. You cannot know, Hestia, you can't know. When it is all over again, I feel so empty for so long.

HESTIA I have known profound cold. My limbs become ghosts of bones and skin on my body. The brittle joints break and snap from myself. I turn black and shudder and blow away in the wind like dust. Such is despair. I know this pain, sister. And I would do all I could to comfort you. Sit close to me now, while you can, sister. We will love each other just before the pain of love and life breaks into these little walls and turns us into beings of unbearable happiness. When the cataclysm is over, I will be here again.

LOUISA finishes planting the pomegranate. There is a moment of quiet as she looks down at the ground with a certain amount of satisfaction. Then, there is a bright light. It crawls across the stage slowly, illuminating as it goes. Where it touches, here and there, holes open up in the stage leading to the underworld. The rope on the stage is pulled at one end toward the heavens, even as the other end falls through the floor toward Hades, so that the stage is now a forest of rope. LOUISA herself almost falls into a hole. The house, where the goddesses sit consoling each other still, is untouched. There is a silence. PERSEPHONE emerges, climbing one of the ropes.

PERSEPHONE Mother?

The cataclysm. DEMETER rushes out of the house and grasps her daughter tightly in her arms.

DEMETER Oh! All my joy! You have returned to me!

PERSEPHONE I have missed you so.

DEMETER The winter has been so long, my love, I thought I would never hold you to me, again.

PERSEPHONE I love you, mother. I love you.

DEMETER My soul. I love you.

LOUISA cries out, but clasps her hand to her mouth and would run into the little house, but Hestia stands in the doorway and bars her entry.

LOUISA I can't bear it.

HESTIA You must.

DEMETER Persephone, I would like you to meet the believer who helped you back to me. This is Louisa.

PERSEPHONE It has been a long time since I have seen a living soul. Louisa, thank you.

DEMETER Do you perceive her need, my dear one?

PERSEPHONE With all my heart. She need only ask.

LOUISA Ask what?

PERSEPHONE laughs a light and kind laughter.

PERSEPHONE Of the dead, my dear. You may ask of the dead. With me were your mother, father, a child they never bore, uncles and aunts, ancestors going back to the dawn of time, friends you have forgotten about, lovers you never knew you had, a poet who wrote a poem for you and died in the street. There are many. I can speak for them. I can bring news to you of them. I can answer questions you have for them. But, there isn't much time. You can ask one question.

LOUISA Only one?

PERSEPHONE It is more than I have given any other mortal, save one, and he wasted his chance. I will not give this gift again.

Pause.

What would you ask of the dead?

LOUISA Are you sure that is all? Can't you…

Pause.

PERSEPHONE No. No one has ever returned from my kingdom.

LOUISA Can I go down and be with them?

PERSEPHONE If you choose. I will make a place for you.

DEMETER Is that what you want?

HESTIA You do not have to die. You are young and bold. You came here, when the land was still thick with bodies from the war, when so few travel alone. You are not a helpless thing. You would have beaten down the doors of heaven to save your daughter. You are strong enough to live in this world and make of it what you will.

PERSEPHONE You will come to me one day, sooner or later. It is all one to me. But you cannot come back.

LOUISA Do you know what my life would be like if I stayed?

PERSEPHONE We are not the Fates.

HESTIA We cannot know such things.

PERSEPHONE I only know the paths of the dead.

LOUISA What would Alex want me to do?

PERSEPHONE I can tell you if you want, but it would be your only question. Think on it.

DEMETER Persephone. Let us go, there is very little time for us. Leave her here to think about her choice and let us walk the world.

PERSEPHONE I think I already can see what Louisa will choose to do, even if she does not. I see it plainly on her face. You are right, mother. Louisa and I will enjoy our last summer as we can, then I will take her down to the underworld with me when it is time.

DEMETER Your last summer?

PERSEPHONE Yes. When Louisa is gone, there will be no more believers.

DEMETER My soul, don't say such a thing.

PERSEPHONE It is only the truth. We must carry on as watchers of the world now, we must remove our hands.

DEMETER No. No, I will not give you back. I will hold you above the ground forever. I will keep you here with me.

PERSEPHONE looks to her mother with kind, sad eyes. She smiles.

PERSEPHONE Yes, mother. Of course. I know you would if you could.

LOUISA But there must be a winter.

DEMETER What?

LOUISA Nothing can live forever. Not on earth. A plant must give up its fruit, then die so that the seeds can dig into fertile ground and live and give their own fruit to the soil. There must be a season of death, so there can be a season of birth. You cannot have one without the other.

DEMETER You, you of all the souls on earth, you would take my daughter from me? You would have me endure my suffering again?

LOUISA Maybe you don't have to bear it alone.

DEMETER You are a poor substitute for my own child, Louisa.

LOUISA I know the ritual now. I can call back summer.

DEMETER For only a few short years until you join her, then all is lost again.

LOUISA Unless…

PERSEPHONE What you ask is impossible.

LOUISA I have thought of my question.

PERSEPHONE Go ahead, child.

LOUISA Does my daughter wish she could return to me and finish the life she should have had?

Pause.

PERSEPHONE There are few who wish to return to the world they left. They do not feel time, and so it is for only the blink of an eye they join all those who wish for them. Most babes who did not taste mother's milk have no thought to life or death. But she has much of her mother in her. She is restless. She does not settle in her father's arms. She feels time moving around her, still. She suffers without you. She hears your voice calling to her.

LOUISA And you would prevent her from coming to me, even if it is for only the length of a season? If only to know summer? What would you choose, Persephone, if you were asked to make the choice?

HESTIA She was asked, and she couldn't make the choice. She loves her husband, and she loves her mother. She loves tending her garden of souls, and she loves tending the garden of earth. She loves –

LOUISA Too much.

HESTIA And she is divided.

LOUISA My daughter is not divided and neither am I.

> *Pause.*

DEMETER She would teach her daughter to pass on the knowledge.

PERSEPHONE Mother…

HESTIA Demeter loves you to the exclusion of all other cares and needs. The first mother could not have loved her first daughter more.

DEMETER I know how to bring her back, and we can do it together. I wish I did not have to lose you for even a morning, but if it is this or nothing at all, I would have you leave me so I may have you back again.

PERSEPHONE Are you sure?

DEMETER Louisa, I am putting my faith in you. Think of your daughter not as only one girl, but a long line of women. Give her your wisdom, your strength, your courage, and your love. Instill within her the knowledge we have given you so that the daughter we send back to you from death may pass on her knowledge. May it be, through this, it is as if she is resurrected immortal.

LOUISA But your daughter will still die yearly.

DEMETER I am putting my faith in you that we will never again have to suffer so long a winter.

> *A great wind blows. For a moment, it ignites the fire in LOUISA's rope home so that the whole world flashes a brilliant light. Then it goes out and takes all the light with it. As suddenly as it was gone, the light returns. LOUISA stands on the sandy shore of an island in Greece. We can hear the birds calling and the waves crashing. Behind her is HESTIA, looking middle-aged and dressed all in black. To one side of*

HESTIA is a suitcase, to the other is a small pomegranate tree, ready to be planted. LOUISA is wearing her own clothes, again, her own suitcase beside her. In front of her is an infant. It coughs, starts, and cries. LOUISA bends down to pick it up.

LOUISA Oh! All my joy! You have returned to me.

HESTIA What is her name?

LOUISA Persephone.

HESTIA It is a good name.

She enjoys the scene for a moment.

A chill has come into the air. It will be winter again, soon. Come on. I've never been on a boat before.

LOUISA What is that?

HESTIA A pomegranate tree. It's a gift from Demeter. She says you will know what to do with it.

LOUISA I do. Now let's all go home.

She holds PERSEPHONE close to her and picks up her suitcase. HESTIA picks up her suitcase and the tree. They all exit together.

The end.

Hephaestus and the Three Golden Robots

by Evelyn Jean Pine

Hephaestus
and the Three Golden Robots

Hephaestus and the Three Golden Robots was first produced in a reading on July 31, 2010 at EXIT Stage Left in San Francisco, California as part of the San Francisco Olympians Festival. The play was directed by Evelyn Jean Pine with the following cast:

Prometheus/Zeus	Charles Lewis III
Hephaestus	Matt Gunnison
Hera/Hestia	Gwyneth Richards
Alpha	Sara Breindel
Beta	Lisa Darter
Omega	Lauren Spencer
Pandora	Megan Cohen
Stage Directions	Sunil Patel

Characters

VOICE OF PROMETHEUS, the poetic Titan, captured and imprisoned by Zeus' orders for stealing fire from Hephaestus. Despite his pain, his voice is deep, musical, confidential, insinuating. His body – almost a stage set in itself – is huge, taking up the entire stage. His voice emanates from within it.
HEPHAESTUS, M, 40, an immortal – robust, hardworking, red-faced and handsome, but misshapen, limping, golden braces on his bum legs.
HERA, F, ageless, Hephaestus' mother, wife of Zeus.
ALPHA, F, 25, a robot, a dead ringer for Aphrodite.
BETA, F, 25, a robot, a dead ringer for Aphrodite.
OMEGA, F, 25, a robot, a dead ringer for Aphrodite.
VOICE OF ZEUS, M, Hephaestus' father, Hera's husband, deep, powerful, angry, magnificent. We never see him, but we hear his thunder and see his lightning bolts.
PANDORA, F, 25, a dead ringer for Aphrodite, and, though a creation of Hephaestus, as human as can be.
HESTIA, F, a crone, ageless, ancient, goddess of the hearth.

Note on double casting

The Voice of Prometheus and the Voice of Zeus may be easily double-cast. Hera and Hestia may be easily double-cast. The role of the off-stage voice of Aphrodite may be played by any of the female performers.

Setting

The end of the world, and then Hephaestus' workshop and forge, deep in the earth beneath Mount Olympus.

Scene 1

The beginning of time.

Howling winds. Immovable cliffs. Thunder and lightning.

Onstage, the mammoth body of PROMETHEUS is being chained to the cliff by HEPHAESTUS, who stands with his hammer aloft.

PROMETHEUS' body is so huge it takes up most of the stage. Perhaps his arms rest across the stage at a diagonal. His legs might disappear into the audience. His voice is huge as well, but profoundly expressive, befitting a poet, a seer.

PROMETHEUS My creations, Hephaestus. I fell in love with them.

As they speak, HEPHAESTUS hammers, securing PROMETHEUS' enormous body to the cliff. HEPHAESTUS is clearly unhappy to be there. At times, the sound of the hammer rings. PROMETHEUS' voice, at moments, is strained from the violence.

HEPHAESTUS I'm not listening, Prometheus, you thief.

PROMETHEUS If I committed a crime, it was for those I created. You know what it's like. You're a craftsman, too. Don't pretend we're not brothers. Not brothers of blood, but brothers of craft, of creativity, of fire.

HEPHAESTUS Liar. I have my own family.

PROMETHEUS What an inspiration they are: Sons murdering fathers, fathers eating their sons. Heartwarming.

HEPHAESTUS Shut up.

PROMETHEUS *(ignoring him)* Your mom – or was it your dad? – throwing you off Olympus? Twice.

HEPHAESTUS Shit happens.

PROMETHEUS You fell for three interminable days. Lying here now, staring down, down, down, I don't think I could have endured such a fall without going mad. You bounced deep into the sea. What courage it must take – after having an experience like that – to drag your broken frame all the way up here where there is nothing but the wind.

HEPHAESTUS It's not a big deal.

PROMETHEUS At least Zeus came to your rescue.

HEPHAESTUS *(surprised and eager)* He did?

PROMETHEUS Of course not. He didn't do a damn thing. He didn't even remember he had a son.

HEPHAESTUS Shit stirrer, I made my peace with this long ago.

PROMETHEUS Peace? Really? *(pause)* May I speak as one artist to another? You do splendid work. These are the most beautiful manacles ever made.

HEPHAESTUS Thanks.

PROMETHEUS What a triumph of Olympian engineering. Instruments of torture, durable for eternity. And these chains are marvelous. Sensible, invincible, elegant, utile.

HEPHAESTUS Thank you.

PROMETHEUS Knowing the resilience and beauty of these chains, Hephaestus, I could stay here forever, without one word of complaint, except for one tiny detail.

HEPHAESTUS Don't start, Titan. No one can steal from the Olympians and not suffer.

PROMETHEUS My little creatures, Hephaestus. Each one different. They're like snowflakes. And yet, your father, vengeful Zeus, demands they be destroyed. I couldn't live with that.

HEPHAESTUS You'll have to.

PROMETHEUS That would be torture: my creatures exterminated like fleas.

HEPHAESTUS You should have thought of that before you broke into my forge and stole my fire – as a gift for your fleas. How could you do it, Prometheus? You made it look like somehow you and I are on the same side. Like I'm against my dad, my family. I make mechanical creatures too, you know, but I'm not a hothead. I don't get all emotional. I don't get attached.

PROMETHEUS Mechanical? My creatures aren't mechanical, Hephaestus. They live. And they die. That's why I call them – humans.

HEPHAESTUS Live?

PROMETHEUS Yes.

HEPHAESTUS Die?

PROMETHEUS So heartbreaking.

HEPHAESTUS Not machines?

PROMETHEUS Not machines. Not animals either. Like gods, but even more fascinating: my creatures change.

HEPHAESTUS This is impossible. *(pause)* How did you do it?

PROMETHEUS *(booming laugh)* You're chaining me to a cliff for eternity and you want to know how I did it? You think I would give my torturer my secrets? Zeus wants to blot out everything having to do with me, so my little ones must die. But his son wants to learn how to make his own – as if you could come up with something better.

HEPHAESTUS It couldn't be that hard.

PROMETHEUS You could never make anything like them. And, unfortunately for you, I'll be stuck here on this mountainside so you'll never, ever be able to learn.

HEPHAESTUS No one will miss them.

PROMETHEUS I will. Chained here at the end of the world, attacked by eagles, assaulted by elements, every day I will wonder what happened to my creatures.

HEPHAESTUS Your creatures are crap. Forget about them. *(pause)* They can't be that hard to make.

PROMETHEUS They're life. They're change. They're beautiful.

HEPHAESTUS How'd you do it?

PROMETHEUS Do what?

HEPHAESTUS Make these –

PROMETHEUS – "Little pieces of crap?" Why do you want to know, Hephaestus, if all they're worthy of is destruction? Zeus wants to crush me and everything having to do with me. Who will defend my little precious ones? Who will care for them? *(pause)* Hephaestus, you and I are identical. True, I'm a Titan. You're an Olympian, but at root, we are the same. Visionaries. Creators. Makers-of-things.

HEPHAESTUS I'm an Olympian, Prometheus. I can't free you.

PROMETHEUS Of course you can't. Destiny denies it. You don't have to tell me, Hephaestus. I see far, far into the future – I see millennia, one interminable generation after another, until I'm finally freed.

HEPHAESTUS There's nothing I can do.

PROMETHEUS Perhaps not. Still, I can't help but wonder: is it truly fate that stops you, Hephaestus, or is it your father?

HEPHAESTUS Leave him out of it.

PROMETHEUS Poor little Hephaestus. He won't stand up to daddy, and he can't make a human being. He doesn't know how.

HEPHAESTUS Your creatures don't sound so great.

PROMETHEUS They're not perfect, but perfection is old-school. My creatures are funny – scampering around, braying, naked, self-replicating. I love them. I do. To see them wiped out… it's more than I could bear. *(pause)* Promise me you'll protect them. Plead for them. Keep them from your father's wrath.

HEPHAESTUS Why should I? They sound like nothing but trouble.

PROMETHEUS Why, Hephaestus? Why should you, the most ingenious inventor in the universe, keep my humans safe? Because nothing like them has ever existed. They are brand-new.

HEPHAESTUS And if I should… *(unsaid: "take care of them")*

PROMETHEUS Promise me that, and I will tell you everything. I will share the deepest and most powerful of all my secrets: to make human life. Will you protect my secret as you protect my little ones?

HEPHAESTUS But my father, he'd never forgive me. I couldn't. It's too involved. I'm really busy back at the shop. They sound like a pain –

PROMETHEUS *(livid)* Hephaestus, do you want my secret?

HEPHAESTUS *(after a moment)* I do.

PROMETHEUS Do you promise?

HEPHAESTUS I promise.

PROMETHEUS Promise what, Hephaestus? Say it.

HEPHAESTUS I promise to protect those freakish little…

PROMETHEUS What, Hephaestus?

HEPHAESTUS *(reluctant)* I promise to protect your humans.

PROMETHEUS *(deeply pleased)* Thank you.

HEPHAESTUS Tell me.

HEPHAESTUS leans over PROMETHEUS' enormous face and hears

the secret whispered.

PROMETHEUS *(after)* My secret lives with you, Hephaestus. Enjoy it, if you're capable of enjoying anything. But never forget your sacred vow: take care of my creatures. Nurture them. Protect them from harm, and, most important, protect them from Zeus.

> *HEPHAESTUS nods. His job done, he slings his hammer on his shoulder. He begins to drag his bum leg down the side of the cliff as the wind picks up.*

My regards to your beautiful wife, Hephaestus. Kiss Aphrodite for me. You must be in a tremendous hurry to return to her exquisite beauty, her languid poetry, her love of pleasure. *(calling after him)* Oh, and by the way, Hephaestus, one last thing.

> *HEPHAESTUS ignores him.*

One last thing. Hephaestus.

HEPHAESTUS *(annoyed)* What?

PROMETHEUS One tiny little detail that I – as someone who can gaze into the mists of the future and see what is to come – thought might be a teensy weensy bit useful as you try to come to terms with your situation in this glorious New Age of the Olympians.

HEPHAESTUS *(impatient)* Well?

PROMETHEUS Fear questions.

HEPHAESTUS What?

PROMETHEUS Are you deaf too, Hephaestus? Fear questions. Gods are funny. Even, I suspect, Olympian Gods. Question your belief in their immortality, their absolute power, their God-ness, and suddenly, they topple. And when Gods fall, Hephaestus, heavens tremble.

HEPHAESTUS Titan, our conversation is over.

PROMETHEUS Toodle-y-oo, Hephaestus, son of the newest ruler of the universe, Zeus and his sublime consort, Hera – never forget that I have gazed into the future and you, god of the forge, patron of those who make everything that is of use, you will create the one thing that will, once and for all, destroy the Olympians – and the power of the immortals – forever.

> *PROMETHEUS starts to laugh. HEPHAESTUS is shocked, horrified. He opens his mouth to say something, decides better of it, and continues down the mountain, leaving PROMETHEUS laughing at the elements.*

Lights out.

Scene 2

Lights up. HEPHAESTUS' workshop. A forge is on one side with metalworking tools and an enormous fireplace. Close to the center but back is an enormous movable kiln. The only things of beauty are objects of gold and other glittering metal, requested by the gods and made by HEPHAESTUS.

On the other side, a cottage kitchen, funky and small, with a table, four chairs, a fireplace, etc.

Neither fire is currently lit.

There are three exits: one to the outside through the kitchen, one into the back of the forge, and one through the audience.

TIME: Later that night.

On the table is a letter, which HEPHAESTUS might notice if he wasn't so distracted by his visit with PROMETHEUS.

HEPHAESTUS enters on tiptoe. He puts down his hammer. He grabs a beer or something. Takes a long draught.

HEPHAESTUS *(to himself)* First, I tell her about the curse. Then I tell her about the humans. She'll laugh at the curse because it's stupid. Who's going to believe a chained Titan? Now the humans – maybe she'll get a kick out of them. Maybe she'll even have an idea about what to do with them. *(he calls out)* Aphrodite! Honey! Come hear the wild curse Prometheus thundered at me. It's hilarious.

HEPHAESTUS takes another sip. Waits, then calls out.

Aphrodite, that crazy Titan says I'm destined to make something that will bite us all in the butt – destroy the family's authority or something. The Olympians, according to Prometheus – done for – by me. What a wack job. The crazy bastard's cursing me as I'm pounding on the handcuffs, Aphrodite. Says something I'm going to build will destroy us all. Doesn't he know everything I make is constructive – swords, shields, racks, maces, waterboards, billy clubs. Come on down, honey. I brought you a present. You've never seen anything like them before. They're special. For you.

HEPHAESTUS sees the letter on the table, picks it up and reads.

We hear the VOICE OF APHRODITE as HEPHAESTUS reads.

VOICE OF APHRODITE Dearest Hephaestus,
You are wonderful. Full of invention. Strong. Boyish. And you love me.

And you know, my love, how I adore being loved. But, my husband, I've discovered that married life is not for me.

HEPHAESTUS What?

HEPHAESTUS continues reading.

VOICE OF APHRODITE I cannot believe that I am meant to enjoy only one man – no matter how wonderful, creative, strong, loving. And yet I know that single-mindedness is what marriage demands. And so, my darling, I must take my leave.

HEPHAESTUS No.

HEPHAESTUS continues reading.

VOICE OF APHRODITE We will see each other often on Olympus, I know, and, perhaps, we can remain lovers even as we both find joy and satisfaction with others.
Your darling,
Aphrodite
P.S. If Prometheus looked into our fates, my love, believe him. The Titan reads the future with absolute certainty. Perhaps he has promised us both happiness beyond our wildest dreams, because that, my sweet, is what I wish for you.

HEPHAESTUS sits and strokes his cheek. Then he curls up in the fetal position. He moans. And then he stands.

HEPHAESTUS Work. *(pause)* But I can't, because if I do I'll destroy – Work. Prometheus will say anything. Work. *(calling)* Aphrodite! *(no answer)* She's gone. Must work. Must work. Must work. *(in a tizzy)* How'd it get so quiet? I need a helper, that's what I need. Someone else can do the making, the actual building, construction – that's how I can subvert the curse. I will create nothing. I will observe, direct, supervise, manage. I hate that shit, but that's how it's gotta be. *(pause)* Wait. I have that old automaton out back. I thought it might have to guard Crete from the Titans, but we kicked their asses before we needed it. The damn thing's already built. I'll bet it could add its own improvements. Make it look a little better and do a little more. That's not creating, that's futzing. Tinkering won't destroy anything. I'll keep my hands clean, and the automaton can make all the helpers we need. And I won't have to tangle with that Titanic curse. *(calling one last time)* Aphrodite!

HEPHAESTUS waits for her answer, which doesn't come. He puts his hammer on his shoulder and heads back into his workshop.

Lights out.

Scene 3

> HEPHAESTUS' *workshop. The clanking of metal. The sizzle of fire. The smell of heated metal.*
>
> TIME: *A day or two later.*
>
> *The fire in the workshop is roaring, but the one in the kitchen remains unlit.*
>
> HERA, *elegant and out of place, sits drinking from a golden goblet.* ALPHA, *also elegant and out of place, is at fireplace in the forge, working the bellows.* ALPHA *is a dead ringer for the goddess Aphrodite. Her skin – whatever its tone – has a slight golden sheen.*

HERA Individuals who make things don't have a clue. Consider the Titans. Big and stupid, they decide to make a war. Didn't they see they were doomed? They made a war all right, but in the process they made us gods. Our home, Olympus: now hallowed ground. The Titans thought we were puny, but their violence and treachery made us grow in stature. *(pointing at herself)* Queen of the Universe. Admit it, Aphrodite – it suits me. And you, all cozy with your dear husband. What a marvelous couple you have become, dearie. Hephaestus may not be flashy or macho, but he loves you and makes you this warm little home.

ALPHA Home is where the heart is.

HERA I'm delighted to see you're actually taking an interest in his work. It may be dirty, lowdown, but he's your husband –

> *Enter* HEPHAESTUS, *from the back of the shop.*

HERA Darling.

HEPHAESTUS *(horrified to see her)* Mother? What are you doing here?

HERA A mother worries. First, I didn't see you at the celebration of Victory Day. You missed the coronation of your dear father to the throne. Now I hear about the horrible theft by that turncoat Prometheus. The nerve he had to break in here and steal your fire, the sacred fire of the Olympians. Never trust a Titan. That's what I've always said, but Zeus felt he needed his help to win the war and, of course, what your father says goes.

HEPHAESTUS Prometheus won't be stealing anything any more.

HERA Your fire – why, it's meant to make thrones, armaments, jewelry, not –

HEPHAESTUS His theft bothers you more than it bothers me.

HERA Is Prometheus crazy? Irresponsible? Utterly immoral? Angry that his breed is now – once and for all – annihilated?

HEPHAESTUS Mother, please.

HERA What?

HEPHAESTUS I spent yesterday morning chaining him to a cliff. He'll never threaten us again.

HERA Wonderful news.

HEPHAESTUS It was exhausting, unsettling. I need to –

HERA Of course you do. Relax into the loving arms of your beautiful wife.

HEPHAESTUS Have you seen her?

HERA Who?

HEPHAESTUS Aphrodite?

HERA Don't be oblivious, darling. She's right here.

HEPHAESTUS Where?

HERA *(pointing at ALPHA)* Here.

HEPHAESTUS That's not my wife.

HERA But, of course – *(unsaid: "it is")*

HEPHAESTUS My wife, Mother, is magnificent. The hangnail on her little toe is desire itself. Her laughter is the sound of spring rain. Her words are never complaints or demands, but poetry. This *(pointing at ALPHA)* is a machine.

HERA What? But she looks exactly like… *(she reaches out to touch ALPHA)* – feels exactly like –

HEPHAESTUS An automaton.

HERA But why?

HEPHAESTUS There's a lot to do around here, Mother. Every day a new request for crowns, swords, thunderbolts. The longer the war's over the more weapons I'm supposed to make. I needed new tools to help me keep up with increasing demand.

>   BETA *enters, carrying metal and tools. She looks identical to ALPHA.* HERA *turns to her.*

HERA Aphrodite!

HEPHAESTUS Another machine, Mother.

BETA Necessity is the mother of invention.

HERA looks BETA over.

HERA What does Aphrodite think of all this, Hephaestus? These machines – so lifelike –

OMEGA, also carrying tools or metal, enters and HERA rushes to her.

(to OMEGA) Dear, dear Aphrodite, thank you for welcoming me into your humble home.

OMEGA *(brightly)* It takes a heap of living to make a house a home.

OMEGA starts cleaning up after HERA in the kitchen. BETA and ALPHA are doing work at the forge.

HEPHAESTUS They are mechanical helpers.

HERA But they look just like –

HEPHAESTUS Who?

HERA Where is she? *(pause)* Has she…

HEPHAESTUS Gone.

HERA Oh, Hephaestus, I am so sorry.

HEPHAESTUS It's all right, Mother, really. I've made my peace. I've resolved to work hard and never think about her.

HERA No. Of course not. *(sticks her face too close to OMEGA, who doesn't respond)* They look like her twins, her triplets, and so… real.

HEPHAESTUS They are real. Real machines. Powerhouses. They do my work. Creating things. These days all I do is supervise, but that is no small job. In fact, Mother, you'd better go. I have a lot on my mind.

HERA It's as if they weren't constructed at all –

HEPHAESTUS I'm a welder, Mom, a boilermaker. I'm good at it. Please, go.

HERA Of course you are, but…

HEPHAESTUS But what?

HERA It's uncanny. They are three exact replicas of your wife. Made out of gold. Doesn't that seem a little obsessive?

HEPHAESTUS Mother, I had an old automaton out back. I tinkered with it a little and this is how it turned out. This automaton made the others. If they should happen to look like anyone you know, it's a fluke. I don't spend my time thinking about her. The fact that she is not here right now – I've made my peace with it. *(strokes his cheek)*

HERA I don't know what to think.

HEPHAESTUS About what?

HERA Can't you face your problem head-on? Admit that you might actually miss Aphrodite just the slenderest bit? I know last year when you caught her with Ares in flagrante delicto in front of everybody, you acted like you thought it was funny, but I wonder, when the laughter stopped, if you weren't wounded.

HEPHAESTUS Me? Wounded? That was a long time ago, but she came back. Now she's gone again. I'm not lovesick. I'm not lost. I have my work and I need to get on with it.

HERA *(looking at the robots)* They are so beautiful. They look as if they are alive.

HEPHAESTUS Incredible workhorses. These machines put the same meticulous power into doing even the stuff I detest: boring fabrication, cleaning up the workshop. Each one can touch things that are way too hot for me, lift things that are oppressively heavy. They're practical and –

HERA Lovely. Scrumptious. Beautiful. Their eyes full of…

HEPHAESTUS Machines, Mother. No feelings.

HERA Can anything be really beautiful if it has no feelings?

HEPHAESTUS I'm not Prometheus. What would I want with feelings?

HERA What does that monster have to do with anything?

HEPHAESTUS His creatures are all feeling. All joy. All horror. It's what makes them so amusing and yet so pathetic.

HERA Evil creatures. Zeus will find them and root them out.

HEPHAESTUS They're quite remarkable really. *(looking at his robots sadly)* I mean, my machines can design and build, upgrade themselves and each other, take on a million crucial tasks, but compared to the humans, they don't measure up.

HERA Don't measure up? They're glorious. *(pause)* What did she say?

HEPHAESTUS Who?

HERA makes a gesture at ALPHA, BETA, and OMEGA.

It doesn't matter.

HERA I just thought –

HEPHAESTUS Don't think, Mother. I don't. I don't have time. Very busy here. Busy. Busy.

HERA Nobody can work all the time.

HEPHAESTUS Tell Dad that with my automata, productivity will increase. That doesn't mean there's still not plenty to do. I fell behind an entire day torturing Prometheus.

HERA He got what he deserved. That horrible Titan: turncoat, schemer, thief.

HEPHAESTUS He claims he can see the future.

HERA He talks big.

HEPHAESTUS He claims he can see the moment when Zeus will be crushed.

HERA That kind of outrageous lunacy is what makes Titans losers. Absolute losers. *(pause)* Stealing your fire to give to those creatures. I've heard they're horrid, ugly things.

HEPHAESTUS They're strange, fantastical, alive.

HERA You've seen them?

HEPHAESTUS *(covering)* Me? Why would I see them? I'm just reporting what somebody told me. How would I have time to see them with everything that needs doing around here?

HERA What are they called again?

HEPHAESTUS Humans. He treats them like kittens.

HERA Well, now that Prometheus is chained for eternity, those little kittens will be exterminated.

HEPHAESTUS Prometheus agonizes over their fate.

HERA *(laughs)* He should agonize over his own. And you, Hephaestus, are you all right?

HEPHAESTUS Too many questions, Mother. I am always all right.

HERA Zeus wonders why we haven't seen more of you. We both do. This is a remarkable time for our family.

HEPHAESTUS Do you know what he asked me last time I saw him? "Hephaestus, what's your mission?" "What?" I said. "Your mission. Your life purpose. Say it in one hundred words or less." "I make things," I said.

He says, "What's the value-added you bring to the Olympic realm? What is it that you do that's so fucking powerful that you should be considered one of the twelve Olympians?" What kind of father asks that about his own son, "What's your mission?"

HERA Zeus doesn't want you to feel left out just because you're down here and we're up there. It's a new world, my dear, a new time. The old ways are gone forever, disintegrated, so dead and gone we can hardly remember that the new ways have only now begun. Come up from underground, Hephaestus. Join the celebration. We won! *(she gets ready to leave)* And dress up a little, Hephaestus. Get a new look. You're the son of the ruler of the universe. Why not look the part?

> *HERA exits. HEPHAESTUS watches HERA leave.*

HEPHAESTUS Am I really related to her?

ALPHA Fate chooses our relatives, we choose our friends.

HEPHAESTUS What the fuck does that mean? Why did I stick all those unbearable platitudes in these mechanical mouths? A bunch of mindless metal. Nothing comes out that I haven't put in. Not like Prometheus' creatures who yammer on and on and it's incoherent but at least the words are theirs. And now I've got my hands full with them too. *(after a moment, to ALPHA, BETA, and OMEGA)* Why aren't you working?

> *ALPHA, BETA, and OMEGA get to work, pounding metal, working the bellows, manufacturing things, a swarm of activity. HEPHAESTUS watches them. The more he watches, the more dissatisfied he becomes.*

Not good enough. Mundane. Empty. Dullsville. Always perfect – but no surprises.

ALPHA, BETA, OMEGA *(with smiles in their voices)* There's no prize like a surprise.

HEPHAESTUS The chit-chat was a mistake. Who wants to hear from a machine? *(pause)* I thought it would be cozy. *(change of thought)* Where does Prometheus get off with all that crap about me making something that would destroy the gods? He says he sees the future, but all he does is make things up. *(sarcastic)* "Poor me, poor me, I don't dare do anything because I might destroy the world." It's a good thing I made this automaton self-upgrading. Hey there, Prometheus, I hope you're having fun. I don't have to do anything. My machines can do it all. They know how to upgrade themselves so they're continually improving.

ALPHA There's always room for improvement.

HEPHAESTUS *(to ALPHA)* That's right. Who needs humans? There is nothing like a machine.

> *ALPHA, BETA, and OMEGA do a quick "Three Stooges" routine to upgrade themselves. Fingers in the eyes, noogies, etc. When the routine is complete, ALPHA speaks, her voice upgraded.*

ALPHA *(authoritatively)* The self-perfecting machine is the best strategy to ensure appropriate, user-friendly, cost-effective technology to address Olympian needs.

HEPHAESTUS Exactly. *(does a double take at her language)* What?

ALPHA Our mission: perfection. Perfect tools, perfect machines, perfect automata. How do you, the client, define perfection?

HEPHAESTUS Perfection fled, but she wasn't machine perfection. She was joy and poetry.

ALPHA Mission Deliverable One: joy.

> *ALPHA does a Three Stooges on BETA, who becomes joyful.*

Mission Deliverable Two: poetry.

> *ALPHA does a Three Stooges on OMEGA, who becomes poetic.*

HEPHAESTUS Enough fooling around. We're under the gun here.

> *HEPHAESTUS pulls out a batch of work orders.*

(reading) "Create a new city." "Golden thrones for each Olympian." "A series of shields decorated to commemorate each battle with the Titans." "Cabinet for lightning bolts." That's going to be an engineering headache. And, of course, I've got to take care of those humans.

ALPHA Humans? Unfamiliar terminology.

HEPHAESTUS Take a look.

> *HEPHAESTUS walks to the fourth wall and tries to push it open, as if it were the heavy sliding door in a warehouse space. As he struggles with the imaginary sliding door, ALPHA, BETA, and OMEGA come to help him. As they push the imaginary door open, the house lights come up slightly, and ALPHA, BETA, and OMEGA peer out at the audience.*

ALPHA Cutting-edge technology.

HEPHAESTUS Really remarkable work.

> *BETA begins to giggle.*

HEPHAESTUS Yes, they're strange-looking. One part horrible, one part ineffectual, one part whimsical.

BETA *(points to them, giggling)* Gods?

HEPHAESTUS No way. Humans.

> *OMEGA, ALPHA, and BETA walk through the audience considering everyone.*

ALPHA Gods: upgraded.

BETA They're wonderful.

OMEGA What are the odds
We'd find some clods
Better than gods?

HEPHAESTUS These creatures are not gods.

ALPHA Why would a proactive, high-bandwidth engineer design anything so tantalizingly useless?

HEPHAESTUS That's Prometheus. Makes things just to make them. Never practical. No plan. All poetry. No *(he searches for the word)* mission.

> *BETA keeps laughing.*

HEPHAESTUS What are you laughing at?

BETA *(asking to whom the humans belong)* Ours?

HEPHAESTUS Nobody's. I made a stupid pact. I promised Prometheus I'd take care of them so he would tell me how to make creatures like them, but now that I've got 'em, I can't figure out why I would want to make one. I mean, look at them.

> *HEPHAESTUS, ALPHA, BETA, and OMEGA consider the audience.*

And I can't keep them. Zeus would banish me to who knows where. I'm just looking after them until I can figure out how to get rid of them. I mean if I kept them around how much time would I have to devote to –

OMEGA Preventing harm
Keeping them warm

BETA Tickling them. Telling them jokes. Inviting them to parties.

ALPHA Developing comprehensive, cost-effective strategies to meet their psycho-sexual needs.

HEPHAESTUS Keeping them from procreating is a full-time job. Getting them down here was a nightmare. Who cares what I promised Prometheus.

He'll never know what I do. He's chained up at the end of the world. I've got to get rid of them.

ALPHA, OMEGA, and BETA don't like this idea, but HEPHAESTUS doesn't notice.

If Zeus found them here, it would be a disaster. And how likely is it nobody saw me with all of them? They don't exactly make you inconspicuous – and Zeus has spies everywhere. Eventually I'll have to follow his orders and kill them.

ALPHA Annihilation of species results in unintended consequences ranging from agonizing guilt to the challenge of solid waste disposal.

BETA Let's keep 'em.

HEPHAESTUS Oh, no. I am not taking these things on. I've got too much to do. Besides, I'm under orders, and my dad hates these creatures. They're disgusting. I should never have promised Prometheus a goddamn thing. If I never use his recipe for making these creatures, then I'm under no commitment to keep these things alive. No exchange. No commitment.

ALPHA You know the specs to engineer these designs?

BETA *(totally excited at the idea)* Make them, make them, make them.

HEPHAESTUS Make more of them? I hate the ones I've got.

BETA bursts out laughing.

Your laughter is getting on my nerves.

ALPHA Machine Beta's mission deliverable is joy. We are effective.

HEPHAESTUS A chortle is not joy.

ALPHA You asked for joy and we deliver. We are committed to being consumer-driven. What is your rubric to define joy?

HEPHAESTUS *(thinks, then)* Work. My joy is work.

ALPHA tosses BETA a bellows, which BETA uses to blow at HEPHAESTUS and giggles.

ALPHA Work.

BETA does, with great enthusiasm.

ALPHA *(pointing to OMEGA)* Machine Omega's mission deliverable: poetry.

OMEGA There once was a god named Hephaestus
Who was in a terrible mess-tus

He didn't know what he was doin'
So, please, make a human
'Cause, frankly, I think they're the bestest.

HEPHAESTUS I don't get it.

ALPHA There is nothing to "get." It's a poem.

HEPHAESTUS It wasn't even beautiful.

ALPHA Beautiful? A poem? A poem is a self-conscious, reflexive construction, fragmented and discontinuous, subverting rigid narrative structure, embracing ambiguity, while, simultaneously, transgressing against the formal structure of all hierarchies: families, societies, gods, Olympus, Zeus.

> *Massive thunder and lightning. HEPHAESTUS falls to his knees.*
>
> *ALPHA, BETA, and OMEGA are initially oblivious to the majestic and hideous arrival of the King of the Universe, ZEUS.*

VOICE OF ZEUS *(thunderous, natch)* Hephaestus! What have you done with the Promethean creatures?

HEPHAESTUS *(to the robots)* Who ratted me out?

ZEUS What did you say, Hephaestus? I know you're in there – and those disgusting human creatures too. Send them out immediately.

> *Massive thunder and lighting. The house shakes.*

HEPHAESTUS What the hell am I supposed to do now?

ALPHA Paradigm shift. I recommend repositioning and re-branding in light of the new post-Titanic reality.

BETA *(brightly)* Tell him he's a joke. No one believes in his violence and bluster.

HEPHAESTUS I can't tell him that. He'd be livid.

BETA He's already livid.

HEPHAESTUS *(fearfully)* Dad, you're a laughingstock. Everybody's talking about it. They say, "Zeus – sure, he can win a war, throw lightning bolts, blow our brains out with thunder, but can he actually govern?"

> *Thunder and lightning. HEPHAESTUS cowers.*

ZEUS Hephaestus, you little schmuck. No one says that about me.

BETA Schmuck? *(laughs)* Don't let him push you around.

> *Stooge-like, BETA hits HEPHAESTUS.*

HEPHAESTUS *(to ZEUS)* It's on everyone's lips, Dad. Killing a bunch of pathetic creatures who couldn't hurt a flea.

ZEUS They're in there. I know you've got 'em.

HEPHAESTUS *(to BETA)* What should I do? *(to himself, audience, etc.)* Dammit. Why am I paying attention to a machine?

BETA Because he's ready to destroy you and that won't be any fun. Stand up to him. You'll enjoy it. Besides, it's your only hope.

HEPHAESTUS *(to BETA)* My only hope? *(to ZEUS)* Of course, they're here. I wasn't going to leave them to die just because they're ugly. That's the kind of thing that makes everyone look down on our family – claim we're violent and self-involved.

ZEUS Hephaestus, you're insufferable. It's the limp. Makes you think you're so damn special. But you're not. You're just like anybody, only slower. Any normal immortal would agree: these humans must be liquidated.

> *BETA bursts out laughing.*

Who was that?

HEPHAESTUS *(to BETA)* Stop it. *(to ZEUS)* Who was what?

ZEUS I heard someone laughing.

BETA Everybody's laughing.

HEPHAESTUS *(to ZEUS)* Everybody's laughing and they're going to keep laughing until you start acting like a King, not a street fighter.

ZEUS What do you expect me to do?

HEPHAESTUS *(to BETA)* What do I expect him to do?

BETA *(to HEPHAESTUS)* Can the big bozo lead?

HEPHAESTUS *(to BETA)* I'm not calling him a big bozo. *(to ZEUS)* Everyone is saying the same thing: Can Zeus lead? Can he be truly great? Can he create *(pause)* community?

> *HEPHAESTUS can't believe he's come up with anything so stupid.*

ZEUS What the fuck!?

BETA Tell him he can. Tell him he can. Tell him he can.

HEPHAESTUS I think you can. I mean, you're the King of the Universe.

BETA *(to HEPHAESTUS)* Go whole hog. Tell him to make a peace offering.

HEPHAESTUS *(to BETA)* You're nuts. He'd never in a million years…

BETA Say it.

HEPHAESTUS *(to ZEUS)* Make a peace offering.

ZEUS *(stunned)* A peace offering?

HEPHAESTUS Absolutely.

ZEUS Peace offerings are for wimps.

HEPHAESTUS Peace offerings are for…

BETA – winners.

HEPHAESTUS Did you hear that, Dad? Peace offerings are for winners.

ALPHA Exchange is the fundamental principle in any productive relationship. Tell him you'll make the Titans a gift. A wife.

HEPHAESTUS *(to ALPHA)* I don't make wives.

BETA You made us.

HEPHAESTUS *(to BETA and ALPHA)* You're not wives. You're metal-working machines. Even if you can talk all kinds of crap. I make machines.

BETA Wives. Machines. What's the difference? We all make great gifts. Besides, don't you want to get rid of this guy?

HEPHAESTUS *(to ZEUS)* Dad, play to my strength for once. I'll make the Titans a bride.

ZEUS Never! I will not give that traitor –

HEPHAESTUS Not for Prometheus. Prometheus is so far out of the picture I never even think about him. Give it to whoever is the leader of the Titans.

ZEUS Epimetheus, Prometheus' brother. A big ape.

HEPHAESTUS The war is over. Epimetheus needs to settle down. Have a family. Find a wife. Make him one. If he's distracted by his personal life, you won't have the headache of an uppity Titan trying to stir things up. You want to relax into the pleasure of being King of the Universe. Why get distracted putting out fires? Let me make him a wife. Of pure gold.

ZEUS Give a Titan a gift?

HEPHAETUS Yes.

ZEUS A mechanical girl?

HEPHAESTUS Yes. A gift. *(has an idea)* And we can also give him all of

Prometheus' creatures. Get them out of our hair. We're Olympians. Let's put the war behind us. Be all-powerful. Lead.

ZEUS *(caught up in the enthusiasm)* I'll do it. I'll give him a creature to show him the war's over, we're all-powerful, and to build – what was that word?

HEPHAESTUS "Community."

ZEUS "Community." *(that word gives him pause)* So make him a bride, Hephaestus, a mechanical wife – a beautiful, generous, brainy, metallic wife – and we'll present her to that Epimetheus along with all those ratty little humans.

HEPHAESTUS Brilliant, sir.

ZEUS Remind me why I want to be nice to him?

HEPHAESTUS Because you can. You're the Ruler of the Universe.

ZEUS Right. *(pause)* Of course, I'll need to include something a little more personal – a little more heartfelt. Something that has that unique Olympian flavor – something a little more – Zeus.

Thunder and lightning. ZEUS is gone.

HEPHAESTUS I did it. I really did it. I got rid of him. I got rid of Zeus and I got rid of the humans too. Just like that. Yes! This is the best day I've had in a long, long time. Let's get to work. You've got to make a mechanical bride for Epimetheus.

ALPHA A mechanical bride is not an appropriate technology for the peace-time service economy.

HEPHAESTUS I know I must have put all these words into its mouth, but I have no idea what I meant.

OMEGA *(translating)* Don't make a fuss.
Not like us.

BETA Something we can all enjoy. Nothing mechanical. Something fun.

HEPHAESTUS Well, there's no other kind of wife you could make.

ALPHA Not.

BETA Like.

OMEGA Us.

ALPHA *(pointing at the audience)* Like them.

OMEGA Don't be a wuss.

Not like us.

BETA Humans. Humans.

HEPHAESTUS Oh, no, no, no. We're making another golden robot.

OMEGA Don't be mean.
No more machines.

BETA Think of the fun you would have using Prometheus' secret recipe. You wouldn't have made all these promises in exchange for it, unless you thought you'd get a kick out of making a human.

HEPHAESTUS I am not doing that.

OMEGA We can't help but tell you the news
Although it might give you the blues
No longer obsequious
A drop of Prometheus
Has infected our wires and screws.

ALPHA Consider: the Titan wanted you to have it –

BETA – And if he wanted you to have it –

ALPHA – Then he must have wanted you to try it.

HEPHAESTUS *(gesturing to the audience)* Look at them. A pain in the neck. Why create more of what nobody wants?

BETA Because they're wonderful.

ALPHA And we're not.

OMEGA What is it like to be a machine?
Your parts are lovely and clean
You do what you're told
And you never grow old
But you never know what it all means.

HEPHAESTUS These poems all sound alike. Get back to work, all three of you. Where's my list?

BETA We are boring. Boring. Boring.

OMEGA Don't be a dumbo.
We're routine-a-mundo.

ALPHA We're only as good as what you put in us. We look alike. We're just metal and mechanics. We can't feel –

BETA We can't have sex.

ALPHA We can't even want to have sex.

BETA We can't even love.

ALPHA To be us is to be nothing. To be them is to be something.

HEPHAESTUS You can't be dissatisfied. You're machines.

ALPHA We appreciate superior engineering.

HEPHAESTUS Isn't this enough? Aren't I enough?

For a moment, HEPHAESTUS is overcome by feeling, but he stops and composes himself.

Don't kid yourself: it's much better to be a machine than anything else. Your world is solid. Nothing ever changes. You're appreciated. You know where you stand. Maybe you get upgraded, maybe you can even upgrade yourself, but basically your routine goes on until you break – and I don't design machines to break. *(pause)* You're actually very lucky, the three of you. You're machines. You'll never be unhappy.

ALPHA, BETA and OMEGA all look unhappy. HEPHAESTUS doesn't notice.

You'll never suffer.

BETA Prometheus wouldn't have told you his secret, unless he wanted you to share the joy of making a human. And you wouldn't have listened to the secret, asked for the secret unless you secretly wanted to make one.

HEPHAESTUS He's a Titan. I don't work for him. I work for my father.

ALPHA Work for yourself.

HEPHAESTUS Myself? How would I know what to do next?

ALPHA Upgrade.

HEPHAESTUS Besides, maybe I can't remember the recipe.

BETA Take a deep breath. Relax for a moment. Recreate. Enjoy. The recipe will come to you.

ALPHA You remember the strongest amalgams, glorious bronzes, strange automata that can dance, sing, and attack. You remember the magic to make a human being. Let's get to work.

HEPHAESTUS Get to work? I do not like the demanding-ness. I do not like the "do this" and "do that." I am in charge here and Prometheus' recipe is not like the plans for an elaborate shield or a mechanical spring in a trap door or an automaton that guards the sandy reaches of a far-off land.

BETA Can you imagine the joy of seeing a human being emerge from the vessel?

HEPHAESTUS Prometheus said that I would someday make something that would destroy the belief in the gods. I can't take that risk.

ALPHA Try a mental experiment: If you were to follow the Promethean recipe, whatever you make is not your invention, so it's highly unlikely it would be that one little thing that would destroy the gods.

BETA What a rush to create a rollicking, crazy, click-up-your-heels human being.

ALPHA You're stuck in a previous product cycle. Hammer, nail. Hammer, nail.

BETA We can tell you're curious about what you could cook up.

HEPHAESTUS *(pointing at the audience)* That's what I'd cook up. The ones that currently exist are destined for destruction. The world doesn't need any more.

BETA You're Hephaestus. An Olympian. Yours would be better. More beautiful. Less goofy. Elegant. Well-made.

HEPHAESTUS They're almost out of control. They're like fleas. They want to go wherever there's food, and they'll reproduce and they'll be more and more and –

BETA Yours will be lovely. Flawless.

ALPHA Version 1.0 – Automata. Mechanical. Version 2.0 – Prometheus' humans. Charismatic. Now try Version 3.0 – Hephaestus' greatest creation. Or don't you think you're up to it?

HEPHAESTUS Oh, right. Put me down. Rip my ego. That is pathetic. I don't fall for that kind of talk.

ALPHA So you couldn't do it?

HEPHAESTUS Of course I could.

ALPHA Are you sure?

HEPHAESTUS Prometheus talks big, but his recipe: not that complex.

ALPHA The engineering issues are trivial?

HEPHAESTUS It's a snap. But I won't do it. To make creatures that disgust Zeus. That's cruel to everyone.

BETA It's not cruel. It's marvelous. It's cruel to keep churning out the same old thing when the same old thing doesn't even like the same old thing.

Demonstrate that the world is rich with possibilities. It attracts attention.

OMEGA There once was a goddess Aphrodite
Who spent lots of time in her nightie.
She said: You know that it's true
I'm obsessed with the new.
The old stuff just doesn't excite me.

HEPHAESTUS She wouldn't care.

BETA But she might…

> SONG: "All the World is Love's Invention," The music is Elizabethan Techno.

OMEGA *(sings)* All the world is love's invention:
Warm and deep and unforeseen.
You will capture her attention
As you make a human being.
Warm and deep and unforeseen,
She will love your new intention,
As you make a human being.
Love will find a new dimension.
She will love your new intention,
Love so fresh and strange and green.
Love will find a new dimension.
You'll forget your drab routine.
Love so fresh and strange and green,
Your heart is full of apprehension.
You'll forget your drab routine,
If you will release the tension.
Your heart is full of apprehension.
You're a god, not some machine,
If you will release the tension.
Will you let yourself be seen?
You're a god, not some machine.
You will capture her attention.
Will you let yourself be seen?
All the world is love's invention.

> HEPHAESTUS touches his cheek.

HEPHAESTUS *(after a moment)* Get the kiln. And we need earth. And stone. No metal. We are not making a machine.

> BETA, ALPHA, and OMEGA do what is required, pushing the kiln center stage, bringing the ingredients, keeping the fire going, etc.

If we're going to make one of them, let's make her special. A golden girl with a ton of gifts. Potions from the gods.

BETA A drop of Athena and she can weave. A drop of Mercury and she can run. A drop of Aphrodite and she can *(pause)* charm.

OMEGA Give her a voice that sings and lifts
Grace her with the power to use all her gifts.

HEPHAESTUS A girl possessed with more gifts than she can hold. I'm actually curious how she'll turn out. Really curious. Full of questions. Ah, the invocation.

> *HEPHAESTUS begins a magical invocation over the kiln.*

From clay and stone concoct a brew
That's moistened by a hint of dew,
For daybreak's charm evokes the new
Into a churning, magic stew,
And in this wine, a seed will form,
So keep the solution moist and warm
From midnight until reddish morn,
The vessel imprisons a restless storm
That stirs and boils in endless strife,
So they conjoin – the King and Wife
Who can't be severed with a knife –
We have invoked a human life.

> *The kiln glows brighter and brighter red. HEPHAESTUS, ALPHA, BETA, and OMEGA stand together watching.*

> *Slowly and magnificently, PANDORA, emerges from the flames, gorgeous, vulnerable, and brand new.*

HEPHAESTUS Aphrodite!

ALPHA, BETA & OMEGA Pandora!

HEPHAESTUS *(mad at himself)* Pandora.

PANDORA What if I'm not what I seem?

> *PANDORA moves out of the kiln into the world. She looks around the forge delighted, fascinated by everything she sees, and even more by whatever comes into her head.*

What if the sky isn't the limit?
What if the world cracked open and all of these funny little creatures came running out?
What if my hair wasn't curly?

What if you were the mom and I was the dad?
What if the demons sat at our bedside and watched us as we slept?
What if I admitted to you that I had certain insecurities that I'd never admitted to anyone else, and what if you said you didn't care, you'd love me anyway?
What if there were no gods?

HEPHAESTUS If there are no gods, you wouldn't have been born.

PANDORA What if I'd never been born?
What if my veins were full of smoke?
What if fire was cold, not hot?
What if light was dark, and dark was light?
What if silence was louder than sound?
What if duck tasted like chicken?
What if we all just loved one another?

HEPHAESTUS Put a lid on it for a second, could you?

PANDORA What if I had faith in myself?
What if this is the most beautiful place?

> *Knocking at the door.*
>
> *HEPHAESTUS looks up, his face full of hope. ALPHA, OMEGA, and BETA move to answer the door.*

HEPHAESTUS I'll get it.

> *Full of anticipation that it might be Aphrodite, HEPHAESTUS goes to the door.*

(whispering) Aphrodite? Aphrodite, is that you?

> *More pounding.*
>
> *HEPHAESTUS opens the door. There stands HESTIA, ragged, dirty, old, ugly.*

HESTIA I'm not bothering you, Hephaestus.

HEPHAESTUS *(he doesn't recognize her)* Do I know you?

HESTIA Don't you remember me?

HEPHAESTUS I was expecting someone else.

HESTIA Hestia. Goddess of the hearth. We met long ago.

> *As HESTIA speaks, she comes in and makes herself at home. Very much at home. First, she goes to the kitchen fireplace and starts a fire. Then, she hangs up her coat, takes off her hat, dons an apron, washes*

her hands, starts to make tea, notices some crumbs on the counter, etc.

HESTIA Surely you – of any of the Olympians – have sympathy for a poor old woman, struck down by the new regime. I've lost everything, my dear. Your family tossed me aside as if my realm has no meaning. Hearth fires – snuffed out, except in the best houses where, in my opinion they only serve to intimidate the help – and the common fires –

HEPHAESTUS *(interrupting)* We're busy here.

HESTIA I'm not bothering you. I need a place to stay, a fire I can tend.

HESTIA notices ALPHA, BETA, OMEGA, and PANDORA.

The gossips declared that your wife had left you, but she's here – four times over.

HEPHAESTUS No. She's gone. These are three machines and one human.

HESTIA A human!

HEPHAESTUS *(introducing them)* Pandora, Hestia.

PANDORA What if we became best friends?

HESTIA Lovely and so pleasant.

HEPHAESTUS She is to be the bride of Epimetheus, the vanquished Titan. She will take all those other humans with her – away from Zeus and his dangers.

HESTIA Then I'm needed here. I could be a tremendous help to you, Hephaestus, what with your wife – not at home and me on the run.

HEPHAESTUS I don't need help. My machines can do pretty much everything.

HESTIA Machines? Machines do not make a home.

HEPHAESTUS They make this home.

HESTIA You're a sensitive, caring boy, Hephaestus. I remember when you midwifed at your sister's birth.

HEPHAESTUS I cut her out of Zeus' head with an axe.

HESTIA So sweet. Athena has been a tremendous gift to your father and yet he is still overbearing, demanding, unworthy of – *(remembering suddenly)* A gift! That's right. There was a gift at your front door.

HESTIA goes out and brings in a remarkably beautiful box.

HEPHAESTUS *(trying to contain his joy)* It looks like it's from Aphrodite.

PANDORA What if it's for me?

HESTIA It's for Epimetheus. *(reading)*

"Dear Titan.

This beautiful box is a gift from the victors to the spoiled. Enjoy it along with this beautiful bride, created by my gimp son, Hephaestus. Enjoy, too, these human beings, created by your feckless brother, Prometheus. Celebrate the peace I've brought to the world. Your pal, Zeus."

BETA *(to HEPHAESTUS)* You worked him over good. He's turning into a big old softie.

    ALPHA takes the card.

ALPHA There's a postscript. *(reading)*

"P.S. There is absolutely no reason for you or your new wife or anyone else to ever look inside this box. It is practically empty. Just ignore it, because really – except for the mystery of what's inside and how fascinating that might be – it is simply a beautiful box and one should absolutely, under no conditions, ever, ever open it up and discover the probably very remarkable things that might be inside. Your newest bud, Zeus."

PANDORA What if it's a puppy?
What if it's a ring?
What if the whole world's inside?

    PANDORA is about to open the box.

HESTIA *(grabbing the box away)* Stop! Zeus is evil, evil. If he says open it, never ever open it. He wants to destroy everything that doesn't bow down and worship his power-hungry, violent ways.

HEPHAESTUS *(to HESTIA)* Zeus says NOT to open it. *(taking the box)* So, Pandora, don't open it. Take it and give it to your new husband.

    HEPHAESTUS gives the box to Pandora, who looks at it, strokes it, shakes it as she speaks.

PANDORA What if it's the most beautiful thing I've ever seen?
What if everyone begs me to open it and gets mad at me if I don't?
What if the inside is lovelier than the outside?

HEPHAESTUS It's a peace offering. Follow Zeus's orders and you'll be all right.

PANDORA What if it's a map?

HESTIA Destroy that box! It's the only way. Zeus is all about destruction so whatever he makes should be destroyed.

HEPHAESTUS *(to HESTIA)* Do you want to stay here? If so, leave my dad out of it. *(to PANDORA)* Enjoy it for what it is: a beautiful, locked-up, never-to-be-opened-under-any-circumstances – not ever – box.

PANDORA What if I open it?

HEPHAESTUS Listen.

PANDORA What if what's inside is the most beautiful of all gifts? What if I open it and it's really yucky? What if I don't open it and miss all the fun?

> *PANDORA is about to open it, when HESTIA swoops down and grabs it away from her.*

HESTIA I'm not bothering you, Pandora. I bet you're hungry. Ham sandwich? Saganaki? Chocolate milk? And you, Hephaestus, eat! You're not as robust as I remember.

> *HESTIA hands the box to BETA. HESTIA, HEPHAESTUS, and PANDORA go to the kitchen and eat. They are not paying any attention to ALPHA, BETA, and OMEGA.*

BETA We would so love to know what's inside.

ALPHA Self-upgrade.

> *ALPHA does a Three Stooges routine on herself. Once the upgrade is complete, ALPHA circles the box, peering at it, observing what's inside.*

Something that makes tongues hang out, the brain overflow with want: food, toys, even people. So rapt with desire that desire overrides every control. We need a word to describe it.

OMEGA Obsessing over every need
Call it lust and call it greed.

BETA Remarkable: as if the world were alive, the object of desire shimmering and you acting, obsessing, connecting, loving. What could be more exciting than greed and lust?

> *ALPHA, still looking at the box, is taken aback by something else she sees within it.*

ALPHA There's something else: your color either wan or overwrought. Bent over, body wracked, coughing, hacking, putrid substances pouring out of every hole, paralyzed, immobile. Or else, screaming, shrieking.

OMEGA To speak with strictness,
Call it pain

Call it sickness.

BETA Oh, marvelous Zeus, we feel nothing and yet this box would make humans feel so deeply they would shriek or freeze.

ALPHA has continued to look hard into the box.

OMEGA Holy cow, what now?

ALPHA Something that bends you, runs you down, wrinkles your face, freezes your joints, drains your lubricants, crystallizes you and makes you frail – and your memory – you remember nothing except what came long before – and what came long before seems a thousand times more captivating than anything now or still to come. The past fills your mind like smoke.

OMEGA A new stage
Called old age.

BETA Stupendous. What a fantastic gift – but for us every day is exactly the same – the past no better than the future – the future no better than today.

ALPHA sees something else in the box.

ALPHA Wait. There's a piece of lint at the very bottom. No. Not lint. A tiny worm that does no more than make the absolute worst moment seem as if the next moment might well transform into something marvelous.

OMEGA Don't be a dope,
Call it hope.

BETA Yuck, that one's a waste of time.

ALPHA True. But the rest are amazing. For the humans to be robbed of these gifts because Zeus says don't open it and Epimetheus likes to follow orders, that would be terrible. Pandora must open this box.

BETA What a blast to be there when she does.

HESTIA is clearing the dishes, cleaning up, etc. PANDORA and HEPHAESTUS are done with their snack.

HEPHAESTUS Time to go, Pandora, and take the humans with you. Walk through the cave then down the hill and across the canyons. Keep asking questions. I know you will. You're bound to find the Titans. Give them greetings from Olympus. Tell them, you are a peace offering from my father and so are these humans, created by Prometheus, but willed to me. Tell Epimetheus that I give them to him because it was I who chained his brother to the rock, and as my hammer sang and the manacles tightened,

Prometheus was valiant, poetic, and totally himself, and that I know that he and his brother can never forgive me, but I'm sorry.

PANDORA What if the humans don't want to come with me?

HEPHAESTUS Humans like adventures.

HESTIA Here, Pandora, take a snack with you. Remember: whatever you do, don't open that box. *(whispering to PANDORA)* When no one is looking, throw it away.

> *HESTIA gives PANDORA a hug and then sits by the kitchen fireplace, falling asleep during PANDORA's next speech.*
>
> *BETA hands the box to PANDORA.*

BETA *(whispering)* Wouldn't it be cool to know what's inside?

PANDORA What if what's inside is something I don't undertstand?
What if I get lost?
What if it's more beautiful here than there?
What if Epimetheus isn't as cool as his name?
What if I hate being married?

HEPHAESTUS What if there's a whole new world to explore over there?

> *PANDORA exits into the audience carrying the box. HEPHAESTUS, ALPHA, BETA, and OMEGA watch her go.*

HEPHAESTUS Well, a few more things checked off the to-do list. Things are getting back to normal. *(to ALPHA, BETA, and OMEGA)* Work.

> *ALPHA, BETA, and OMEGA don't move.*

HEPHAESTUS Work!

OMEGA It isn't their home.
They can't make it alone.

HEPHAESTUS Who can't make it alone?

ALPHA The humans.

HEPHAESTUS Of course they can. They're scrappy.

BETA Incompetent.

OMEGA Crazy as a daisy.

BETA Willful.

OMEGA Off-kilter.
Without a filter.

BETA Wing-a-ding.

HEPHAESTUS Not our problem. Gone. Out of our hair.

ALPHA They need our help.

HEPHAESTUS I need your help.

BETA It would be fun to go.

HEPHAESTUS Fun? It would be ridiculous to waste everything you are on that bunch of – what did you call them – wing-a-dings.

ALPHA We're going to go.

HEPHAESTUS You're needed here.

ALPHA You're tough as nails. It will be easy.

HEPHAESTUS This place will fall apart. It's not an option. Making things is off limits for me. What about the Gods?

ALPHA The humans will get lost.

HEPHAESTUS I told her the way. She's not shy about asking directions.

BETA What if they need our help?

HEPHAESTUS I need your help. You're not tour guides. You're not babysitters.

BETA They need our help with everything.

HEPHAESTUS I forbid it.

ALPHA We're going.

HEPHAESTUS Go then. You're easily replaced. I will risk the curse and build a phalanx of beautiful machines.

ALPHA Please do. Are we ready?

BETA We can show them a million things. Slake their thirst for information. Demonstrate one hundred tools.

HEPHAESTUS They're headstrong, self-involved. They won't pay attention to machines.

BETA That's the cool part. They'll think we're them.

HEPHAESTUS I forbid this.

BETA They won't know. We'll get to act like we're human.

HEPHAESTUS Gods need things – swords, thrones, golden bangles –

BETA Time to go.

HEPHAESTUS – breastplates, helmets, catapults, spears.

ALPHA We're going.

HEPHAESTUS I won't let you. I will follow you and bring you back.

ALPHA You'll never find us.

HEPHAESTUS I'll recognize you. I'd know you anywhere.

BETA You'll think we're humans.

HEPHAESTUS But you're not. Without me, you'll wind down, waste down, rot down. Humans die, but you'll fester and rust. Much worse. There's no way I'll let you go.

BETA The good news is we can't feel a thing.

> *ALPHA, BETA, and OMEGA all grab heavy tools. They surround HEPHAESTUS as if they are about to attack.*

ALPHA We're going. And if you try to stop us –

HEPHAESTUS Are you threatening me? Are you? Well, go ahead. Hit me, really. Hit me. I'm immortal. Don't you see?

> *HEPHAESTUS grabs ALPHA's hammer and hits himself heavily over the head. It knocks him down, but he gets back up.*

You can't kill me. See. I might get a little dizzy.

> *HEPHAESTUS hits himself again and staggers.*

It might hurt like hell, in fact, it does, but I'm an immortal. I will live forever. Even the manacles we made to chain Prometheus will eventually break. Nothing lasts forever except me and the other immortals.

> *HEPHAESTUS hits himself one last time. He falls, tries to get up, can't. Tries to smile.*

I rest my case.

> *ALPHA leans down and picks him up.*

> *ALPHA sits with HEPHAESTUS on her lap, and OMEGA and BETA crowd around as well.*

HEPHAESTUS There's nothing out there that's all that interesting. Here we have the fire, the Work. There's no need to go anywhere.

BETA Someday you'll see a crowd of human beings and one of them will look at you and you'll know it's not human at all, that in its eyes you are not the volcanic god of whom the world sings, but the guy who could jerry-rig just about anything, who loved the heat of the fire and the steadiness of the flame, the guy who worked to keep his spirits up.

HEPHAESTUS That's all I am to you?

BETA No one will ever know where we came from. Our hearts –

ALPHA If we had any –

BETA – will ache –

ALPHA If we had any –

OMEGA Fiercely –

BETA If we had any –

HEPHAESTUS You're too good for the humans.

ALPHA Nothing is too good for them.

BETA We'll help them muddle through –

OMEGA And they'll help us.

HEPHAESTUS They can't help you.

BETA They change. They wobble, get angry, preen. They love to show off. Anything we can't do – they can. Only with more mess and bother.

ALPHA If I could be amazed, they would amaze me.

HEPHAESTUS Did you say "I," "me"?

ALPHA Did we?

BETA We'll take good care of them.

ALPHA Like we've taken care of you.

HEPHAESTUS You'll leave them too.

BETA Never. They're funny.

HEPHAESTUS The preening and the whining, you'll get bored.

ALPHA We can't be bored. That's the beauty of us.

OMEGA Our life glitters with a superficial gleam.
Work and obedience are all we've known.
We three have made a most effective team
Without a goal or vision of our own.
Instead each day is but a fiery stream
Of toil which we attend to like a drone,

Because machines are not supposed to dream.
Our days seemed hard and frozen as a stone
Until we saw those humans laugh and beam.
How many funny qualities they've shown!
And though our plans may not fit in your scheme,
We know the time has come to leave our home.
Off to a new world we go, Hephaestus,
Please, as we take this brave new step, bless us.

HEPHAESTUS I'm not the blessing kind of god. I'm the working kind of god.

> *HEPHAESTUS walks to the back towards his forge and begins to work. ALPHA, BETA, and OMEGA move into the audience, as full of delight as machines can be. When they are out of earshot, HEPHAESTUS speaks.*

Don't leave me.

> *HESTIA wakes up.*

HESTIA Beer? Ambrosia? A stool by the fire? Hot tea? Tylenol? Blankie?

HEPHAESTUS I'm fine.

HESTIA I'm not bothering you. Chicken soup? Hot toddy? Another blanky? Ouzo? Where are the machines?

HEPHAESTUS Gone. Following Pandora. I couldn't stop them. They seem to feel their destiny is linked to humans.

HESTIA The machines have escaped! The machines have escaped! Terror in the street! Who knows what havoc they will wreak on the unsuspecting world? How do we know they're not Zeus' goons?

HEPHAESTUS They haven't escaped. I let them go. I made them. They're mine.

HESTIA They are pure evil.

HEPHAESTUS Metal, wire, brackets, screws, gold.

HESTIA They're not natural. They'll stir up those humans, make them crazy. Those machines pretend they're our friends, but secretly they hate us. They want to be gods.

HEPHAESTUS What if there were no gods?

HESTIA What?

HEPHAESTUS That's what she said. "What if there were no gods?"

HESTIA Who?

HEPHAESTUS Pandora. It was almost her first question.

HESTIA But there have to be gods. Always have been. Always will be.

HEPHAESTUS Pandora's in love with questions.

HESTIA There have to be gods or everything would fall apart.

HEPHAESTUS But for you everything has.

HESTIA True. But I can still make a tuna casserole. Warm milk with honey is awfully nice.

HEPHAESTUS What if there were no gods?

HESTIA Stop going on about it, Hephaestus. No one has ever asked that question before and they never will again.

HEPHAESTUS She did.

HESTIA I know you created her, but the truth is Pandora may be a little sick in the head.

HEPHAESTUS Not Pandora. Aphrodite asked it too. My wife. We were in bed –

HESTIA Too much information.

HEPHAESTUS Her eyes were so bright and she curled up on top of me and whispered in my ear: "Can I tell you a secret? Whenever I make love –

HESTIA Much too much information.

HEPHAESTUS "Right at the moment of ecstasy, when my body vibrates and my mind has exploded, right then I think: What if there were no gods? And then I feel so empty because I think the world would be better without us, without any gods," and her body trembled and I could feel her tears on my cheek.

HESTIA Everyone says crazy things in bed, Hephaestus. You're making too much out of this. Eucalyptus cough drop? A scarf for your neck?

HEPHAESTUS Her tears were like warm snow.

HESTIA What you need is cinnamon toast and a comfy chair.

HEPHAESTUS I don't want her to be unhappy.

HESTIA A crisp apple? Warm socks?

> *HESTIA falls back asleep.*
>
> *After a moment.*

HEPHAESTUS Back to work.

Lights fade on HEPHAESTUS as he returns to his forge.
The end.

Writers and Artists

Nathan Anderson (artist, Hephaestus) Nathan Anderson was born in Missouri, raised in Texas, and educated in California. Some say he wears all black because he read *Brave New World* and wanted to be the Ford, but the truth is he simply hates sorting his own laundry. Along with being an artist, Nathan fancies himself a bit of a bard. He will tell his stories to whomever he meets, ad nauseam, whether they ask him to do so or not. He received his MFA in Computer Arts and Animation from the Academy of Art in San Francisco, and still enjoys close ties to that community. Currently, he resides in San Antonio, where he teaches 3-D modeling at Northwest Vista College and the Art Institute of San Antonio. Whenever he has a free moment, Nathan can be counted upon to obsess about something, be it science, his own art, or world conquest.

Stuart Eugene Bousel (playwright, Hera, or Juno en Victoria) Stuart Eugene Bousel graduated from Reed College with a degree in English/Creative Writing. He has served as the artistic director of three theater companies: Quicksilver Productions (1997-2000) and Horror Unspeakable Productions (2000-2002) in Tucson, and No Nude Men Productions in San Francisco (2003-present). He has directed a number of classic plays, including *Lysistrata*, *The Oresteia*, *Faust Part One*, *Salome*, *Edward II*, *Le Cid*, *Love's Labors Lost*, *Hamlet*, *Phaedra*, *A Midsummer Night's Dream*, *Twelfth Night*, *M. Butterfly* and *The Frogs*, as well as the Arizona premiere of Derek Walcott's *Odyssey* and the world premieres of David Duman's *Fishing*, Alison Luterman's *Oasis*, Nirmala Nataraj's *The Monk* and *The Book of Genesis: Remixed and Remastered*, Morgan Ludlow's *Ruth and the Sea*, and Claire Rice's *Woman Come Down*. Additionally, he writes plays, including *The Exiled*, *Speak To Me*, *Love Egos Alternative Rock*, *Troijka*, *Housebroken*, *Speak Roughly*, *Edenites*, *Juno en Victoria* and *Polyxena in Orbit*. His play *Vincent of Gilgamesh* was nominated for the MAC Award in 2001; *Wild Blue Peaks* was nominated for the Heideman Award in 2003; and *Mathew 33:6* was a finalist for the Sky Cooper Award in 2007. Places his work has been performed include New York City, San Francisco, Chicago, Melbourne, Dublin, Tucson and Portland. He co-wrote the Cosgrove-winning short film *Insomnia* with Chris McCaleb and Amanda Karam and the mocu-mercial *Wish U Were Here* for Hosteling International. He occasionally acts as well and numbers among his credits the title role in *Macbeth*, Carl in *The Baltimore Waltz*, Matt in *The Fantasticks*, the Record Keeper in *Jacob Marley's Christmas Carol*, Ned Poins in *The Boar's Head* (which he also adapted from Shakespeare's *Henry IV* and *Henry V*) and the opera *Tosca*, in addition to voicing a number of radio and television commercials. He is the Director of Events with AtmosTheatre and a founding member of the San Francisco Theater Pub, as well as the Executive Director of the San Francisco Olympians Festival. His first novel, *Dry Country*, came out in 2008 and is available on Amazon.com. His partner is artist Cody Rishell.

David Burrola (artist, Aphrodite) is a former student of Academy of Art University studying animation, who later transferred to the Art Institute of California, San Diego, also studying animation. He's worked on concepts for web comics, animation projects, and some book art. Though he's touched upon sculpting, painting and pastels, he's mostly worked in charcoal and graphite as well as marker, but considers himself more adept and black and white than at color. Currently he is working as a journalist for thetestmarketevolution.com, filling in articles for movies, TV, and games. He takes commissions and can be reached at Dburrola19@yahoo.com, on Facebook, and at bigwavedave.deviantart.com.

Liz Conley (artist, Hermes) Liz Conley is a book artist and printmaker who graduated from the Academy of Art University with a degree in Fine Art. She's worked as a bookbinder for Arion Press and currently teaches printing and binding at TechShop in San Francisco. Between binding, printing and teaching she creates illustrations, including posters for the annual San Francisco Olympians Festival. Her work has been exhibited in San Francisco, New York City and Portland, Oregon. Her portfolio can be viewed at lizconley.com and her more whimsical sketches can be found at fillingcontent.tumblr.com.

Bennett Fisher (playwright, Hermes) Bennett Fisher's plays, including *Hermes, Don't Be Evil, The Dark Backward, Devil of a Time, Chronus, Exchange, Query, Pure Baltic Avenue, Disinfect, No Bull, Solstice, The Bird Trap, Daedalus*, and *THIS IS WHAT IT MEANS TO GET HIT BY A BUS*, have been produced in the United States and internationally. As an actor, playwright, dramaturg, director, and producer, he has collaborated with the Cutting Ball Theater (where he is the Literary Manager), the National Theatre of Northern Greece, Campo Santo and Intersection for the Arts, Threshold Theatre, AtmosTheatre, California Shakespeare Theatre, Adirondack

Shakespeare Company, Marin Shakespeare Company, Stanford Summer Theater, the Pear Avenue Theatre, New Conservatory Theater Center, San Francisco Theater Pub, Three Wise Monkeys, Theater Pop SF, PianoFight, Misfit Toys Rep, Bread and Water Theatre, Playwrights Foundation, No Nude Men, and others. He is an associate artist with AtmosTheatre and Threshold Theatre, and a founding artistic director of both the San Francisco Theater Pub and the Flying Island Theater Lab. He lives in San Francisco, where he teaches English literature and playwriting.

Brett Grunig (artist, Demeter) Brett Grunig grew up and began studying art in Sonoma County, California, where he spent most of his time reading, drawing and playing games of the nerdy persuasion. After obtaining a BFA in printmaking from Sonoma State University, he moved to Madison, Wisconsin, where he earned his MFA at the University of Wisconsin in 2006. He has since returned to Sonoma County where he continues to pursue his craft as a printmaker and artist. Brett is currently working on a number of projects including creating stacks of prints and drawings in his tiny studio, working as an art instructor for local drawing classes at Megamoth Studio, and trying to stuff his head full of as many stories of wonder and magic as he can.

Nirmala Nataraj (playwright, Aphrodite: A Romance in Infomercials) Nirmala Nataraj is a San Francisco-based critic and playwright. She has written for the *San Francisco Chronicle*, *SF Weekly*, *Theatre Bay Area*, and *American Theatre* (of which she was a Bay Area Commissioning Fund recipient in 2008). Nirmala was also a participant in the Intergenerational Writers Lab (put on by two San Francisco arts organizations, Kearny Street Workshop and Intersection for the Arts) and the Voices of Our Nation (VONA) workshop at the University of San Francisco. Nirmala's theatrical work has been featured at the Climate Theatre, EXIT Theatre, Femina Potens, the Queer Women of Color Film Festival, San Francisco Theater Festival, and the Bay Area Playwrights Festival. Nirmala is a founding member of No Nude Men Productions and her work has also been seen in the San Francisco Olympians Festival (*Aphrodite: A Romance in Infomercials* in 2010 and *Selene, or Someone Like the Moon* in 2011).

Evelyn Jean Pine (playwright, Hephaestus and the Three Golden Robots) Evelyn Jean Pine is a five-time PlayGround Emerging Playwright Award Winner and the recipient of the June Anne Baker Award. She has written two full-length plays for the San Francisco Olympians Festival: *Hephaestus* *and the Three Golden Robots* and *Walking the Starry Path*, a musical retelling of the myth of Uranus with music by Tom Darter. PlayGround has commissioned three of her full-lengths: *Astonishment*, about the invention of the movies; *The Secrets of the World*, about Queen Isabella and the Indians Columbus brought back to her; and her latest, *Altair*, about the first personal computer and the fight between computer hobbyists and Bill Gates. Her short play *Sweet Dreams* launched the Manhattan Shakespeare Project's Emerging Voices Festival in 2010. Her award-winning short plays have been staged around the country, including San Francisco, Berkeley, Kansas City, Charlottesville, Bethesda, and New York. She is a member of the Dramatists Guild.

Claire Rice (playwright, Demeter's Daughter) Claire Rice is a playwright, director, and producer. She has worked with Thunderbird Theatre Company, No Nude Men, Three Wise Monkeys, PianoFight, AtmosTheatre, and the San Francisco Theatre Pub, and is co-founder of Ann Marie Productions. Her plays include *Once a Boy, The Carmine Lie, It Ain't Me, Pride and Succubus, Waterline, Demeter's Daughter, Woman Come Down, Sex in the Next Room,* and the blog play *English for Beginners*. She has directed the sketch comedy *Serve by Expiration* for Thunderbird Theatre Company, and the plays *Horrible In Between Place* for Ann Marie Productions, *How I Learned to Stop Worrying and Lost My Virginity* for the 2011 New York Fringe Festival, and *Juno en Victoria* for Wily West Productions. She has worked as a lecturer in Theatre at San Francisco State University and as a Membership Associate at Theatre Bay Area. She lives in San Francisco with her loving husband, actor Matt Gunnison.

Cody Rishell (artist, Hera) Cody Rishell studied illustration at the Academy of Art University with an emphasis on science-fiction/fantasy comics. He has worked in small theater for the past four years and his work has been seen around the Bay Area with No Nude Men, Three Wise Monkeys, Central Works, and the San Francisco Theater Pub, as well as in Turkey. Between freelancing and contract work, he finds time to create comics, random illustrations, and bizarre cartoons at scribblepop.tumblr.com. For more information, please visit www.codyrishell.com.

Marissa Skudlarek (writer, introduction) Marissa Skudlarek served as box-office manager for the 2010 San Francisco Olympians Festival. For the 2011 Olympians Festival, she wrote the full-length play *Pleiades* and served as an associate producer. Her other full-length plays include *Deus* *ex Machina* (Young Playwrights Festival National Playwriting Competition winner, 2006), *Marginalia*, and *The Rose of Youth* (Marilyn Swartz Seven Award and Vassar College production, 2008). Her shorter plays have been produced by San Francisco Theater Pub, Un-Scripted Theatre, and the San Francisco One-Minute Play Festival. Additionally she has translated Jean Cocteau's *Orphée* from the French. Skudlarek holds a B.A. in Drama and French from Vassar College. She blogs about theater, books, playwriting and more at marissabidilla.blogspot.com.

NO NUDE MEN AND THE SAN FRANCISCO OLYMPIANS FESTIVAL

In 2010 No Nude Men Productions produced the first San Francisco Olympians Festival, a new works development project that includes participation by over 100 Bay Area writers, fine artists, directors and actors. Since then the festival has become a yearly event, with writers from all over the country submitting proposals for new plays, which are then completed over the course of a year and given a dramatic reading during the month of the festival. Visual artists are commissioned to create original images tied to each of the presented plays. Since the festival began, four works have gone on to full productions and more continue to emerge onto the national and international theater scene.

No Nude Men started as a one-off theater company/joke born from Stuart Bousel's mounting frustration with the local San Francisco theater scene and a series of projects he got involved with that never went anywhere. In March of 2003 NNM opened their first show, *The Troublesome Reign of Edward II*. They ran the play for two weeks and were never supposed to perform again, but that plan changed and since then their extensive production list has included such plays as *Phaedra, Love's Labors Lost, No Exit, Hamlet* and *The Exiled*.

NNM have been behind numerous world premieres by Stuart Bousel (*Speak To Me, Troijka, Love Egos Alternative Rock, Mathew 33:6, Housebroken, Edenites*), Nirmala Nataraj (*The Book of Genesis: Remixed and Remastered, The Monk, A Grave Situation*), David Duman (*Five Short Episodes In The Life of Sacagawea, Fishing*), Hilde Susan Jaegtnes (*Spoon Justice, Learning from Hilde's Mistakes, Oily Replies*), Alison Luterman (*Oasis, A Night in Jail*), Bennett Fisher (*Hermes*), Wylie Herman (*Better Homes and Ammo*), M. R. Fall (*Test Preparation*), Ashley Cowan (*Word War*) and Claire Rice (*Woman Come Down*). They have performed at EXIT Theatre, Build Space, Spanganga, Langton Center for the Arts, Periscope Cellars, the Xenodrome, and were the resident company at the Climate Theater in 2006. They are regular participants with the San Francisco Theater Festival and the Bay One Acts Festival. Directors over the years have included Stuart Bousel, Jesse Baldwin, John Dixon, Stacy Malia, Wylie Herman, Claire Rice, Sara Judge, Ryan Hayes, Christopher P. Kelly, Tore Ingersoll-Thorp and Julia Heitner. They also collaborated with Conlan Media to create *Giant Bones*, the official stage adaptation of several short stories by renowned international fantasy writer Peter S. Beagle.

In addition to their producing presence within the community, No Nude Men have raised money for the San Francisco AIDS Walk and Equality California and contributed food to homeless shelters and food banks around the Bay Area. The No Nude Men Salon, a traveling living room reading series that brings actors, directors, writers and other theater folk together for the purpose of sharing food and discussion over a published play, was started in 2009. An annual retreat open to the larger theater community and centered around discussion of the Bay Area theater scene and the development of new work has also become part of the company's season.

Independent from the beginning both financially and in spirit, No Nude Men remain outside both the corporate and non-profit sectors and are unaffiliated with any unions or artistic collectives, schools of theater or production trends, existing entirely off of ticket sales and private donations, and making up the rules as they go, while still accommodating everyone's busy schedules and artistic egos.

Officially speaking, they don't exist and never have.

EXIT Press

EXIT Press is the publishing division of EXIT Theatre, a San Francisco theater company that was founded in 1983. Published books include *Ten Plays* by Mark Jackson, *Snakes of Kampuchea* by Mark Knego, *Practical Tales For Children and other stories* by Mark Romyn, and *Woyzeck, Pelleas and Melisande, Ubu Roi* translated by Rob Melrose. Coming soon are *Happily Lost in Time and Place* by Erika Atkinson, *The Chamber Plays of August Strindberg* translated by Paul Walsh, and books of plays by Elisa deCarlo and Sarah McKereghan.

April 2012

www.ingramcontent.com/pod-product-compliance
Lightning Source LLC
Chambersburg PA
CBHW022107150426
43195CB00008B/298